THE STRUGGLE

10 YEARS LATER

This title is a true story. However, some names have been changed to protect individuals' privacy. Many of the events in this title occurred while the author was under the influence of drugs and alcohol, so the details may not always be completely accurate.

ISBN 979-8-9852911-1-7 (Trade Paperback)
ISBN 979-8-9852911-0-0 (Hardcover)
ISBN 979-8-9852911-2-4 (E-book)
ISBN 979-8-9852911-3-1 (Large Print)

Library of Congress Control Number: 2021923077

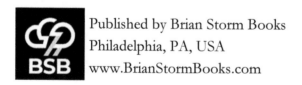 Published by Brian Storm Books
Philadelphia, PA, USA
www.BrianStormBooks.com

Book cover designed by Ismail Ben
www.bookconsilio.com

<u>Warning:</u>

The book you are about to read contains graphic details that may upset some readers. If you are sensitive to **substance abuse, suicide, vulgar language, physical violence, murder, or prostitution**, this may not be the right book for you.

This book is dedicated to those who have gone through or are still going through "The Struggle" of substance abuse.

We all have a story to tell...

Preface

I originally wrote this story in 2012, when I had two years clean and sober. Now, 10 years later, I decided to rewrite it. Not only because I have grown as a writer, but because a lot has happened in the past 10 years. It's still the same story, only restructured and reworded so that it flows better, with a few new chapters to show how my life has drastically changed in the past 10 years.

I wrote this book to share my experience, strength, and hope for recovery from drug addiction and alcoholism. You will read about how I used drugs and alcohol to fit in and have fun with my friends. Over the years, I became a person I never thought I would become. I hope this book opens the eyes of both addicts and non-addicts and gives a better understanding of how addiction can affect anyone.

I tried to be 100% honest in my writing, but the time frames and details may not always be completely accurate. This is because drugs and alcohol have taken a toll on my memory. However, I tried my best to write it exactly as I remembered. Either way, I hope the true message of my story can reach whoever reads this.

I pray that my story can offer hope to those still suffering from addiction and/or alcoholism and let them know it is possible to recover from this disease. You will read some graphic details in this book, but if I could go back in time, I wouldn't change a thing from my past. Everything that happened to me has made me the person I am today, and I realize how truly blessed I am to be alive.

If this book can open just one person's eyes or save one person's life, I know it has served its purpose. If you are stuck in "The Struggle" of addiction or alcoholism, please know that help is available. Even if you don't believe in yourself, just know I believe in you. If I can do it, then I know you can too.

1

Chapter 1

I was defeated. I couldn't go on living any longer. I was tired of what my life had become. I was tired of looking in the mirror and seeing a monster staring back at me. I was tired of not recognizing myself anymore. My eyes were bloodshot, my cheeks were sunken in, and I could see the bones in my rib cage. I had not shaven for days, and I really needed a haircut. I saw the evil in my eyes and felt the demons deep in my heart. I hated the person that I had become.

It was a bitter cold day, sometime in January of 2009. I waited for my brother to step into the shower, which was my cue to make a move. I heard him turn the water on, so I crept into his room and stole some cash from his wallet. I had about $100 left from my unemployment check, but a drug addict can never be too greedy. I found $100 in my brother's wallet, so I figured he wouldn't notice if $40 went missing. I snatched two crisp $20 bills, grabbed my jacket, and headed for the door.

My first stop was at the liquor store to get a bottle of Bacardi. This was my last drink, and I didn't want to short-change myself by drinking the cheap stuff. The next stop was "North Philly Badlands." A neighborhood known as Kensington was one-stop shopping for all the drugs I could ask for. I parked the car down the street from a well-known drug corner, and a young Spanish dealer shook his head no as I approached him.

"Five minutes, papi," the young Spanish dealer said.

Damn! I don't have the patience to wait five minutes. I want what I want, and I want it now! I jumped back into the car and drove to another spot.

"Dope, powder, rock. How many papi?"

"Five dope and two powder."

After a quick hand-to-hand exchange, I was back in my car, tucking the drugs into a small hole in the roof. Now it was time to get my needles.

I approached the busy corner of Kensington and Somerset, a hotspot for needles and a wide variety of other drugs. I told the scruffy addict that I needed a set of works ("works" is street slang for syringes). I saw a cop, so I kept walking and remained calm as if nothing was wrong. He passed by me without even looking, so I ran back to the corner to get my works.

"I got zannies and E too," the addict mentioned.

I always heard mixing uppers and downers could make your heart stop. Plus, the ecstasy would make me feel so good. So, I copped four Xanax and one E and then kept it moving. Now I'm off to my final stop. I couldn't have an end-of-the-world party without a little weed, and if I was going to get weed, I might as well go all out and mix it with some good old PCP. I drove to another sketchy corner, got out, and walked to the young dealer.

"Two wet and two weed," I told him.

He reached inside the window of an abandoned house, more commonly referred to as a "bando," and once again, I made the hand-to-hand. I quickly jumped in my car and headed back to Tacony, the small neighborhood in Northeast Philadelphia where I grew up.

I decided to spend my final moments at Keystone Park. I sat on a bench at the basketball courts. The same basketball courts that my friends and I used to hang out at, but I was all by myself this time. The friends I used to have just didn't know me anymore; nobody did. Besides, I wanted to be alone. I didn't want anyone to try anything stupid, like save my worthless life.

I took a gulp from the bottle of rum and chased it down with my Xanax and ecstasy. Most people would take the pills first, followed by the drink, but I always did everything backward; maybe that's why I was an addict to begin with. I cracked open the blunt and dumped the tobacco onto the same ground where I used to play basketball. Then I emptied the weed and PCP into the blunt and rolled it up. It looked perfect. I was always good at rolling blunts. It's probably one of the few things I was ever good at. I put the flame to the tip and began smoking. I could finally relax.

As the Xanax kicked in, I opened the bottle of Bacardi. I took a swig and emptied the heroin and coke into the cap. That's when I realized I didn't have any water to mix my concoction. With no water to mix my drugs, I asked myself, "What would MacGyver do?" So, I filled the syringe with rum and squirted it into the cap with the coke and dope. I pulled the plunger out of the needle and mixed the shot that would make me sleep forever.

By this point, I was pretty fucked up. The ecstasy kicked in, and my bottle was half empty, but I knew there was still work to be done. Truth be told, I was excited to see what was waiting for me on the other side. Anything would've been better than the life I was living. I pulled off my belt, wrapped it around my arm, and stuck the needle in my vein. I slowly pulled back the plunger until I saw blood and injected the deadly mixture in one quick shot. Ahhh… That's the feeling I was looking for. Now I just had to wait as I slipped into permanent sedation.

An hour had passed, and I was still breathing. I sat on the park bench in confusion. I didn't understand how I was still alive. The uppers, downers, hallucinogens, and everything else should have made my heart explode. That's when I realized I couldn't do anything right; not even kill myself.

It was time for plan B. There were train tracks not far from where I was sitting. I stood up and stumbled my way to the tracks. It was only 50 yards away, but I fell twice before I could get there. I sat in the middle of the tracks and waited for a train to take my life. I heard a loud thunder from up above. When I looked up at the sky, a few cold raindrops smacked me in the face.

"If you really exist, let's see you prove it!" I shouted to the sky.

I didn't know if God was real or not, but that didn't stop me from feeling angry at him. If he loved me, how could he let me suffer like this?

I sat there for a while, wondering where the train was. I couldn't wait any longer. I wanted to end my pain and see my mother again. I knew she was in heaven but wasn't sure if I would end up there or not. No, my bet was I'm going someplace much worse. Still, it was a better alternative to the life I had been living.

As I got deep into my thoughts of death and the afterlife, I heard a phone ring from my coat pocket. Who would call at a time like this? I looked at the caller ID and saw it was my ex-girlfriend, Penelope. We had broken up a couple of months earlier. I missed her and still loved her at the time, so I immediately picked up the phone. I was so drunk and high that she could barely understand the words I mumbled. I don't remember the conversation much, but she must have said something that made me change my mind.

After I hung up the phone, I wiped the tears from my eyes and got myself up off the ground. As I walked off the tracks, I tripped and banged my knee on the steel rail, but I was so doped up that I barely felt it. I got up and continued to stumble off the tracks. I only made it about 20 yards before the deafening sound of a train whistle pierced my eardrums. I turned around to see a train speeding past at a frightening speed. It couldn't have been more than 60 seconds since I stepped off the tracks. I was literally 60 seconds away from death.

I began to wonder why Penelope called on that particular night. Why at that exact moment? At first, I thought it was just a coincidence, but looking back, I now realize it wasn't. God must have wanted to keep me around for a reason.

Chapter 2

Let's rewind back a little bit. I want to explain how I got to the point of suicide because being in that state of mind doesn't just happen overnight. I didn't come from a broken home or experience any childhood trauma. My parents weren't addicts. Nobody had ever sexually abused me or anything like that. I could go on and on with the reasons people come up with. Look, I can't tell you why I became an addict, but I can tell you how I became one.

My family was actually kind of normal. We weren't poor, but we weren't rich either. We were just an average family that lived in a small row home in Philadelphia. Sure, we had problems, but what family doesn't? My parents were some of the nicest people you would ever meet. Well, my dad was unforgiving at times, but that's only because I was always getting into trouble. He was a Philadelphia police officer who was very strict because he wanted us to understand that there were consequences for our behaviors. But for some reason, it took almost 30 years to realize what he was trying to teach me.

My mom was one of the happiest people in the world. Her bubbly personality put a smile on everyone's face she came into contact with. But she did have an angry side to her that very few people ever witnessed. Of course, I was one of the people who could bring that side out of her. But all in all, she was a very loving person that was quick to forgive me for all the nonsense I put her through.

I was the youngest of four siblings. My brothers, Mike and Shawn, and my sister, Kim, were all born a year apart. Being a few years younger, I constantly tried to fit in with them. But no matter how hard I tried, they were always tougher, faster, and smarter than I was. I felt as if I could never measure up to them.

I grew up Catholic, so I had always believed in God. My mom went to church every week, and when we were younger, she used to drag us there with her. My parents even sent me to a Catholic school, Our Lady of Consolation, which was a block away from our house. You might find it hard to believe while reading this story, but I was even an altar boy at one point.

My siblings gave me the nickname "Brain" when I was in first grade. I earned this name by acing a spelling test, but I somehow misspelled my own name. I spelled it "Brain" instead of "Brian," and the name has stuck with me ever since.

I met my best friend, Sean, when I was three years old. A couple of years later, I met two other childhood friends, Ioana and Alicia. The four of us were joined at the hips. We did everything together; rode bikes, played knock-knock zoom-zoom, built snowmen, and all the other stuff that young kids do. Unfortunately, one by one, they all moved away. It hurt the most when I said goodbye to Sean, though. He was my right-hand man.

To make matters worse, Sean moved all the way to Florida, which made it impossible for us to ever see each other. I eventually made new friends, but it just wasn't the same. I felt like I didn't fit in with them, like I wasn't good enough. Whenever I played sports with the neighborhood kids, I was always one of the last to get picked. I also got bullied at times, but not nearly as much as some of the other kids. Most of the time, it was because I was afraid to stand up for myself. I had it in my mind that my older brothers would fight all my battles for me.

I was always trying to fit in and be one of the cool kids. I guess that's what made me take my first sip of alcohol at age 12. My friend Anthony broke into his dad's liquor cabinet and stole a bottle of vodka. I didn't want him to think I was too scared to drink or for him to make fun of me, so I took a sip. It was nasty. I couldn't stand the taste, and my chest felt like it was on fire, but I took another swig anyway. Even though I hated the taste, I loved the effect that alcohol had on me. It made me feel invincible. It made me feel free. It made me feel alive.

Remember when I said I always felt out of place, like I wasn't good enough? Well, when I was drunk, those insecure feelings faded away. Alcohol gave me the confidence to talk to girls, crack funny jokes, and just feel normal. It made me feel like I had a sense of belonging. It all came down to me not liking who I was, and alcohol made me feel like I was a different person. So naturally, I wanted to drink again to achieve that same feeling, but at 12 years old, getting my hands on booze was a real challenge. I tried to ask my older siblings to get me alcohol, but they always denied me because I was too young.

After a few years, my older brother Mike finally changed his mind and decided I was old enough to drink. I guess 14 was the family drinking age, or at least that's what it seemed. Once he got me alcohol, it was easy to convince my other siblings to buy it for me. If all else failed, I would just pay one of the bums from the neighborhood to buy me a 40-ounce.

My friends and I had many places in the neighborhood to get drunk. But our favorite spots were the basketball courts, the train tracks, the river, and on the corner with my older siblings and their friends. But the slickest spot was right on our friends' front porches. I used to pour liquor into a soda bottle so that their parents would never suspect a thing, but they would catch me every once in a while. Especially when I got so drunk that I pissed in a neighbor's flowerpot and the entire neighborhood saw me do it. Things like that got me banned from hanging out at some of my friends' houses. But whenever that happened, we would all just migrate to another friend's house and do the same shit over again.

At one point, we started drinking at our friend Theresa's house, on her back deck. The back deck was elevated above street level, directly above an alleyway. It was a sweet spot to drink for a while until I fucked it all up. After a night of heavy drinking, I decided to piss off the deck into the back alley.

"What the fuck!" a voice screamed from below.

I looked down and saw Theresa's neighbor standing below in the alley, screaming, cursing, and dripping with piss. Needless to say, we were never allowed back after that. This is just a glimpse of what life was like in my early drinking days. Honestly speaking, I don't remember any of this actually happening. I just remember my friends telling me about it the next day. Most of the time, I would laugh it off and not even care about the people I harmed. In my mind, I was just living life and having fun.

Chapter 3

My brother Mike introduced me to hip-hop music, and I fell in love the moment I heard it. I would use the tape deck to record songs off the radio and then play them back so that I could write down the lyrics. Once I had the lyrics written, I would study and memorize them. It's funny how I could never apply this concept to my schoolwork, though.

In the early 90s, Weird Al Yankovic was pretty popular, and believe it or not, he was the reason I started writing my own hip-hop songs. I was a huge fan of how he turned popular songs into parodies, and I loved his music so much that I decided to try it myself. I already had the lyrics from Dr. Dre's "Nothing but a G Thang," so all I had to do was change a few words to create my first song, "Nothing but a Big-Mac." When I spit it to my friends, they absolutely loved it. So I decided right then and there that I wanted to be a rapper.

Eventually, I began writing my own original songs. To me, it was more than just writing a few rhymes on a piece of paper, though. I loved piecing the words together like it was some sort of puzzle. It felt amazing to know that I created something out of nothing. It felt even better to witness my friend's reactions to that creation. Writing rhymes gave me a natural high that turned me into a rap-aholic. There was no stopping me after that; hip-hop was my first real addiction.

Before Eminem changed the game, being a white rapper made me an outcast. Everybody took me as a joke. My classmates laughed at me, told me I'd never make it, and even compared me to Vanilla Ice. After a while, even the teachers joined in on the fun. But I didn't care what they thought about me. I just wanted to prove them wrong so I could laugh in their face when I finally made it.

I loved listening to hip-hop just as much as I loved writing it, and listening to it is what sparked (pun intended) my curiosity about smoking weed. Some of my favorite artists taught me "How to Roll a Blunt" and take "Hits from the Bong" long before I'd ever take my first puff. Don't get me wrong, I don't blame music for my drug use. I made my own decisions. It's not like Snoop Dogg held a gun to my head and made me smoke weed.

My brother Shawn and my sister Kim both smoked weed back then but thought I was too young, so they never let me smoke with them. I don't know if it was because they were afraid my parents would find out, or maybe because they actually had morals. Thankfully, my sister's boyfriend, Danny, didn't have any morals. Danny would always get beer for me. He was one of the few people I knew who was old enough to buy it legally.

One night, while driving back from the beer distributor, Danny asked if I smoked weed. I told him I had never smoked before but had always wanted to try it. He cracked a smile, pulled a joint out of his cigarette pack, and lit it up. I was expecting it to give me the most incredible feeling ever, but by the time we were finished, I didn't feel a damn thing. I thought Danny played a joke on me and gave me fake weed or something.

I was somewhat disappointed but thought to myself, "Well, at least I have the beer." Danny popped the trunk so I could grab the booze, and that's when it hit me. The street lights got brighter, and the world moved in slow motion. I lost control of my emotions and began to laugh hysterically. I loved the feeling that weed gave me, and I wanted more!

The next night, I convinced my old heads to get me some weed. They were hesitant at first but reluctantly brought me along for the ride to North Philly to get the good shit. I had never been to North Philly before, so it seemed like a different world to me. I grew up in Tacony, which wasn't exactly a nice neighborhood, but it was nothing compared to North Philly. Run-down houses and open market drug corners told me we were dead smack in the ghetto.

I'm not going to lie. I was scared shitless. We were the only white people around, so we stuck out like a sore thumb. Adrenaline pumped through my veins as I waited in the car for my old head to get back from buying the weed. When he finally came back, a sense of relief ran through my body, accompanied by a euphoric feeling that gave me a natural high. See, it's not only the drugs that are addictive; just buying them can be an addiction of its own.

None of my friends had ever smoked weed before, but they all wanted to try it. So when I showed them the weed I bought, their eyes lit up like Christmas trees, and smiles jumped onto their faces like young children on Christmas morning. I felt like Santa Claus as I rolled my first joint, and even though I spilled weed everywhere and had to use three rolling papers, it was still smokable in the end. The stoned look on my friends' faces told me they loved weed just as much as I did.

Smoking weed was an expensive habit for me at 15 years old, but I had a paper route that made it a little more affordable. Back then, I had to knock on customers' doors every week to collect the money for the newspapers. The paper cost $3 a week, and I usually got a dollar or two as a tip. So all I had to do was knock on a couple of doors, and I would have enough money to buy myself a bag. It was like my own personal ATM that I used to support my growing habit.

My parents were strict and used to punish me a lot as a teenager, so I rarely smoked and drank with my friends on the weekends. The only time I could leave the house was to go to school or deliver my newspapers. So I used these opportunities to get drunk and high since I couldn't go out with my friends on the weekends. It was kind of ass-backward to get drunk and high during the week, only to stay sober on the weekends, but I did what I had to do.

I started getting drunk while delivering my newspapers after school but never had enough time to finish my beers. I didn't want to waste too much time because I knew my parents would get suspicious. But I didn't want to waste the beer either, so I always tucked it into my bag. That way, I could keep drinking while continuing my paper route. Hiding beer in the newspaper bag worked for a while until I accidentally threw a beer bottle onto a customer's porch. I was so drunk that I mistook it for a newspaper. It wasn't until I heard the glass smash that I even realized what I had done. I was afraid the customer would question me about it, but he never did. I guess I got lucky with that one.

Eventually, my parents caught me drinking while delivering newspapers, so they started giving me a strict time limit. Now my only option was to drink and smoke before school. I tried to drink beer in the morning but just never had a taste for it. Mixing cereal with malt liquor didn't sit well in my stomach. Weed, however, was the perfect before-school activity.

I didn't want everyone in my school to know that I smoked weed, so I always sprayed myself with cologne before I got to class. But when I burped a cloud of weed smoke in the middle of class one day, it was hard to deny that I was a pothead. The teacher thought someone lit a joint in the classroom but couldn't prove anything. I later laughed about it with my friends, but my virgin lung classmates viewed me as some sort of weirdo.

The good thing about smoking in the morning was that I would be completely sober by the time I got home from school, so my parents never suspected a thing. After a few months of staying out of trouble, I was finally let off punishment, which called for a celebration. The first day I was allowed back out, I got a case of beer and met a few friends down by the river. We were having a blast, at least until the cops busted us. On the way to the police station, I couldn't help but think of the irony; I got arrested for celebrating my freedom. Once we got to the police station, we had to call our parents. The irony struck again when I had to tell my dad, who was a cop, that I got arrested. He picked me up from the station and got the charges dropped for all of my friends, but when I got home, he beat my ass. I can't say I didn't deserve it.

After a few more months of punishment, my parents finally let me back out for good behavior. Even though I got arrested the last time I was at the river, it didn't stop me from going there to get drunk once again. This time I was drinking with my sister, her boyfriend Danny, and a couple of my other old heads. Danny and I were so drunk that we could barely walk, but he wanted to teach me how to drive. At 15 years old, I couldn't pass up the opportunity to drive a car.

Kim agreed to let us use her car as long as we promised not to leave the parking lot. But after Danny taught me the basics, I pulled out of the parking lot and onto the road, where I ran a stop sign and almost hit another car. I got scared after that, so I circled the block and went back to the river. When we reached the parking lot, I stopped the car, and we both got out. A moment later, my sister and her friends started screaming and pointing at the car. I turned around and saw the car rolling toward the river. Apparently, I never shifted the car into park. Thankfully, Danny was able to stop the vehicle before it plunged into the river. I can't blame my sister for never letting me drive her car again.

Chapter 4

When I turned 16, I got my first real job at McDonald's. I wasn't planning on retiring as a head cashier or anything, but it was a good job for a teenage pothead, especially since most of my co-workers smoked just as much as I did. Around the same time I started working at McDonald's, I noticed some of my classmates coming to school with red eyes and cases of the munchies. Most of them used to make fun of me for smoking weed but were now sitting next to me, stoned out of their minds. I couldn't help but laugh at their hypocrisy.

One day, while sitting in class, a light bulb went off in my mind. I knew a lot of people who smoked weed. There were plenty of potheads in the neighborhood, plus all my co-workers and classmates. So I saw an easy opportunity to make money, and with my first real paycheck from McDonald's, I bought an ounce of weed and started selling it. They say that a monkey shouldn't sell bananas, and even though that may be true, in the beginning, I was actually making a little money. However, it seemed like the more I sold, the more I smoked, and the more I smoked, the more I dug into my own pockets. It got to the point where I was handing my paychecks over to my dealer every week.

When it came to me selling weed, it wasn't all about the money. Remember how I told you about the adrenaline rushes I got when buying drugs? Well, the same went for selling drugs. Not to mention, supplying weed to my customers made me feel as if I was needed. It gave me a sense of purpose like I was someone important or something. But eventually, it all had to come to an end.

My dealer got his hands on some new shit that smelled delicious, so I bought two ounces and rolled a fat blunt to test the new product. I was so high when I got home that I left the weed in my coat pocket when I hung it on the rack. As I walked away, the coat fell, and the weed spilled onto the floor—right in front of my parents. My parents had found a nickel bag or two on me in the past, but this time was different. This time it was two ounces. They flushed it down the toilet and punished me for a year straight. I had to put the weed business to a stop, at least for now.

Once I stopped selling weed, I felt like something was missing from my life. I was used to having those adrenaline rushes every day. Every time I made a sale, it felt like a natural high, but now that I wasn't selling, there was nothing at all. It was only a matter of time until I found something to fill that void, and what I found was a drug that very well could have been created by the Devil himself.

The first time I tried Xanax, also known as zannies, I didn't really know what to expect, but I fell in love the moment I felt it. The only problem was that Xanax released my inner demons. Before being introduced to zannies, I was a pretty honest person. Even though I technically sold drugs, I never ripped anyone off or did any shady shit. People generally trusted me, but once zannies were in my system, all bets were off. Xanax gave me a "Fuck the world" attitude and turned me into a thieving snake bastard who would stab my best friend in the back just for the fun of it.

The Xanax era of my life is a giant blur to me. The thing I remember most is waking up every morning and trying to figure out what happened the night before. I often woke up with empty pockets, wondering what had happened to all my money. Other times I woke up with money that wasn't mine and stuff that didn't belong to me, with no memory of where any of it came from.

Mixing alcohol with zannies intensified the effects, making it difficult to walk without falling all over the place. This made me an easy target for crooks on the prowl. But somehow, someway, I was always able to defend myself. Many people attempted to mug me in this condition, but nobody ever succeeded. In some cases, I probably should have just given them what they wanted.

On one Xanax-fueled night, while walking home at 4:00 a.m., a carload of thugs drove past me. What caught my attention was how this car was crawling at such a slow pace. I looked over as it rolled by and saw six faces staring back at me. The car quickly pulled over at the corner, and the doors opened up. I knew it was about to go down. When I reached the corner, six guys were crossing the street toward me. I knew what they wanted: the book bag strapped to my back. They probably assumed I had something valuable in it, but the only thing in my bag was my rhyme book, and NOBODY was ever going to steal my rhymes.

I took a drag of my cigarette as the first guy approached. When he got close enough, he asked if I had a light. I knew this trick, so I was just waiting for it. When I handed him my lit cigarette, he took a swing, so I quickly dodged the punch, regained my balance, and then flicked the lit cigarette at his face. This threw him off guard, leaving him wide open for a right hook to the chin. He dropped like a fly, but the remaining five thugs surrounded me. I wasn't about to fight five people at once, so I turned around to run but tripped over a trash bag and fell flat on my face.

These guys haven't even touched me yet, and I was already getting fucked up. I got up as quick as I could, but it was too late; they had me surrounded. My fist swung at anyone who came close enough, but for every punch I threw, I had six more coming back at me. I was holding my ground, bobbing and weaving, swinging left, right, left, right. I somehow knocked one or two of them down, but my legs suddenly gave out on me, and I found myself kissing the concrete.

I must have gotten struck hard, but my adrenaline was pumping so much that I didn't even feel it. I got back up and started swinging again, but then BAM! My legs buckled from beneath me as I took another hit to the back of my head. I found myself on the ground once again, this time getting kicked repeatedly.

"Get his bag, get his bag," someone yelled.

I flipped myself over so that I was lying on my back. I figured it would be harder to get my bag if my body weight was leaning on it. But I couldn't just lie there and do nothing while these dudes kicked my head in. So one by one, I kicked them all in their kneecaps. A few of them tried to get the bag, but I wasn't rolling over for them. BAM! I'm hit again. I thought to myself, "How is someone punching me this hard?" I was on the verge of giving up until a passing motorist stopped.

"Hey, get off of him. I'm calling the cops," the motorist shouted.

Next, a neighbor opened their door to see what the commotion was, and that's when they called it quits. As they walked back to their car, I noticed one of them holding a tire iron. Those heavy hits that brought me to my knees suddenly made sense now. It wasn't a fist, but a tire iron, smashing against my skull; no wonder why I went down so quickly.

I got home around five in the morning and immediately looked in the mirror. To my surprise, I didn't have a scratch on me. But when I felt the back of my head, my blood-covered hand told a different story. It scared me shitless, and I wasn't sure if I should go to the hospital or not, so I woke up my mom to get her advice. My mom didn't think I needed stitches but insisted on calling the police. I didn't want to get the cops involved, but she called them anyway.

Xanax brings all types of demons out of people; for me, that demon was a kleptomaniac. I would steal anything I could get my hands on. It didn't matter if it was a candy bar from the store, a friend's wallet, or a pencil from my teacher. Whether I needed it or not, I would steal just for the thrill of it; just to see if I could get away with it. Eventually, I started breaking into cars and robbing people with a pellet gun.

It was only a matter of time before my dad found that pellet gun in my room. He took it off me and locked it in his closet, but I figured out the combination to the lock and stole it back the next day. When I broke into the closet, I found a colossal-sized coin jar filled with quarters. I felt like I hit the jackpot! I could easily take a few dollars without him even noticing.

After a while, stealing became second nature to me. I didn't have to be high anymore. I was stealing every chance I had. Sometimes my friends would all chip in a few dollars apiece and send me to go get an ounce of weed. You can imagine how mad they were when I came back with nothing but a big bag of oregano. I played dumb and acted like I was angry, hyping them all up to go find the fuckers who ripped us off. We drove around for hours looking for the person who robbed us when all they had to do was look in the passenger seat. Stealing from the people closest to me didn't faze me one bit. I had no remorse. In fact, I loved it. It felt like it was some sort of game. I just wanted to see how much I could get away with. How far could I take it before someone actually caught me?

At this point in my life, one of my favorite things to do was go to the mall, pop some zannies, and steal anything that wasn't tied down. My favorite store to steal from was Sears. It was so easy because they had an escalator that led to a separate store underneath. They shared the same building, but they were completely different stores. I would take the escalator to the other store and walk right out their front door.

Most of the time, I stole random shit from Sears that I didn't really need. But one day, I went there specifically for a basketball. I was trying to find a clever way to steal the ball because I knew I couldn't stuff a basketball down my pants with no one noticing. I mean, I could've tried to convince everyone that I had the hugest balls in the world, but I had to be realistic here.

Usually, I would have taken the ball off the shelf, gone down the escalator, and exited through the other store, but I didn't do that. No, I walked right out the front door with the basketball still in the box. I made it halfway through the parking lot before a security guard grabbed me by the collar.

16

"Do you have a receipt for that ball?"

The security guard brought me back to the store and gave me a chance to get rid of any drugs before the police came. I wasn't holding anything, but I thanked them for the opportunity because I usually would've had drugs on me. When the police finally arrived, they searched my pockets and found $150.

"Why'd you steal the ball? Why not just pay for it?"

I didn't feel like explaining to the cop how I got a thrill from stealing, so I just shrugged my shoulders and exercised my right to remain silent. He continued searching my pockets until he found a pack of cigarettes. He dumped the cigarettes onto the table, and a nickel bag of weed fell out. The security guards looked at me in disbelief. I was so high that I had forgotten it was even there. The cop threw me in the back of the paddy wagon and took me to the 15th district police station. Once inside, he started asking me all sorts of questions.

"What is your mother's occupation?"

"She works at a deli."

"What is your father's occupation?"

"He's a cop."

Silence filled the room. The cop took off his glasses and stared me down like he was going to punch me.

"Your father is a cop, and you smoke weed?"

I almost burst out in laughter until I realized the cop wasn't joking. It took me years to understand the embarrassment my dad must have experienced every time I called him from a jail cell. That day when I called my dad, he told me there was nothing he could do to get me out, but deep down inside, I knew he could have. I think he was just trying to teach me a lesson.

The lesson my father was trying to teach me actually worked. I spent that Saturday night in jail, contemplating my recent life decisions. I knew that if I hadn't taken Xanax, I would have never tried to steal a basketball like that, so I told myself I was done with taking them. Surprisingly, I was able to stop taking zannies with no problems. All it took was a lot of heavy drinking and a steady cloud of weed smoke.

Chapter 5

Throughout most of my high school years, I felt like an outcast. I went to a Catholic school, so most of my classmates didn't hang on the corner, do drugs, and listen to rap music like I did, at least not at first. This made me an open target for mockery, especially after they found out I was a rapper. I was constantly getting into trouble at school, too. It was mostly minor things that would have landed me a day or two in detention, but my teachers knew I was a rapper, so they made me spit a rhyme in front of the class instead of punishing me. They knew that the other students busted on me for it, so they figured the ridicule was punishment enough. But I'm glad my teachers made me spit rhymes in front of the class because it helped me overcome stage fright after a while. In fact, I actually enjoyed rhyming in front of a crowd. It got to a point where the more people that were there, the better I would perform.

By senior year, more and more people became interested in my rhymes. It was partly because I was getting better, but mainly because this was the year Eminem became famous. He changed the game and made it socially acceptable for white kids like myself to become rappers. Two of my close friends I met in high school, Drew and Craig, weren't part of the hip-hop crowd I usually hung out with. They didn't really like rap, but what brought us together was our mutual love for weed. We smoked every day after school, and even though they didn't like hip-hop, they always loved hearing me spit a rhyme after smoking a blunt. Craig always had this really potent weed that he stole from his dad. I always begged him to sell me some, but he never budged because he was afraid of stealing too much and getting caught. Besides, he smoked with us for free every day. What more could I ask for?

I lived two and a half miles away from school, so my mom gave me money for bus tokens every week. But she didn't know I walked home with Drew and Craig every day, so I always used the token money to buy weed instead. My mom also gave me lunch money every once in a while. Most kids used their lunch money to buy lunch, while others forked theirs over to the bullies. But I chose a different path and gave my lunch money to the dealers. I had to suffer the consequences when lunchtime came, though, and everybody was eating except for me. So, with my stomach rumbling and no money to eat, I started going around the cafeteria, begging people for loose change. Some of my classmates would offer me a quarter, but only if I spit a verse for them. Word got around, and my rhymes became

18

even more popular. So I started standing in the lunch line every day, rapping for spare change until I had enough money to eat.

As you already know, my parents punished me throughout most of my high school years, so it was rare for me to leave the house. However, there were times when I didn't want to leave, like when my parents went on vacation. My friends and I loved when my parents went away because it gave us a place to drink and smoke weed without cops busting us. It also allowed us to record rhymes on the computer with a cheap microphone I had bought. I recently found a demo album that we recorded, and all I could do was laugh at how terrible we sounded.

By this point, my siblings were old enough to drink legally, so they hung out at the bars a lot. But that didn't stop them from chilling with their little brother every once in a while. One night, while my parents were away, my brother Shawn was partying with us at the house. We were having a good time until Shawn pulled out a bag of coke and asked if we wanted any. I was furious because I had never done coke before and swore to myself I never would, so I told him to get the fuck away from me with that shit.

A few nights later, I found Shawn's ID on the floor in the laundry room. I was still mad about the other night, so I stole his ID and used it to buy alcohol. It worked most of the time, especially in the local bars. Sometimes I didn't even need the ID because they wouldn't card me. I even started hanging with my other brother, Mike, in the Prince Café, a hole-in-the-wall bar right down the street from our house.

One of my closest friends and next-door neighbor, Mark, found out I was hanging in the bars and presented me with a business opportunity. Mark was the go-to guy when I needed ounces of weed and other party supplies. Mark's proposal was for me to sell coke for him in the bars. At first, I was hesitant because I never did coke, but Mark brought up a good point: I didn't do coke, which is why I would be good at selling it. I would actually make money instead of sniffing up all the profits. So, I agreed to work for him and began hustling coke in the bars every night.

Hanging in the bar every night meant I was drinking a lot more. I was drinking so much that I even fell back from smoking weed for a while. I figured since I wasn't smoking weed anymore, I might as well sell it again. And if I'm going to sell weed, I might as well sell Xanax too. I wasn't even old enough to drink, yet all the bartenders knew me by name. Some of them even bought coke from me, so they didn't care if I sold it as long as I kept it discreet and made all of my transactions in the bathroom.

Everything seemed good for a while. Selling drugs became like a full-time job for me. I made enough money to drink for free every night and even bought myself a pager, so my customers could get in touch with me if I wasn't at the bar. I told them my hours of operation were 24/7, and some of them took me up on my word, paging me at six in the morning to get a bag of weed or coke before they went to work.

Getting drunk in the bar every night was always a good time, but I started to blackout more than I would like to admit. Sometimes my mom woke up to find half-naked girls sleeping next to me on the couch. I didn't even know their names or remember talking to them, let alone bringing them home. It was embarrassing for my mom to see me like that. There were also plenty of nights when I embarrassed myself in front of my friends, too.

A perfect example would be after I broke my ankle playing basketball. I had to get around on crutches for a few weeks, but I didn't let that slow me down when it came to drinking. One night, I was drinking vodka at my friend Kenny's house, and on my way to the bathroom, I knocked his TV over and almost broke it. When I finally got to the bathroom, I fell backward into his bathtub while pissing. I tried to grab the shower curtain to stop myself from falling, but it snapped right off of the hook. I was lying in his bathtub, covered in piss. Between my broken ankle and being pissed ass drunk, I couldn't get myself up and had to scream for help. My friends heard me, but they couldn't open the door because it was locked. They were forced to break the door down so they could get me out. Needless to say, Kenny never invited me back to his house after that night.

Chapter 6

My best friend, Sean, moved to Florida when we were younger but then moved back again when we were teenagers. Only this time, he moved to New Jersey, right across the river from Philly. Sean drank with me a lot, but he never did drugs. He didn't even like the fact that I smoked weed. He was extremely intelligent and got straight A's in school. We were almost total opposites, but we were still best friends.

Every weekend I went to Sean's house in Jersey, or he came over to hang out in Philly. When he came to Philly, getting drunk was easy because we could just get one of my brothers to buy it for us. But sneaking beer to Jersey was hard since my parents were the ones who drove me. However, it was easy to hide weed in my bag without them noticing. Now, even though I sold weed, sometimes a drought would hit, and I wouldn't be able to find anything.

If I couldn't find weed in Philly, I definitely wouldn't find it in Jersey. Sean lived in the suburbs, so there weren't dealers standing on the corner like they do in the city. One time I got so desperate that I walked into the woods, ripped leaves off of a random plant, rolled them up into a joint, and then smoked it. My theory was this: marijuana was a plant that got me high, so maybe other plants could get me high, too. It wasn't the craziest idea I ever came up with.

Later that day, I started to get really itchy. It started in my hands but then spread to my arms and face. I even felt an itch on the back of my tongue, which quickly developed into a sore throat. It didn't take long to figure out that the leaves I had smoked came from a poison ivy plant. You can laugh, but I was a city boy, so I'd never seen poison ivy before. The sore throat lasted about a week, but the humor of my stupidity will last a lifetime.

Sean and I hung out periodically throughout our high school years. When visiting, I got to know some of his friends from Jersey. After high school, Sean moved away to college, but I continued to go to Jersey to hang out with his friends. One of my friends from Philly, Tom, had a car. So whenever we felt like escaping the city, we just drove across the bridge. It was only a 20-minute ride from our neighborhood, but it felt like an entirely different world. The thing I loved most about Jersey was how it boosted my confidence. It seemed normal to do drugs and get into fistfights in the city, so I kind of felt like I was a nobody. But in the suburbs, I felt like a big shot. They knew I was a rapper who sold drugs, so they looked at me as if I was this thuggish, inner-city gang member or something. It gave me a false sense of pride, which I used to mask my insecurities.

As with all great things, our Jersey trips eventually had to end. It happened one night when Tom and I went to a party. We weren't even there for five minutes before the cops came and broke it up. On our way home, we stopped at a 7-11 to buy some blunts. As we pulled into the lot, it was apparent that this was the local hangout spot; there must have been at least 20 people there. As soon as I got out of the car, a blonde-haired teen approached us.

"Hey man, remember me?"

I didn't have a clue as to who he was. I thought maybe he was at the party we just came from, so I reached out to shake his hand when all of a sudden—CRACK! A sucker punch caught me by surprise as five guys surrounded me, throwing punches from every angle. I tried to fight back, but I didn't stand a chance. After they pinned me to the ground, the blonde-haired kid climbed on top of me and pounded my face in. That's when I noticed the brass knuckles. I guess five verses one wasn't good enough odds for him; he needed to throw in a pair of brass knuckles just to sweeten the deal. Not to mention the four other guys who held Tom down so he couldn't jump in and help me.

After they finished beating me, I got back on my feet and wiped the blood from my leaking nose. When I saw the blood on my hand, I started to laugh deliriously. My abnormal behavior caused them to stare at me as if I were a madman. I stepped to the blonde-haired kid and spit blood in his face, followed by a haymaker to his jaw. But his friends quickly took me to the ground and held me there until I calmed down. After a few minutes, they let us go, and Tom and I got back in the car.

"We're getting everyone from the neighborhood and coming back to fuck these dudes up!"

What I saw next is something I will never forget: a deranged look in Tom's eyes. It was the meanest, angriest look I had ever seen on another human being. He didn't say a word as he reversed the car out of the parking spot. He silently turned the wheel, shifted into drive, and stared at the punks who just jumped me.

"Nah, Brain, we fuckin' 'em up right now!"

Tom suddenly floored the gas pedal, barreling the car toward the unsuspecting punks. Some were lucky and got out of the way just in time, but others were not so lucky. Tom's car crashed into a parked car, which pushed it into another parked vehicle. The blonde-haired kid stood between the two parked cars and got crushed in between.

SMASH! A brick shattered Tom's back window, and glass hit me in the back of the head. Tom quickly maneuvered the car out of the parking lot to escape, but before long, we were being chased by three other vehicles. Tom sped down the main road as the other cars pulled beside us, with punks leaning out the windows, trying to hit us with pipes and baseball bats.

The high-speed chase ended when we approached a red light. Tom slowed down at the intersection, but when he saw a cop across the street, he ran the red light to get the cop's attention. I must admit, that was the first time I was ever relieved to see a cop. The cop pulled us over, and Tom immediately jumped out of the car and pointed at the guys chasing us.

"LOOK WHAT THEY JUST DID TO MY BOY!"

The cop must've felt threatened by Tom's erratic behavior because he drew his gun and instructed Tom to get down on the ground. After the cop placed Tom in handcuffs, I explained how we were being chased by a group of guys who had just jumped me. The cop told me to sit tight and then went back to his car to use the radio. When he came back, he placed Tom under arrest.

"What? We were the ones that got jumped. Why is he under arrest?"

Apparently, it's illegal to mow people down with a car; who knew, right? When an ambulance arrived a few minutes later to examine my face, they strongly suggested I go to the hospital. But I told them I was fine, and it didn't even hurt that much. To convince me otherwise, they gave me a mirror to look at myself. The busted nose was the first thing I noticed on my blood-covered face, followed by the swollen eye that looked like it was about to pop out of my socket. Honestly, I probably should have gone to the hospital, but I didn't have medical insurance, so I decided not to go.

While waiting for my ride, the police informed me they had found the blonde-haired kid who jumped me, and his name was Danny. When I heard the name, I immediately knew who he was and why he had jumped me. We got into a fight a few years earlier. Actually, it wasn't so much of a fight as it was me being a bully. When Sean first moved to Jersey, I bullied a lot of the kids there. I thought I was tough because I was from the city, but I was nothing more than an asshole.

The cops told me if I wanted to press charges, I could, but if I dropped the charges against Danny, Danny would drop the charges against Tom. It was a no-brainer. I didn't want to see my boy face jail time, so I agreed to drop the charges. After that night, Tom and I vowed never to return to Jersey ever again.

Chapter 7

I barely graduated high school, so nobody was surprised when I decided not to go to college. Instead, I hung out in the bars every night and sold drugs. It had its moments, but after a while, it just wasn't enough. I wanted something new and exciting in my life, so my introduction to LSD, or "acid," couldn't have come at a better time. My old heads always talked about taking acid and how much fun it was to see the trails and other hallucinations. After hearing a few stories, I told my old heads I wanted to try it, and the next day, one of them got some for me.

The first time I dropped acid, I took it by myself. It wasn't like I was literally by myself but was just the only one who took it that night. I was chilling with my friends Joe G, Lou, and Vicky, who were afraid to try it at the time. I didn't have the patience to wait for them to grow a set of balls, so I just took it without them. My first experience with acid was nothing like I expected it to be. I didn't see any trails, colorful visuals, or anything like that. There weren't any little blue goblins sliding down rainbows or talking squirrels who gave me inspirational advice like I had hoped. I actually got pissed because I thought my old heads sold me some fake shit.

A half-hour later, I went outside to smoke a cigarette. That's when it hit me. I didn't see any visuals or have any hallucinations, but I felt it: an uncontrollable urge to laugh. I had no clue what I was even laughing at, but I was hysterical. And whenever I thought about how I was literally laughing at nothing at all, it made me laugh even more. This wasn't just a few spurts of laughter, either. No, this was non-stop, sidesplitting laughing that went on for hours and hours. My friends thought I had lost my mind, which made me laugh even more!

After my night of hysterical laughing, my friends became curious and wanted to try acid for themselves. So we dropped some LSD and went to our favorite hangout spot: Keystone Park. Keystone Park was nothing more than a dirty basketball court in a small park next to some train tracks. On any given night, there were 30-40 of us chilling there. The cops rarely messed with us because we respected the neighbors and always cleaned up our mess. No other crews from the neighborhood messed with us either, probably because we never gave them a reason to.

My second experience with acid was vastly different from my first. I stared at a tree trunk for over an hour because I saw miniature aliens building a village on the tree bark. That night, I realized how much I loved taking acid. Not only because of how cheap it was, but because it made me feel like I was in another dimension or on another planet, which allowed me to escape reality.

I started off by dropping LSD only on the weekends, but it became much more frequent after a while. Sometimes I would take acid and stay awake all night, only to drop another hit in the morning and be high again all day. 12 hours later, it would wear off, and I'd take another hit and stay up all night again. Being high on acid for 36 straight hours can give you some of the craziest hallucinations you could ever imagine.

During my LSD phase, Joe G got me a job at the diner he worked at. It was a shitty under-the-table dishwashing gig, but the people who worked there were pretty cool. I felt right at home because most of them got high, just like I did. One day, Joe G and I dropped some acid during work. After it kicked in, we quickly discovered how potent this particular LSD was. I added an entire bottle of dish soap to the sink and put the faucet on full blast. We stood there for about 20 minutes, mesmerized by the bubbles forming in the sink.

As we took in the beautiful view of what we called "Bubble Mountain," our boss walked in and was furious to see the overflowed sink and soap suds piling up on the floor. He yelled at us, but we couldn't stop laughing at him. I thought he was a clown performing for a circus, so when he finished screaming, I started to clap and asked if he knew any magic tricks. Surprisingly, we were not fired. In fact, he promoted Joe G to short-order cook the following week.

Acid is the craziest drug I have ever done. One of the weirdest things about it is how your surroundings can affect the outcome of your acid trip. Ideally, acid should be experienced in a peaceful environment, such as an open field in the middle of East Bumblefuck, where you can look up at the stars and be at peace with yourself. But in the city, these types of environments didn't exist, so the best we could do was the Delaware River.

I had an incredible experience the first time I dropped acid at the river. Everything seemed perfect. The river looked beautiful beneath the night sky as the moonlight reflected off the ripples on the water's surface. I thought I was in paradise, at least up until the sun began to rise. After the sun shed light on my surroundings, I noticed how disgusting it was. Trash and debris littered the shoreline. Styrofoam containers floated next to used tires in the water. The horizon changed from a beautiful night sky to a smoggy backdrop of factories pumping chemicals into the air. The reality of where I lived brought my acid trip to an abrupt end.

Acid trips weren't always fun. I didn't always see cool visuals and have peaceful nights like I did at the river. One night, we dropped some acid and decided to smoke a blunt on the train tracks. As we trespassed onto the tracks, a cop car slammed on its brakes and shined a flashlight on us, so we ran down the tracks and hid behind a utility shed. We realized the cop didn't even try to chase us, so we just stayed at the shed and sparked the blunt. While smoking our weed, a helicopter crossed over the tracks. But it was a reasonable distance from us, so nobody thought anything of it. A few minutes later, the chopper flew over the tracks again; that's when I got worried.

The helicopter came back for a third time and hovered directly above the tracks. As the spotlight crept closer and closer, we knew it would be impossible to outrun it. Our only option was to hide on the other side of the utility shed, opposite the train tracks, with our backs pressed up against the wall.

I wasn't even sure if this helicopter was real or not. It could have been a bird flying around, and the LSD was just making me think it was a helicopter. Without knowing 100%, I had no choice but to act as if it were real. When the spotlight reached us, I could see the silhouette of the shed. My heart was beating so fast that I thought it was going to explode out of my chest. The blinding spotlight and deafening sound of the helicopter left me terrified. I felt myself slipping away from reality, and there was nothing I could do about it.

After the helicopter passed us, we ran farther down the tracks until we reached a hole in the fence leading to another section of the park. We took cover beneath some trees to stay out of the helicopter's sight, which was still circling the area. Everyone else seemed to be relieved that we escaped; everyone except for me. I started to freak out. The sound of the chopper led me to believe I was in Vietnam. I found myself in the middle of a jungle; all my friends had turned into animals. One grew a tail and jumped around like a monkey, while another had wings and flew around me in circles. One of them even looked like a bug, with antennas on his head.

They tried to calm me down, but I couldn't understand their words. The only thing I heard was animal noises. I tried to speak in their native tongue and roared like a lion. When that didn't work, I mimicked a monkey with an "Ooo ooo ahh ahh ahh," but I still couldn't understand them when they spoke. My boy Tony opened his mouth to say something, but to me, he sounded like a barking dog.

Thank God Mark was there because he was the only one who realized that I was spiraling down the rabbit hole. He grabbed my shirt collar with both hands and pulled me toward him until we were face to face. Doing this brought me back to reality for a moment, allowing me to hear his words instead of animal noises.

"We might be animals, but you are a MAN! You are the king of the jungle, so tame these fucking animals!"

He said exactly what I needed to hear. Suddenly, I felt like I was in complete control. The animal noises no longer scared me. In fact, it sounded like a sweet melody. I felt like I was in the Lion King musical as all the animals began singing. Once I snapped back to reality and could communicate with my friends again, I convinced everyone to go to the basketball courts, where life made more sense.

When we got to the courts, a customer of mine stopped by and bought some coke from me. I didn't want to lose the money, so I walked to my house to drop it off, but when I got home, my wallet was missing. I rushed back to the courts, only to find that everyone had vanished, and my wallet was lying on the ground. When I opened it, all my money was gone; fucking snakes!

I didn't care so much about the money but was more pissed that my so-called "friends" would steal from me. I walked around the neighborhood until I found them hanging outside 7-11. They swore up and down that they had nothing to do with it, but the more they denied it, the more the LSD took effect. My friends slowly turned into demons. Their skin glowed bright red, and horns protruded from their skulls. Dark clouds formed in the sky above their heads, and I knew I had to get away. I ran off by myself and spent the rest of the night alone. I couldn't trust anyone, so I avoided human interaction at all costs until the LSD finally wore off.

The people I hung with were exactly like me. I didn't trust them, and I'm sure they didn't trust me either. That's just how our neighborhood was. We were all snakes who lied and stole from everyone we met. We had been stabbing each other in the back for years, but it never bothered me until that night. I was getting sick of the lifestyle I was living, but the lifestyle wasn't sick of me yet.

28

Chapter 8

After I discovered LSD, one of my friends turned me on to PCP, which is sometimes called "wet" or "angel dust." I enjoyed smoking wet, but it made me vulnerable because it felt like I moved in slow motion while the rest of the world moved at a normal pace. This made me an easy target for anyone trying to rob me, so I didn't smoke it too much. That doesn't mean I never smoked it, though; I definitely had a few binges.

The first time I smoked wet was in an alleyway with my boys, Tony and Tim. It tasted very different from weed, with an aroma similar to nail polish remover. After we finished smoking, I felt like I was in an alternate universe. Simple things, such as walking, proved to be a challenge. It seemed as if the laws of physics, for example, gravity, were somewhat distorted. In an attempt to walk, I lifted my left foot as high as I could and stretched it out as far as possible. When my foot finally hit the ground, the horizon shifted to the left. It was like I tilted the entire city with the weight of my foot. I took another step with my right foot, and this time the entire world rocked to the right. All of this happened in slow motion, and it felt like I was stuck in the Matrix. By the time we reached the end of the alley, it seemed as if two hours had passed, even though, in reality, it was probably more like two minutes.

I stepped out of the alley and into the street. Vroom! I almost got hit by a car traveling at the speed of light, but thankfully, Tim pulled me back onto the pavement just in time. I looked to see if any more cars were coming, and after looking both ways, I looked again, and then again. I must've stood there for five minutes before my friends assured me and then reassured me that no cars were coming. I finally grew a set of balls, took a leap of faith, and crossed the quiet, lonely, one-lane residential street.

Shortly after my introduction to PCP, another drug became popular among my friends. MDMA, which is known by many names, such as ecstasy, Molly, E, or even X, was something that I didn't need any convincing for me to try. I heard stories about E long before I could ever get my hands on it. While high on E, one touch from a girl could feel like an orgasm. Needless to say, I was curious to try it, and so were my friends.

Tony's girlfriend was attending Delaware Valley College and had some single friends that wanted to meet us. We saw this as the perfect opportunity to experience E for the first time. We popped our E pills before we got to the college, and they kicked in shortly after we arrived. It was the most fantastic feeling I had ever felt in my life! The feeling of euphoria was intense. It felt like someone had permanently glued a smile to my face. My confidence was at an all-time high, so sparking a conversation with the girls was super easy. I kept saying all the right things at all the right moments and had them smiling and laughing all night long. I even spit freestyles about how incredible I felt and how beautiful they all were.

A few moments later, I jumped on the bed and started dancing. One girl, Kristy, joined me, and the sensation of her skin touching mine was amazing. We started making out, and the next thing I knew, our hands were down each other's pants. Meanwhile, our friends were still in the room, but we continued as if they weren't even there.

Our friends eventually gave us privacy, and without going into details, I'm sure you can figure out what happened next. It felt like I was in heaven, and we kept going at it non-stop for an extraordinarily long time. Nobody told me it was nearly impossible to orgasm while high on E. We finally stopped three and a half hours later, as Kristy was exhausted and our friends kept banging on the door. We all had so much fun that night. So much, in fact, that popping E instantly became part of our weekly routine.

I met up with Kristy at her college once or twice after that, and every time I was there, I couldn't help but think how beautiful the area was. It was in the middle of nowhere, surrounded by farmlands, the perfect place to drop some LSD. So one night, I convinced my boys to get some acid and take a trip to her college. But I knew Kristy wouldn't want all my friends to visit because she had work the next morning. So instead, I called and asked if just me and Tim could come hang out with her, to which she happily agreed.

Me and seven of my boys dropped acid before piling into two separate cars and making our way to the college in East Bumblefuck, Pennsylvania. I kept thinking about how this poor girl had no clue what she was in for. She was expecting just two of us, but all eight of us greeted her when she answered the door. She was pissed at me for lying to her but let us into her dorm anyway. However, she quickly regretted it because we were being loud and obnoxious all night. Around 2:00 a.m., Kristy turned off the lights and tried to fall asleep, but leaving us in total darkness made the LSD kick in even more.

I sensed how aggravated Kristy was getting, and it started to affect my high. Her voice sounded like nails on a chalkboard, and the room shrank to the point where I began to feel trapped. I tried to convince my friends to check out the nearby farmlands, look up at the stars, and all that other hippy shit people do while high on acid, but they didn't care about that stuff.

Joe G was the only one willing to come with me, so we ventured out to escape the chaos brewing in the room. The dorms were surrounded by farmlands, so we decided to go cow-tipping. We were city boys who had never seen a real live cow before, so we thought it would be a funny story to tell. We walked around for a while but couldn't find any cows. The only thing we could find was a vegetable farm. The rows of crops seemed like something you would see on TV. Being from the city, we thought we walked onto the set of Green Acres. We stumbled across a sign, and I couldn't believe my eyes when I read it. I thought the LSD was causing me to read words that weren't really there, but Joe G confirmed that he also saw the sign.

The sign read, "Do not eat these vegetables! They are scientific tests and are not edible!"

We were baffled by what was going on. We couldn't control ourselves when we began rolling around on the ground, dying of laughter. I was tempted to eat a tomato just to see what it tasted like but was afraid I would grow a third arm or fish gills or something. We continued to admire the view surrounding us. We were used to the city, with its dirty streets and graffiti-covered brick buildings, so the pleasant, open landscape was a nice change of scenery. The entire area was beautiful, and neither of us wanted to leave, but the sun was rising, and it was time to go home.

A couple of weeks later, someone invited us to another college party, but all of our friends who had cars were stuck working that night. However, it was Pete's birthday, and his grandmother had just given him her old car as a birthday gift. The only problem was that Pete didn't have a license yet. He also didn't have insurance or registration, but Pete didn't care about that kind of shit, and honestly, neither did we. He knew how to drive, which was good enough in our book.

We made it to the party, drank all night, and headed home around 3:30 a.m. The plan was to drop Tony off first, but we came to a red light two blocks before we got to his house. Pete, drunk as shit, said "Fuck it" and drove right through the red light. As we crossed the intersection, we noticed two cop cars that were initially hidden from our view. Obviously, they saw us run the red light because one of them followed us.

"Yo, lemme out here. I'll walk da rest of the way," Tony said.

"Gimme a minute. I wanna lose these cops first," Pete responded.

Pete stopped at the stop sign and turned the corner. Once we were out of the cop's view, he floored the gas pedal. The cop was a block behind us by the time he flashed those red and blue lights. Pete was speeding recklessly through the neighborhood, running stop signs as if they weren't even there. We begged him to stop before he killed us, but we might as well have been talking to a brick wall.

Pete whipped the corner onto the main artery and ran every red light we came across. As we approached one of the red lights, I saw a car crossing the intersection, but before I could warn him, BOOM! The other car spun around in a 360-degree fashion. It didn't even faze Pete; he just kept on driving. A couple of blocks later, we reached Frankford Avenue and Levick Street, one of the busiest intersections in the neighborhood. With police still hot on our trail, Pete didn't hesitate to fly right through the red light, almost hitting another car in the process.

After narrowly avoiding another accident, Pete cut the wheel and escaped through the parking lot of a shopping center. When we exited on the other side, there were no cops behind us, so we tried to convince Pete to pull over and let us out, but he wouldn't listen.

When we reached the next intersection, the flashing lights suddenly appeared behind us once again, and just like before, we flew through stop signs that seemed to be invisible to Pete. After a few blocks, the red and blue lights faded in the rear windshield, so Pete made one last attempt to lose them. He tried his best to maneuver around the corner, but the speed at which we were going made it impossible to make such a tight turn, causing us to crash into a parked car. We all piled out of the totaled vehicle and made our escape. As I ran in what seemed to be slow motion, I once again noticed the familiar glow of those infamous red and blue lights. I turned my head to look and saw four cop cars, not even a block behind me. I knew I had to do something slick if I wanted to stay out of jail.

When we reached the intersection, some of my friends ran straight, while the rest turned right, but I turned left. I dashed around the corner, out of the cop's view, and threw the baseball cap I was wearing behind a bush. Next, I shoved my t-shirt down my pants and hoped that the wife beater I wore underneath would be enough to throw them off from my original description. I then stopped running and walked at a normal pace. I walked as if nothing was wrong; as if I wasn't just involved in a high-speed chase with the law. A cop car turned the corner, pulled beside me, took one quick look, and then sped off. They were searching for a guy with a baseball cap and a black t-shirt; I was wearing neither. Plus, I wasn't running, which led them to believe I wasn't the guy they were looking for.

I made another left at the next corner, walked halfway down the block, and another cop car approached me from behind. They drove beside me and followed at the same pace I was walking until I finally looked over at them. They were watching my every move, so I just shrugged my shoulders and kept walking as if nothing was wrong. A moment later, they sped off down the street.

When I reached the end of the block, a few neighbors were standing on the corner, observing the police activity at the scene of the accident. I noticed another cop car was approaching, so I used this opportunity to my advantage and blended in with the crowd. Standing only a block away from Pete's crashed car, I played dumb and approached one of the neighbors.

"Yo man, what happened?"

"Some drunk assholes crashed a stolen car."

The car wasn't stolen, but I couldn't let them know that I knew that. So I just shook my head in disgust and agreed with him. Another cop car passed by us, but they didn't even look at me this time. As far as they were concerned, I was just another neighbor looking at the car crash. I waited a few minutes until it was safe enough to leave without raising suspicion. On my journey home, cops passed by me left and right, but none of them tried to stop me.

The next day, I realized that I hadn't heard from any of my friends yet. So, I gave Tony a call.

"Yo, what happened? Did you get away last night?"

"Nah, man, they caught me. What da fuck happened to you?"

"Wait, if they caught you, then how you out already?"

"They had nothing to charge us with. Pete was the only one who got charged."

"Damn, they caught Pete too?"

"They caught everyone! Everyone except you! How da fuck did you even get away?"

I explained how I ditched my hat and shirt and just walked away like nothing happened. Tony couldn't believe that it actually worked. Honestly, I could barely believe it myself. A crazy night like this would probably make most people reconsider their lifestyle choices. But for me, it wasn't even enough to slow me down.

Chapter 9

By the time I was 20 years old, my parents had realized that my life was going nowhere. I kept jumping from one dead-end job to the next, with no real goals for the future. They knew I liked computers, so they convinced me to enroll in an internet programming course at a computer training school. As much as I hated school, I knew I needed a good-paying job and figured this school could help me get one. It was easy at first but soon became difficult because of my one-track mind and short attention span.

I began the course with good intentions and tried to be responsible by only partying on the weekends. I was really interested in learning about computers and wanted to focus on my schoolwork so I could get good grades. At first, everything was going as planned. I was even studying every night, something I had never done in my life. But it wouldn't be long before all of my plans came crumbling down.

One of my classmates was a major pothead. He invited me to smoke a joint one day after school, and I gladly accepted his offer. But the weed he had was garbage, so I rolled up some of the weed I was selling. My weed got him high as fuck, and he instantly became one of my best customers. Once word got out at school that I sold weed, a lot of my classmates started buying from me. In fact, I was selling more weed at school than I did at the bars. Here I was trying to better myself, yet I was doing the same shit I was trying to get away from.

It wasn't long before my classmates and I started a daily ritual, where we sat at the bus stop every day after school and smoked a few blunts. I figured that if they smoked weed every day and got good grades, then I could, too. But being the addict I was, smoking after school wasn't enough, so I started smoking before school, too. In a matter of weeks, I went from a straight A student to a C student, but none of that mattered when life came to a screeching halt.

One day, I came home from school to find my brother Shawn in tears. Shawn had always been an attention seeker, so I wasn't sure if this was just Shawn being Shawn or if something serious had actually happened. Regardless, he was still my brother, so I wanted to make sure he was OK.

"Shawn, wassup, bro? You aight?"

"Something's wrong with Mom. She's in the hospital."

Shawn was known to exaggerate at times, plus he was a pathological liar, so I couldn't believe anything that came out of his mouth. I assumed my mom just went for something minor since he couldn't give me any details, so I just patted him on the back and told him everything would be OK.

Later that day, my dad came home and told me what had happened. My mom was getting ready for work when she suddenly collapsed. Her eyes rolled to the back of her head as she began spurting out random numbers and letters; it turned out that she had a brain aneurysm. My dad saw the confused look on my face, so he explained what a brain aneurysm was: a tiny blood bubble in her brain. And in my mom's case, the blood bubble ruptured. This took my whole family by surprise. My mom was only 49 years old and in near-perfect health. She never drank, did drugs, or even smoked cigarettes. My mom was a good-hearted person who even attended church every Sunday. So, I began questioning God by asking, "How can you allow something like this to happen?"

The reality of the situation didn't really hit me until I saw my mom lying on that hospital bed. They shaved half her head, revealing an incision where they cut into her skull to operate on her. They hooked her up to all types of tubes and machines and put her in a drug-induced coma, so she wasn't awake or able to talk to us. The heart rate monitor made a beeping sound every second or so, which made me realize how fragile life really was.

That entire week was hell for my family, but we stuck together day and night, waiting for a doctor to bring us some good news. Since my mom was in the ICU, they only allowed two visitors at a time, and even though she couldn't respond, we still talked to her because we knew she was listening. That was probably the worst week of my life. Each day, her condition deteriorated more and more. Even though I was hoping for the best, I was prepared for the worst.

My mom was in the hospital all week, so when the weekend came, I planned to get extra shitfaced to escape the reality of what was happening. That Friday night, I partied as usual, but that Saturday night was a little different. As I was getting ready to leave the house, the phone rang. It was my boy Sean asking if I wanted to go catch a movie. Shrek was playing in the theater, and although I was hesitant at first, I ultimately agreed to go. I'm glad I went because it was just what I needed. I hadn't laughed that hard in a long time. But I kept getting annoyed throughout the entire movie because my pager was blowing up. I didn't recognize the number but assumed it was one of my customers trying to get some weed or coke, so I just ignored it.

When I finally got home, I called the number on my pager to find out it was my cousin Chris. He told me to stay put because he was coming to get me. It didn't take a brain surgeon to realize why my cousin was coming to scoop me up. I only saw Chris at family gatherings, so why else would he pick me up so late on a Saturday night? A few minutes later, when I heard the horn honk, I went outside to find not only my cousin Chris but also my cousin Tommy in the car with him. Now I definitely knew something was up, so I didn't even give them a chance to say hi.

"Is my mom dead?"

"I'm going to be honest with you, pal. She ain't going to make it through the night," Chris said with sorrow in his eyes.

Although my body was physically in the back seat of the car, my mind was elsewhere. I felt like a fucking zombie. I didn't know how to react or what to expect. All I knew was my mom was going to die, and I was scared shitless. When we got to the hospital, my dad told us that the doctors could technically still save my mom, but she would be a vegetable for the rest of her life. My mom would have never wanted that, so my dad had no choice but to pull the plug. I'm glad I went to the movies that night instead of the bar. The fact that I was sober on a Saturday night was more than just a coincidence; it was more like a miracle. I am so grateful I had a clear mind when I said my final goodbyes to my mom, but being sober did not make it any easier.

I held my mom's hand and told her I loved her, and even though she couldn't say it back, I knew she loved me too. As I spoke my last words to her, I noticed a tear rolling down her cheek. That single teardrop broke my heart, and it still breaks my heart to write about it now. I don't think I have ever seen my dad cry before; it's hard for him to show emotions. But that night, I saw tears in his eyes for the first time ever. Between losing my mom and watching how it affected my dad, it turned out to be the worst night of my life. My mother was pronounced dead shortly after midnight on June 3rd, 2001. Her life was cut way too short. When we got home, my dad tried to offer me some good advice.

"Don't go drowning yourself in alcohol. It won't bring her back."

I should have listened to my dad, but like everything else he tried to teach me, I had to learn the hard way. All the drinking in the world didn't bring her back, and it didn't make the pain go away either. In fact, the more I drank, the angrier I became at God. My mom was the most righteous person I have ever known. She didn't have a bad bone in her body, so how could God let this happen?

To make matters worse, my sister was eight months pregnant with my niece, Caitlyn. A part of me died when I realized my mom would never get to meet her granddaughter. This led me to think about other things my mom would never witness, such as me graduating from computer school or eventually getting married. Sadness, fear, and anger ruled those dark days, but nobody around me would ever know because I hid my feelings behind a fake smile. On the inside, I was an emotional wreck. But instead of facing those emotions, I dealt with them the only way I knew how, with drugs and alcohol.

On the day of the funeral, a massive crowd of people came to pay their respects to my mom. The line went out the funeral home door and stretched all the way around the corner. I never realized that my mom touched so many lives. I heard so many beautiful stories about my mom that day, and everyone had nothing but great things to say about her. They loved how her smile could light up a room and bring joy to everyone around her. I didn't realize it until after she was gone, but my mom was one of my best friends. She was the most incredible woman I had ever known, and I missed her already.

When my mom died, I was still selling coke, but I didn't let her death interfere with my hustle. It's not like selling drugs came with funeral leave or vacation days. I knew that if I stopped meeting my customers, even for just a few days, then they would find new dealers. Up until this point, I had never used cocaine, which was why I was good at selling it. When I was younger, I promised myself I would never touch hard drugs like coke and heroin. But after losing my mom, I didn't give a fuck about anything anymore. This included stupid little promises I made to myself, as if I lived by some moral code. I didn't have time for that after-school special bullshit.

I never planned to snort my first line of coke; it just kind of happened on a Tuesday afternoon while I was taking a shit. I didn't even think twice about it. I emptied a bag of coke onto the back of the toilet, rolled up a dollar bill, and took my first sniff. It hit me quicker than a speeding train, and I immediately fell in love with it! I had an instant burst of energy and felt like I could accomplish anything. A million thoughts and ideas ran through my mind, and I loved every second of it.

Cocaine wasn't cheap, so I barely used it at first. I was more concerned with drowning my sorrows in alcohol. Some nights, I would drink an entire bottle of Bacardi 151 by myself. Other nights, Tony and I would split a half-gallon of vodka. I hadn't even reached the legal drinking age yet, and already I was a full-blown alcoholic.

Drinking heavy liquor often came with blackouts, but finding a solution to my blackout problem didn't take long at all. One night, at the bar, I snorted a little coke, which helped me to stay awake and drink all night without passing out. This started a new trend for me. I would stay out all night and party right into the morning hours. This wasn't a problem on the weekends when I could sleep in. But during the week, when I was still drunk and high from the night before, my classmates became concerned. They tried to talk to me, but it was useless. No matter how hard they tried, nobody could get through to me. I didn't even care about school anymore. Every day I just sat there, staring at a blank computer screen as everyone else took notes and did their work. I felt like a lost soul.

I don't know how it happened, but I somehow graduated with the rest of my class. Maybe the teachers felt bad for me and just decided to let me graduate; who knows? What I do know is that my family was very proud of me, but I felt ashamed because I knew I didn't deserve it. So I did what I always did. I pushed those feelings of shame and guilt deep down inside and buried them with more booze and drugs.

After graduation, I got a temp job at a small company that edited websites. It was supposed to be a three-month gig, but I did such a good job that they kept me on for an extra couple of months. However, the position eventually ended, and I was right back where I started. After months of searching for a new job in the computer field, I concluded that my diploma from DPT Business School was worthless.

My dad kept on hassling me to find a new job. So I stopped looking for the perfect computer job and settled for one at Kinko's. Working with a Xerox machine was probably the closest I would ever get to working with computers, anyway. The job was a lot better than I expected it to be. For the first time in my life, I actually loved my job. All I had to do was help customers make copies and ring their orders up. It was the easiest job I ever had, and I felt right at home because my co-workers partied just as much as I did.

A few weeks after starting my new position, I showed up at work one morning with a nasty hangover. So my co-worker handed me a small white pill with the number "512" imprinted on it.

"What's this?"

"It's a Perc. Just take it. You'll feel a lot better."

Without hesitation, I swallowed my first Percocet, or "Perc," for short. Honestly, I didn't know much about Percs. I knew they were painkillers, but whenever I heard the term "painkiller," I always thought of aspirin or Tylenol, which didn't do shit for hangovers. So, it surprised me a few minutes later when my hangover slowly faded away. Not only was my headache gone, but I also felt this strange sensation. It felt like a thousand kittens kneading their soft paws on my chest, which came with a super intense euphoric feeling throughout my entire body. A burst of energy made me feel like I was ready to take on the world. I'd been searching for this feeling my entire life, and I finally found it.

After I started taking Percs, I got caught in a vicious cycle. Every night I'll go out drinking and snorting coke, and then I'd pop a Perc in the morning to get rid of the hangover. I'll go to work, come home, and do it all again. I didn't know it at the time, but Percs are highly addictive. Unbeknownst to me, I was slowly forming a physical dependency on opioids. A few weeks later, one or two Percs just weren't cutting it anymore. I reached the point where I needed three or four just to feel normal, even if I didn't have a hangover. I couldn't afford it anymore, so I stopped taking them, but this made me feel like shit! My stomach would hurt, I would feel weak, every muscle in my body ached, and my anxiety would go through the roof. I didn't know it was withdrawal, though. I just thought I was getting the flu or something. So, I convinced myself to take more painkillers just until the flu was over, and then I'd stop. I didn't know I was only making things worse.

Eventually, I figured out that it wasn't the flu but the Percocet withdrawal that was making me sick. This gave me even more of a reason to stop taking them, but it was easier said than done. Since I couldn't deal with the withdrawal symptoms, I tried to ease the pain by replacing the Percs with other drugs. So I would wake up every day, snort some coke, pop an E pill for breakfast, and then smoke a joint on my way to work. I honestly didn't think anything was wrong with living like this; it all seemed normal to me. As long as I woke up and went to work every day, then who was I bothering, right?

Even though I replaced Percs with other drugs, I couldn't completely stay away from them. No matter how hard I tried, they kept calling my name. I knew I would never be able to stop, so I told myself I would be OK as long as I didn't do them every day. So, I started a cycle where one day I would do Percs, the next day a little coke, the next day an E pill, and then repeat the process all over again. I really thought I had it under control, but little did I know I was just digging myself into a deeper hole.

Because I wasn't taking Percs every day for my hangovers, I started missing a lot of work. On the days when I did make it to work, I would show up late and still smell like booze from the night before. Sometimes, when my friends dropped me off at work, I would sit in the parking lot to finish my last beer or snort my last line before starting my shift. I just wasn't thinking rationally anymore.

I was out drinking and snorting coke one night with a friend when I suddenly remembered I had to go to jury duty in a few hours. My friend offered to drive me since I was giving her free coke all night. On our way there, we hit a lot of traffic on the highway and began snorting lines off the dashboard. I'm sure other drivers saw us, but we just didn't care. When I arrived at the Criminal Justice Center, I saw people emptying their pockets and waiting to go through the metal detectors. Fuck me! I forgot I had to empty my pockets and slide my belongings through the machine. Usually, it wouldn't be an issue, but I just happened to have an ounce of weed in my pocket that day. How could I be so stupid? I didn't know what to do; cops were everywhere. I was sweating bullets. It's not like it was just a nickel bag or two. It was an entire ounce, worth about $100, so I couldn't just throw it away. Instead, I took my chances and emptied everything except the weed from my pockets. I passed through the metal detector and time stood still as I awaited that dreadful beeping noise, which would give the officers a reason to pat me down.

To my surprise, the officer waved me through. But as I walked away, I felt someone tugging at my arm, followed by a stern voice.

"Hey, you!"

Paranoia took over as adrenaline pumped through my heart. This is it; I'm going to jail. Should I just make a break for it?

"Don't forget your belongings, sir."

The officer pointed to the bin full of my personal belongings, and a sense of relief ran through my entire body. I quickly grabbed my stuff and continued on my way.

The lifestyle I lived became too expensive for me to keep up with. I worked a full-time job and sold drugs on the side, but it wasn't enough to support my ever-growing habit. My co-worker and I figured out a way to steal from the register without getting caught, but unlike my high school days, I was no longer stealing just for the thrill of it. This time, I was stealing out of a necessity to support my addiction. But eventually, I got too greedy and ended up getting caught.

Soon after I lost my job, I also lost a good friend, Tony, aka T.O. He was best friends with my neighbor Mark. Mark was like a little brother to me, which pretty much made T.O. my little brother, too. T.O. sold heroin with Mark, but when he described what heroin felt like, I suspected he was dipping into his stash. He described it as taking a whole bunch of Percs at once and how a $10 bag can give you the same feeling you would get from $100 worth of Percs.

Part of me thought that T.O. was trying to convince me to buy dope from him, but part of me also thought that maybe he was doing more than just selling it; how else would he know what heroin felt like? However, I didn't like judging people, so I kept my mouth shut. I wish I would have said something, though. I don't know if it would have made a difference or not, but I should have at least tried because later that night, T.O. died from a heroin overdose. DAMN! That was my young buck. He was only 18 or 19; way too young to die. It really fucked my head up.

They say that deaths come in threes, and T.O. was only the first one. After T.O., I lost my uncle, Bill, on my dad's side of the family. His doctor told him he had to stop drinking or else he would die, but he just couldn't stop. He was an alcoholic, just like me. I guess the disease of alcoholism and addiction runs in the family.

At my uncle's viewing, I ran into my cousin Pat. We were close in age and even looked alike, so we were always pretty close. He told me how great things were going for him and how he had met the girl of his dreams and bought a new house. I could see in his face how happy he was. I had never seen him smile like that before. But then, two weeks later, he was lying dead in a coffin. He overdosed on OxyContin, which seemed crazy because nobody even knew he was on drugs.

It seemed like death was surrounding me everywhere I looked. To make matters worse, some of my close friends were getting hooked on crack, while others were getting locked up for selling drugs. I was doing the same things they were doing. I was no different. So it could have easily been me smoking crack or going to jail. By the time I turned 22, I knew I had to stop, or at least slow down a little bit.

I planned to stop getting high by doing nothing but drinking, no drugs whatsoever. It worked for a couple of weeks, but eventually, I slipped up and did some coke one night. This made me realize that if I wanted to stay away from the coke, then I would also have to stop drinking. So, I devised a new plan where I would only smoke weed and do nothing else. Well, that got really boring, really fast. In a matter of days, I ended up popping an E pill and went on an E binge for a while. Well, that got really expensive, really fast. So now, I needed something to replace the E, which led me right back to the Percs again. By this point, I knew I couldn't stop getting high, no matter what I tried to do. It was the first time I ever admitted to myself that I had a problem.

When I came home from partying every night, I passed by the church down the street from my house. This was the same church my mom used to drag me to when I was younger. The same church I was an altar boy at in elementary school. Even though I strayed far away from being the altar boy I once was, I still believed in God. So, I stopped outside that church every night, got on my knees, and begged God for help. I begged him to help me stop getting high. I pleaded with him to help me stop drinking. I promised I would be a better person if only he helped me to change my ways. But the following morning, I would feel like shit. So, I'll take some more Percs and start the cycle all over again. I kept praying for a while, hoping that God would someday answer my prayers. But after years of unanswered prayers, buckets of tears, and scraped up knees, I began to think that maybe God just didn't exist. It was either that, or he just didn't give a fuck about me.

Chapter 10

After many failed attempts to get clean, I finally concluded that I couldn't stop using drugs on my own. So instead, I got myself a girlfriend, hoping she could keep me clean. Her name was Karen, and she had never touched a drug in her life. In fact, she didn't even like to drink that much. She was just an all-around good girl, and we hit it off right away.

I fell in love with Karen in no time, but sometimes I wonder if it was ever truly love. You have to understand that Karen never knew the real me. It was almost as if I was living a double life. She knew I liked drinking and smoking weed, but that's about all she knew. She had no clue that I was a pill-popping, coke-snorting drug dealer. I was so deceptive with Karen that I could have been a Hollywood actor. Every night, after leaving her house, I would call to let her know I got home safe, except I would never go straight home. Instead, I would get drunk and high, often with other girls. I was honest with the other girls, though, and told them I had a girlfriend. Most of them didn't care. In fact, some of them even got off on it. I never understood how I could be honest with random girls I had just met but could never be open with the girl I was supposedly in love with.

It wasn't long before Karen got a glimpse of who I really was. We were chilling at my house one night, relaxing on the couch, when the police suddenly banged on the door. I honestly thought they were looking for my brother Shawn because that was usually the case when police came knocking. But when I opened the door, the police weren't looking for Shawn; they were looking for me.

Earlier that night, I had bought two six-packs for my young buck. He was 16, but I didn't know he was sharing those six-packs with a 12-year-old kid. That 12-year-old drank too much and had to get his stomach pumped. The kid snitched on me and told the cops who they got the beer from. I will never forget the look on Karen's face when she saw me in handcuffs. She was in shock, and after that night, I was surprised that she still wanted to be with me.

When I got to the 15th district, I called my dad, and he came to the station to ask the captain to drop the charges, but the kid's parents weren't going for that. So my dad told the captain that if they pressed charges on me, the kid should get charged for underage drinking. My dad's quick thinking swayed the parents to drop the charges. But when they released me, my dad was so mad that he refused to drive me home.

"Mom would be so proud of you right now," my dad said.

It fucked my head up when he said that, but it still didn't stop me from living the life I was living. Deep down inside, I knew my mom would be disappointed if she saw everything I had been doing, but I had no intentions of stopping; I loved drinking and getting high way too much.

I used to party with these two girls behind Karen's back, Nicole and Vicky. They didn't know each other, but they both threw parties at their houses a lot. Whenever we went to these parties, we would trash their homes by the end of the night. My friends did this more than I did, but I'd be lying if I said I never took part in it. One night, Nicole was giving a blowjob to one of my boys while my other friends lined up outside her bedroom door, waiting their turn. While waiting, they wrote things like "Nicole is a slut" on the wall in permanent marker so her parents would find it. Then they poured vodka in her fish tank and bleach in her flowerpots. I think someone even pissed in her Listerine bottle. They opened Nicole's fridge and tossed a gallon of milk out the window. Then they took a loaf of bread, mayonnaise, pickles, and anything they could find and tossed that out the window, too. It sounds kind of stupid now, but we thought it was hilarious at the time.

There were no limits to the shit we did to these girls. Sometimes, we would break into their houses when they weren't home just so that we had a place to party. Do you want to know the craziest part about it all? They never kicked us out or told us not to come back. I never understood it. No matter what we did, they always wanted us to come back. The last time we ever threw a party at Nicole's house, she invited a bunch of her other friends. We didn't know any of these dudes, so we bought a keg, set it up in her basement, and charged everyone $5 a cup. 20 minutes later, my boy Birdy approached me and whispered in my ear.

"Meet me by the back door in two minutes."

I didn't know what the fuck was going on, but I knew he was up to something shady. So, I finished my beer and headed to the back door to find Birdy standing next to the keg. He opened the door, and I saw Chris's car in the back alleyway, with the trunk popped open. He didn't need to spell it out for me. I grabbed one side of the keg, and Birdy grabbed the other, and together we threw the keg in the trunk, got in the car, and peeled off.

After that, we brought the keg to Vicky's house, had her call a bunch of her friends, and then did the same shit to them. Vicky and Nicole kept calling us all night, talking about how pissed they were and how their friends wanted their money back. We just laughed it off and stopped hanging with them. I kind of felt sorry for these girls. My friends and I were assholes, but we thought we were just having fun at the time.

After a year and a half of living a double life with Karen, I decided it was time for us to break up. I wanted to be free so that I could party and get high all the time. I felt like Karen was holding me back from living how I really wanted to live. So I did what any asshole would have done. I waited for us to get into a fight, blamed it on her like it was all her fault, and then broke up with her for it.

I feel guilty about it now, but at the time, I didn't care that I broke her heart. I was just relieved I could finally get drunk and high without the limitations. There was no more waiting until I left her house so I could snort a line or drink a beer; no more having to sneak away from the party to call and act like I was at home getting ready for bed. After a while, being shady got really tiresome.

Around this same time, my boy Steve got his own apartment, where we would party almost every night. The apartment was on the second floor of a duplex, and his dad lived on the first floor with Steve's half-sister, who was only nine years old. So, we all knew her because she was always outside playing with her friends. Well, one day, she told Steve that her dad's friend asked her to suck his dick. This guy was like 40 years old, so when we heard about this, we knew something had to be done. We couldn't just let this slide. This pedophile needed an ass-whooping.

That night, as we tried to think of a plan to fuck this dude up, Steve's power suddenly went out. We joked and asked him if he had forgotten to pay his electric bill. But when I looked outside, the entire neighborhood was pitch-black. There was a massive blackout; I couldn't see lights anywhere!

"Yo, we should go fuck him up right now. There's no way cops will catch us. They have too much on their plate right now."

Everyone agreed. So, without hesitation, we marched to where this dickhead lived and banged on his front door.

"Who is it?"

"It's Mickey," Tim randomly blurted in a high-pitched voice.

I was trying my hardest not to laugh. We didn't even know anyone named Mickey. But then, to our surprise, the door opened.

46

"Mickey doesn't live here anymore."

When the pedophile unlocked the screen door, I yanked it open, and BAM! Steve sucker-punched him. The pedophile tried to shut the security door, but I jammed it open with my foot. Then I dragged him out of the doorway as Tim and Steve slammed him face-first onto the ground. I kicked him in his lower back toward the kidney area. He tried to get up, but Tim stopped him with a solid kick to the face. Then, Steve stomped the back of his head, which made him curl up in a fetal position. Neighbors came out to see what the commotion was all about.

"Somebody call the cops!" the pedophile screamed.

"Yeah, call the cops. You have a fucking pedophile living next to you," Steve shouted.

We rolled him onto his back and pinned him down as Steve pounded his face in. After we were done, we warned him to stay away from little girls, or we'd come back to finish the job. We took off down the street and headed to Tony's house, just in case the cops came looking for us at Steve's apartment. When we got to Tony's, we smoked a blunt in his backyard to calm ourselves down. As soon as we lit the blunt, we saw a flashlight approaching Tony's gate. The light got closer, blinding us as it shined directly into our eyes.

"Who is that?" Tony said.

"I'm Officer O'Malley from the Philadelphia Police Department. Open this gate right now!"

How did they find us? How did this dude even know where Tony lived? Just then, the gate opened up, and we heard someone laughing.

"I'm Officer O'Malley, and y'all under arrest."

The flashlight went dark, revealing that it was our boy, Rambo! He kept laughing, but the rest of us didn't find it that funny. Rambo had no idea what we had just done, so it made him laugh even more when we told him what had happened. But before long, we all joined in on the laughter. Rambo got us good!

After that night, we never saw that pedophile again. He was smart enough to stop coming around, which was probably best for all of us. He wasn't worth going to jail for. But who am I kidding? Many things aren't worth going to jail for. Yet, I always found myself doing them, especially if it involved money or drugs.

One night, I was in an AOL chat room talking to some girls when I received a private message. This girl asked me for a photo, and after I sent one, she admitted that "she" was actually a "he." But before I could end the conversation, he offered me $300 to sleep with him. I couldn't believe my eyes when I saw the amount of money he was willing to give me. I couldn't turn down an opportunity like this, so I met him in a hotel room. But when I got there, I pulled out a knife and stuck it against his throat. He didn't even try to put up a fight. He was scared yet remained calm. Maybe this sort of thing happened to him a lot, but hey, that's what happens when you offer money to strangers on the internet. Without hesitation, he handed over his wallet; sure enough, he had $300 in it.

I used the extra cash to up my weed game and bought a quarter-pound instead of the usual ounce. After picking up the weed, I realized I had nowhere to bag it up at. My dad was home, so I didn't want to risk doing it there, and Steve was working, so I couldn't use his place either. I didn't know what to do, but I couldn't stay on the streets. If the cops stopped me and found the weed, I would be fucked! So, I went to the bar until I could figure out what to do.

When I got to the bar, I ran into an old high school classmate, Blake. I didn't really remember him, but he somehow remembered me. It's not that big of a surprise, considering that most of my high school years were just one big fucking blur; I have Xanax to thank for that one. Blake's uncle, Groucho, was the bartender at the Prince Café. He got that nickname because he was the spitting image of the actor Groucho Marx. Earlier that night, Blake was looking to score some weed, and Groucho told him I was the one he should see. I explained to Blake that I had weed but couldn't sell him any because I had nowhere to bag it up at. He told me I could bag it up at his apartment if I wanted to, so I gladly accepted his offer.

Once we got to his apartment, Blake introduced me to his girlfriend, Diane. She was cute as shit. I couldn't keep my eyes off her, but I tried my best because I didn't want to disrespect Blake. They both helped me bag the weed, and after we finished, I tossed them a few bags for free, plus I rolled a massive blunt for us to smoke.

Blake quickly became my best customer. He bought weed from me every day and even bought coke a few times a week. Before long, he was inviting my friends over to his apartment every night. Diane was always there too, and the more we hung out, the more I wanted her. Usually, I would have made a move on Diane by now. However, I considered Blake to be a good friend of mine. He even wrote rhymes just like I did. Every night we drank forties, smoked blunts, and went verse for verse with some freestyles. There were plenty of nights when we stayed up all night, snorting coke and talking about how we were going to take over the rap game. But it didn't matter how close Blake and I became, because drugs will make you stab your best friends in the back.

Tim's parents went away for a couple of days, so he invited us all over for a party. We were up all night getting fucked up, but everyone went to bed once the coke was gone. I wanted to keep the party going, even if that meant getting high all alone. The only problem was that I didn't have any money, so there was no way I could get more coke. Instead, I thought about other things that might give me a rush, and the first thing I thought of was coffee. So, I searched Tim's cabinets, found some instant coffee, and snorted a few lines. It burned like hell and made my nose bleed. That's when I called it quits and just crashed on Tim's recliner.

The following morning, or should I say afternoon, I woke up to everyone in the living room smoking a blunt. My head was pounding, and I was thirsty as all hell. I was about to run to the store to grab a soda, but then an opportunity struck.

"Anyone wanna go to the bar and get some six-packs?" Diane asked.

"I'll go. I wanna grab a 40," I replied.

I'm surprised Blake didn't come with us. He must have really trusted Diane. More foolishly, he must have really trusted me. When I left the house with Diane, I honestly didn't have any bad intentions. I really just wanted to get a 40, but when we got to the bar, Diane offered to buy me a vodka and Red Bull. She didn't have to twist my arm. I gladly accepted the free drink and chilled with her for a while. When we were done with our drinks, I stood up to leave, but Diane told me to sit down as she ordered another round and then another one after that.

The entire night, I kept thinking about how much I wanted to kiss her. I tried my best to resist because she was Blake's girl, but after a few drinks, I couldn't control myself. She was telling me a story mid-sentence when I pulled her toward me and kissed her. A moment later, I stopped myself. I knew I shouldn't have done it.

She looked at me with fire in her eyes. I honestly thought she was about to flip out, but that fire in her eyes wasn't anger. It was passion, and

49

she wanted more of it. Diane grabbed my shirt, pulled me toward her, and kissed me back. I knew it was wrong, but in my heart, it felt right. But being the shady asshole I was, it probably only felt right because I knew it was wrong.

After we left the bar, we sat in her car and made out for a while before we finally went back to Tim's house. When we got back, everyone wondered what had taken us so long. Blake even joked around and asked if I had enough room in her back seat—if he only knew.

Diane passed out on Tim's couch later that night. When it was time to go home, Blake tried to wake her up, but she wouldn't budge. So Tim and I convinced him to let her sleep on the couch for the night. He was hesitant at first but agreed to let her be, and then headed home by himself. The minute Blake left the house, Diane woke up. She was just pretending to be asleep so she could go home with me.

Diane stayed at my house for that entire week while she dodged all of Blake's phone calls. I still met him every day to sell him weed and coke, and whenever I saw him, he asked if I had seen Diane. He had no clue we hooked up or anything; he was just worried about her because she just up and disappeared from his life. The rest of my boys knew what was happening, but they kept their mouths shut.

I actually felt bad for Blake. He was a good dude and didn't deserve this. So, I convinced Diane to tell him the truth. He was so upset when he found out, and I felt guilty as fuck for doing him dirty like that. At first, Blake said he just wanted her to be happy, but then rumors spread about how he was planning to stab me. So, instead of waiting for him to catch me off guard, I approached him.

"Yo, you gonna stab me? Then do it now when I'm looking, motherfucker!"

We argued for a hot minute until I apologized for what I had done to him. After I apologized, we squashed the beef and shook hands. But a week later, Blake got jumped by a few guys from the neighborhood. He thought I had something to do with it. I even heard rumors that these guys jumped him because of the beef between us, but I honestly didn't even know who they were. After reassuring him that I had nothing to do with it, he invited Diane and me to a party at his apartment. We thought it would be awkward, but we actually had a good time. Nothing felt weird at all; everything seemed to be back to normal. The only difference was Diane was with me now instead of him.

50

The following day, Diane frantically called me from work. She could barely get the words out of her mouth because she couldn't stop crying.

"Blake is dead!"

"What? We were just with him last night. What are you talking about?"

"He O.D.'d last night!"

"What da fuck? How? All he did was smoke weed last night."

"No, after we left, he snorted some heroin."

I was in shock because I didn't even know that Blake was doing dope. I couldn't help but feel like it was all my fault. If I didn't take Diane from him, maybe things would have turned out differently; I felt so fucking guilty. Diane started eating a lot of Xanax after Blake died, and I mean a lot! She was eating them every single day. At one point, she told me she was pregnant but got so fucked up that she fell down a flight of stairs and had a miscarriage.

A few days later, I was drinking at the Prince with Tim and Diane. Everything seemed fine at first, but halfway through the night, something changed. Tim started acting strange, almost like he didn't want to be there. Diane began acting shady, too. She said she couldn't sleep at my house that night because her dad said she had to come home. Diane's dad had never made her go home before. She never had a curfew or anything like that, so I knew something was up.

I woke up early the following morning and walked by Tim's block. Sure enough, Diane's car was sitting right outside of his house. I couldn't believe it! Why would she do this to me? Why would Tim do this to me? I stepped onto Tim's porch and banged on his door. Tim's mom answered and told me that Tim wasn't home, but I knew she was lying because Diane's car was right there.

When I got home, I called Diane and asked why her car was in front of Tim's house. She tried to tell me she was picking up stuff from Blake's apartment, but couldn't find parking, so she instead parked around the corner in front of Tim's place. I argued with her until she finally told me the truth. She told me she couldn't handle being with me anymore because I reminded her of Blake.

How could I even argue with that? Blake and I looked alike, plus we had so much in common with each other. Even though she had a valid point, it still hurt. I was still angry, felt betrayed, and just sick and tired of everything that was going on around me. I had an awful feeling that everyone blamed me for Blake's death. I even blamed myself for a while. If I had never hooked up with Diane, he might not have been doing so many drugs like that. Everyone looked at me differently after he died; I felt like nobody wanted to hang with me anymore. Around this same time, my boys Eddie and Mark both got locked up for selling coke. I couldn't help but think that I was going to be next. I knew I had to stop selling drugs, but more importantly, I had to stop using them.

With everything going on around me, I needed a solid plan if I wanted to stop getting high. I tried so many times to stop in the past, but it never worked, so this time had to be different. I wanted to get away from all the bullshit. Between Blake and T.O. dying, friends stabbing me in the back, and Eddie and Mark going to prison, I saw my life going nowhere. I knew that if I continued down this path, I, too, would end up dead or in jail.

I figured the best way to solve my problems was to leave the neighborhood and get a fresh start. And what better way to get a fresh start than to join the military? I talked it over with my dad, and he loved the idea! Initially, I planned to join the Army, but my dad convinced me to join the Navy because they had better career choices.

I went to the Navy recruitment office and they took me to take the ASVAB test. The questions on the ASVAB were similar to an I.Q. test, but the way they scored it was completely different. I only needed 35 points to be accepted into the military. If I scored 50 or more points, I could get a halfway decent job, and if I scored above 65, I could get advanced training for a specialized career. Advanced training meant I could become a chemist, electronic technician, or even a nuclear engineer. My score for that ASVAB test was 92. I guess my mom was right all those times when she told me I just needed to apply myself.

Since I could choose any career I wanted, I decided to become an electronic technician. It sounded like the right fit for me since I enjoyed working with computers. There was a six-month wait before boot camp started, and I was told I would get drug tested on the day that I left. I knew I couldn't stay clean for six months on my own, so I continued to get high until a few weeks before the drug test. Staying clean, even for just a few weeks, was going to be one hell of a challenge for me. I honestly didn't know if I could pull it off or not, but I was damn willing to try.

Chapter 11

Two months before boot camp, I started hooking up with this girl, Mary, who used to work with me at Kinko's. It wasn't anything serious, just a friend with benefits type of deal. One night, Mary invited me to hang out and asked if I could bring one of my boys to hook up with her friend Penelope. She wanted us to come to Penelope's apartment to watch a movie and smoke a few blunts. So, I grabbed one of my DVDs, called Mark, and headed over to Penelope's place.

My first impression of Penelope was that she was cool as shit. She had a good sense of humor, a laid-back style, and was sexy as fuck. I was kicking myself in the ass for bringing Mark to hook up with her. Lucky for me, Mark and Penelope weren't interested in one another.

When I got home later that night, I realized I had left my DVD at Penelope's apartment. So the next day, Mary gave Penelope my number so she could get in touch about dropping off my DVD. As I waited outside my house for Penelope, I thought about what I was going to say to her. I wanted her to know that I was interested in her, but I wasn't sure how she would react since I was already hooking up with her friend. When Penelope pulled up outside my house, I started getting nervous. I didn't let it get the best of me, though. I pushed through it and told myself to be honest with her.

"Listen, yo, I like you and was wondering if you wanna hang out sometime?"

"Yeah. I'd like that."

We met up that following weekend, and she turned out to be one of the coolest chicks I had ever met. However, I had to leave for boot camp in a few months, so I didn't want to get too attached. We hung out here and there, but I tried to keep a little distance because I knew I was going away soon; I didn't want to start catching feelings or anything.

I heard that marijuana took six weeks to get out of your system, but after doing some research, I found a loophole. I learned how THC was stored in your fat cells, so it would take less time to get out of your system if you had a fast metabolism. Being the skinny fuck that I was, I had the quickest metabolism imaginable. So instead of stopping for six weeks, I smoked until 10 days before the test; talk about cutting it close.

Five days before my drug test, I tried meth for the first time. I'm not sure if I got some weak shit or just had high expectations, but I didn't like it. When I snorted it, it burned my nose and didn't give me a rush the same way that coke did. It just felt like I drank a bunch of coffee. I ran the streets all night, drinking forties with my boy Jim until we met up with Eddie to cop some coke. Eddie had just moved into a new spot, so he invited us over to check the place out.

A couple hours later, one of Eddie's boys came through with some E. It was my last night of partying before I went to boot camp, so I said "Fuck it" and bought myself one. This was my last chance to get high before I went to the military, so I wanted to party as much as possible. I popped the E pill, and a couple minutes later, the sun began to rise.

I stopped getting high after that night, or should I say morning. I did it the only way I knew how; by drowning myself in liquor. The next four days were a complete blur, but I remember stressing over the drug test. I knew the coke, E, and meth would be out of my system in three days, but I was worried the weed would still show up on the test. I only gave myself 10 days to get it out of my system. What if it didn't work? At that point, I knew there was nothing I could do about it, so I said some foxhole prayers and hoped for the best.

The night I left for boot camp, my dad stayed home and waited for the recruiter to pick me up. While waiting, my dad and I watched TV in the living room. It felt weird to stay sober and hang out with my dad, but it was kind of nice because it was something we normally never did. A little while later, the recruiter knocked on the door. I grabbed my bags, and as I was leaving, my dad stopped me.

"I want you to know that I love you, and I'm proud of you."

Besides graduating from school, I never gave my dad a reason to be proud of me, so these words caught me by surprise, and when I heard them, I couldn't control my emotions. I tried to hold back my tears, but a few of them managed to escape.

The recruiter took me to a hotel outside a military base in New Jersey, where all the other recruits stayed overnight. Early the next morning, they took us to the base, where they checked our weight, height, vision, hearing, and all sorts of other things. When it came time for the drug test, a man in army fatigues made me piss in a cup and then dipped a test strip into the urine. A minute or two later, he informed me I had passed and told me to wait in the next room. Holy fuck! I couldn't believe that I had actually passed! That's when I knew this was really happening; I was really going away and starting a fresh new life. A few hours later, I was on a plane that was heading to Great Lakes, IL.

I'd always heard horror stories about boot camp, and it turned out that they were all true; boot camp was no joke! I quickly adapted from a lifestyle where I could do whatever I wanted to a lifestyle where I was told what to do 24 hours a day. They literally controlled every move that we made. They told us when to eat, when to sleep, when to shower, talk, drink water, and even when to take a shit. I hated it at first and kept getting these obsessive cravings for drugs. I couldn't turn it off. I literally thought about drugs every minute of the day; it was torture.

After just two days, I was ready to go home, but I knew it wasn't an option. So, I did the only thing I could do. I toughed it out and hoped the time would pass quickly. As time went on, I started to get used to it, and eventually, I even began to enjoy it. Sure, it sucked when the petty officer screamed in my face, made me do 50 pushups, and run a mile and a half every day. But I learned a lot of things in those eight weeks. I discovered what loyalty was all about. They taught us that when you are on a ship in the middle of the ocean, and a fire breaks out, you can't dial 9-1-1 for the fire department to come. Everyone on that ship has to chip in and help, or else everyone will die.

They also taught me discipline and helped me to find the courage inside of me. I learned how to face my fears, and no matter how scared I was, to just push through, and everything would work out in the end. For the first time in my life, I felt like a real man. I felt like I was doing the right thing and was proud of myself. This made me realize how dumb I was for getting high, so I swore I would never do drugs again.

Every Sunday, the petty officers gave us some free time to write letters back home and read any letters we may have received. So, every week I wrote letters to both my dad and Penelope. And every week, they always wrote me back. My dad always told me to stay strong and reminded me how proud he was of me. Penelope, on the other hand, got a kick out of teasing me. She always sent sexually explicit letters talking about doing the freakiest shit imaginable. And if that wasn't enough, she ripped pages out of porno magazines and stuffed them in the envelope with her letters. One week, she even sent me naked pictures of herself. She did it to tease me because she knew I was stuck in boot camp with 80 other guys.

On the flip side, she would also write about how she missed me and wished I could come home to be with her. With every letter she sent, my feelings for her grew more and more. Through those letters, I came to realize that I loved her. So I wrote a letter explaining how I felt, and when she wrote back, she felt the same way.

When I graduated from boot camp, my dad drove halfway across the country to attend the ceremony. He was so proud to see me in uniform. I honestly never saw my dad that happy before. We spent the day together, and for the first time in my life, it felt like we had a real relationship. Sadly, we were only able to spend one day with our families before the Navy sent us off to complete our training.

Since I signed up to be an electronic technician, they sent me to a training base directly across the street from the boot camp. I loved the idea of having a little more freedom, but the training was tough. They taught me stuff that I just couldn't comprehend. I was never a big school person but somehow always skimmed by in high school. Skimming by wasn't possible with this type of training, though. It was self-paced training done on a computer, so I needed to know this stuff 100% before moving on to the next lesson. I got through the first half of the training, but I was utterly lost by the time I reached the midpoint.

Christmas was right around the corner, so when Christmas break finally came, I flew home to spend time with my loved ones. I was so happy to see Penelope and even happier to be able to smoke weed again. I made it a point to only smoke that first night, though. I had to go back in a week and possibly get another drug test, so I didn't want to push it.

The following night, I went to the bar with my friends since I hadn't seen them in a while. Halfway through the night, one of my boys offered me some coke. I should have turned it down, but I just couldn't resist. It's funny how quickly I forgot that the reason I went to the military was to get away from the drugs. But just because I was done with drugs doesn't mean they were done with me.

We drank in the bar until closing time, but since we had been doing coke all night, neither of us wanted to go home. So, we went to a sketchy after-hours club on Torresdale Avenue, where we drank and snorted coke until the sun came up. When I finally got home, I ran to the bathroom and prayed to the porcelain gods. As I sat there, puking my guts up, I suddenly remembered why I wanted to stop getting drunk and high.

The following day, I woke up with a massive hangover. So, I got myself some Percs so that I could feel better. Later that night, I was right back in the bar again, getting shitfaced. I had only been home for two days, and already I was diving right back into my old habits. It was almost like I had never left. After that night, I decided I wouldn't get high for the rest of the week. It's not because I didn't want to. It was because I had a feeling the Navy was going to give me another drug test when I got back to the base. That didn't mean I couldn't drink, though. So, for the rest of the week, I got drunk every night and tried to spend as much time with Penelope as I could.

That week flew by, and before I knew it, it was time for me to return to Great Lakes, IL. My dad and Penelope drove me to the airport, and I kept thinking about how I didn't want to go back. After my dad said his farewells, he gave Penelope and me a few minutes to say goodbye to one another. I thought about grabbing her and jumping on the first flight available so we could run away and start a new life together. It didn't matter where we went, as long as we were together. But, I knew I couldn't do that because then I would be on the run for the rest of my life.

I said goodbye to Penelope and gave her a kiss. Tears fell from my eyes because I knew I had to let go of her, even though I didn't want to. Emotions got the best of her, too. She couldn't bear it any longer, so she gave me one last kiss and then left with tears in her eyes. After boarding the plane, I felt so sad and hopeless. And although I think differently today, at the time, I convinced myself that joining the military was the worst decision I had ever made.

When I got back to the base, I resumed my training to become an electronic technician. I was hoping that the Christmas break would have reset my brain and helped me to understand the training a little better, but it didn't. I was just as confused as I was on the day I left, which made me even more depressed. I didn't even want to try anymore. All I wanted to do was go back home. I suddenly felt out of place. I had four bunkmates, all of whom I went through boot camp with and were in the same class as me, yet I couldn't relate to any of them. They were all super-intelligent, goody two shoes who never did a drug or committed a crime in their life. How could I be friends with people like that?

I started spending a lot of time at the bar, which was convenient because it was located right on the base. But even there, among other people who loved to drink, I felt out of place. I never talked to anybody, just sat in the corner, drank my beer, and watched television. I even watched the Super Bowl by myself that year. The Philadelphia Eagles were playing, but they ended up losing, which made me even more depressed. So, I dealt with the pain the only way I knew how — by drowning it in alcohol and hoping it didn't know how to swim.

I talked to Penelope and sent letters as often as possible, but it wasn't the same. I wanted to be with her, and she wanted to be with me. She even told me I could move in with her if I could somehow get kicked out of the military. It sounded like a great idea, so I schemed up a plot.

My plan involved bullshitting a shrink to make them think I was mentally unstable. So, I made an appointment to talk to the psychiatrist on the base. I told her all types of off-the-wall shit, like how I had visions of smacking people with bricks just for the fun of it. But she didn't buy it, so I then fabricated a story about a failed suicide attempt. I told her I tried to eat an entire bottle of ibuprofen but stopped myself because my bunkmate walked in as I was opening the bottle. Looking back on it, I realize that was the lamest so-called "suicide attempt" ever. I forgot that her entire career was based upon examining people, so she saw right through my bullshit.

My mom always said that honesty was the best policy, so when my plan with the shrink failed, I talked to the chaplain and was 100% honest with him. I told him I didn't want to be there anymore and how I just wanted to go home to be with my girlfriend. He basically laughed at me and said that quitting the military wasn't an option. So I told him about another plan I had up my sleeve, which I only wanted to use as a last resort. After hearing my plan, he didn't believe that I would go through with it; he obviously didn't know me very well.

My final, full-proof plan was quite simple. The US Navy had a zero-tolerance drug policy, so I knew I'd get kicked out if I were to fail a drug test. But it's not like the military base had drug dealers hanging out on the corners. Honestly, if they did, I probably wouldn't have wanted to leave. If I knew the right people, I'm sure I could have found something, but as I mentioned earlier, I didn't have any real friends there.

My birthday was fast approaching, and Penelope had already planned to come and visit me. I knew she could get her hands on some weed, so I asked her to smuggle a few nickel bags on the plane when she came to visit. She didn't even hesitate.

When Penelope came to visit, we spent the entire weekend smoking and drinking in the hotel room. But at one point, I brought her onto the military base as a visitor so that she could see the beautiful shoreline of Lake Michigan. As we approached the shore, I began to sweat, which was unusual, considering it was the middle of February and we were just north of Chicago. As we got closer to the water, my heart felt like it was about to fly right out of my chest.

I stopped Penelope, gave her a hug and a kiss, then told her how beautiful she was and how much I loved her. I told her she was the perfect woman for me. The waves crashed against the shoreline as we stared into each other's eyes. It was the perfect moment, so I kneeled down on one knee, pulled out a diamond ring, and asked her to marry me.

"Yes! Yes! Of course!"

I felt like the happiest man in the world, but reality slapped me in the face the next day when Penelope had to catch her flight back home. It was tough to say goodbye to her, especially since she had just agreed to marry me. I had all sorts of mixed emotions. I was super happy, yet super depressed. After saying my goodbyes, I went back to the base and prayed that I would get a random drug test. Two days later, I finally caught a break when I woke up to a petty officer screaming in the hall.

"Wake up! It's time for your drug test! I hope everyone studied long and hard!"

Little did he know that I never studied for anything; I already knew I would fail. A week after I took that test, I received instructions to report to the legal building, where a scrawny petty officer called me into his office.

"Do you know why you're here?"

"No, sir."

"You failed your drug test."

"Thank God," I mumbled under my breath.

"I said you FAILED your drug test!"

"And I said thank God!"

He looked at me with confusion. So I explained how I failed the test on purpose so I could go home. He called me an idiot, and looking back on it now, he was right. I thought I could go home right away, but I found out the hard way that being discharged from the military is not a quick process. They put me on restriction, meaning I couldn't leave the building to go anywhere unless it was to see one of the many doctors they sent me to. They needed to perform all types of tests to make sure I left the military in good health. I didn't mind too much because I knew I was going home, but I grew more anxious by the day.

I knew I had to break the news to my dad, but I didn't want him to know I was getting kicked out for using drugs, especially since the whole reason I joined the military was to get away from them. So, instead, I made up this elaborate story about how I lied on some paperwork, and they were booting me out for it. However, my dad was a cop for 25 years, so I forgot he was a human lie detector. He called some of his old military buddies and found out the truth. He was so disappointed that he basically disowned me and said I wasn't welcome back in his house. I felt so ashamed, and for the next two years, my father and I didn't speak a word to each other.

The day I came back to Philly, I tried to surprise Penelope by having Joe G pick me up from the airport and drive me to her house, but she somehow figured out I was coming home. Nevertheless, she was still happy to see me. After I walked in the door, my friends hung up a sign that read, "Welcome Home Brain!" written with a magic marker in sloppy drunk handwriting. I felt right at home again. We celebrated by drinking liquor and smoking a shitload of weed. I got so plastered that I could barely stand by the end of the night. After everyone left, Penelope and I went to her bedroom, where she climbed on top of me. But in the middle of having sex, I passed out.

"Are you sleeping?"

"Huh? No, no, I just closed my eyes for a second."

She continued to ride me, but I must've passed out again because the next thing I knew, it was morning. I could barely remember anything the next day, but Penelope filled me in on what had happened. I felt bad for passing out on her like that, but luckily, she was very understanding.

Chapter 12

After I moved in with Penelope, everything was going great. Even though I was smoking weed and drinking again, it didn't seem to be a problem like it was before. This was because Penelope lived in a different neighborhood from where I grew up, so I was no longer hanging on the street corners and selling drugs. I still hung out with a few of my old friends but was able to stay away from the criminals and drug dealing lifestyle that I once lived. I thought that the neighborhood I grew up in was the root of all my problems, but boy was I wrong.

Even though I still smoked weed every day and binge drank every weekend, I didn't think anything was wrong with it. In my mind, everything seemed perfect in my life, but it wouldn't be long before those Percocets started calling my name again. Every weekend, I would wake up with horrible hangovers after a night of hardcore drinking. Eventually, I couldn't bear it and began taking Percs to relieve the headaches. I didn't want to make a habit out of it, though, so I only took them on weekends, but that didn't last long at all.

A few months later, I got a job at a copy shop in Center City, Philadelphia. I started out as a copy technician, making copies of documents and architect blueprints. The job wasn't much different from the one I had at Kinko's, except I wasn't operating the cash register this time. A few months after I started my new job, they promoted me to become a delivery driver, which definitely didn't help my addiction.

I absolutely loved driving for a living. All I had to do was load the van with paper products and deliver them around the city. It was super easy, but the part I really loved was how I didn't have a boss breathing down my neck. I also loved how I was making $10 an hour, which was the highest-paying job I ever had. Because (I thought) I was making a lot of money, I got this crazy idea that I could afford to do cocaine again.

Penelope didn't use coke or Percs. She only drank and smoked weed. But she didn't mind if I got high, as long as I didn't get out of hand with it. Yet I still felt the need to hide it from her. At first, I was only using coke and Percs on the weekends when I went out drinking, but after a while, it felt like the weekend couldn't come quick enough. So, I would begin my weekend a day early, on Thursday night. But I wouldn't do Percs or coke on Thursdays because I wanted to save that for the weekends. A few weeks later, I extended my weekend by one day and started going out on Monday nights. Again, I wouldn't use any drugs on Mondays; I would stick to only alcohol, nothing else.

This continued for a few months until I began randomly grabbing 40 ounces and 6-packs here and there during the week. Before long, I found myself drinking every single night. I justified my weeknight drinking by comparing it to how I used to drink. I was now only drinking a few beers a night, not an entire bottle of liquor like I did in the past.

Even though I didn't drink a lot during the week, I would still wake up with hangovers. And since I knew Percs were the perfect remedy for a hangover, I began eating them more and more often. I tried not to take them every day because I didn't want to get addicted again, but since when do any of my plans work out the way I want them to?

One of the benefits of driving for a living was I could make pit stops while out on deliveries, which made it easy to meet up with my drug dealers throughout the day. I thought it was the greatest thing ever because I no longer had to wait until after work to get high. If I felt like shit in the morning, I would just grab a few Percs while making my first delivery.

Joe G worked around the corner from me in a high-rise office building downtown. When he found out I could get Percs during work hours, he would buy me some for going to meet the dealers for him. This allowed me to spend more money on other things, like a bag of coke, to make the workday go quicker.

My increasing drug habit put a financial burden on me, even though I didn't think it was a problem at the time. See, Penelope and I agreed that I would pay the bills, and she would pay the rent. So, as long as those bills were getting paid, I didn't think I had a problem. But because I spent all my money on Percs and coke during the week, I never had money to go out drinking on weekends. But then I got approved for a credit card and discovered I could take out cash advances on it. This is how I hid my drug problem from Penelope for so long. I always had enough money for the bills and to go out on the weekends, so she never realized how much I was spending on drugs.

Since I got approved for credit cards, I decided to try my luck with a car loan. I filled out the application, and to my surprise, I got approved for a loan up to $10,000. I was excited to get my first car, a 1999 Chevy Lumina. The car cost about $5000, but when I found out I only had to pay $60 a paycheck, it suddenly seemed very affordable.

62

Everything seemed to be falling into place. I had a new car, a good job, and an incredible girlfriend, plus I was getting high all the time. But eventually, the drugs put me in an "I don't give a fuck" state of mind. I stopped caring about what people thought of me. I'd be at a red light in Center City, doing lines of coke off the dashboard in my work van. People would see me doing this, and I'd just laugh it off and shrug my shoulders at them. I'm surprised nobody ever contacted my boss, considering that the company name and phone number were all over the van.

Like all good things, my job eventually had to end. It was early in the morning, and I was on my way to my first delivery. I didn't even meet my dealer yet, so I was 100% sober at the time. I was crossing the intersection of Broad and Chestnut when a taxi ran a red light, causing me to T-Bone him. Luckily, nobody got hurt, but the van was severely damaged. As a company policy, anyone involved in an accident had to take a mandatory drug test. I talked to my supervisor and was honest with him, explaining how there was no way I would pass the test. He told me it wasn't up to him, and I had no choice but to take it. So I went through with it, knowing full well I was going to fail.

A few days later, I got called into a conference room. When I walked in, the manager and supervisor were both sitting at the table. As I sat down, I learned they wanted to discuss the car accident with me. I had a feeling that I was about to get fired.

"Did the drug test results come back yet?" the owner asked.

"Yup. It's all good. He's clean." the supervisor stated.

I couldn't believe it. Either the lab mixed up the results, or my supervisor covered for me; I'm assuming it's the latter. I'm still not sure why he did it, but I'm guessing it was because I was honest with him. Or maybe it was because I was a hard worker, and he didn't want to lose me. During the meeting, I learned that I would have to work inside the shop and make copies until they repaired the van, which could take up to two weeks. But it ended up taking more like two months.

Once I started working inside the shop again, I quickly realized how much I hated it. The job was so boring compared to driving on the open road, plus I couldn't meet my drug dealers and get high all day like I used to. I felt like I needed a change, so I began searching for a new job. After sending many résumés, I landed a job interview with a company that paid twice as much as the copy shop, and I nailed it! They seemed extremely interested, so I thought for sure that I had the job. A few days later, while stuck at work with a hangover and no Percs to relieve my pain, I quit my job at the copy shop so that I could meet my drug dealer. Besides, I really thought I was going to get that other job.

It turns out that I was wrong, and the other company hired someone else. So with no money coming in, I had no choice but to live off cash advances until I found a new job. After a few weeks, I maxed out all my credit cards and was still unemployed. Penelope was beyond pissed because I could no longer afford to pay the bills. Luckily, I got a delivery job at Papa John's Pizza, but it didn't pay much, so Penelope agreed to pay for my car insurance. She even started paying for me at the bar every weekend because I couldn't afford it.

After a while, Penelope and I started fighting all the time. At first, it was because I was always broke, but after a while, we began fighting over everything. The fighting had me constantly stressed out, and the only way I knew how to deal with stress was by getting drunk and high. But that didn't exactly help ease the tension between Penelope and me; if anything, it made things worse. The drugs began messing with my head and distorted my perception of reality. I became extremely suspicious of her and even swore up and down that she was cheating on me with Joe G.

The entire time we were together, I always blamed Penelope for our fights. I always pointed the finger at her as if it were all her fault. But truth be told, most of the arguments were my fault. I was always in a bad mood when withdrawing from Percs, so I took it out on her. She never deserved the shit I put her through, and I'm surprised she stayed with me for as long as she did.

Right around this same time, my boy Eddie got out of jail. I used to buy Percs and coke from Eddie, but he was lying low, so he introduced me to his boy Jerry, who sold Percs. Jerry and I instantly became friends; we were always working out deals with each other. That crazy mother fucker loved pizza, and I just happened to work at a pizza shop, so sometimes I'd give him a free pizza in exchange for some Percs. Jerry also gave me free Percs for driving him around so he could meet his customers and/or pick up his scripts.

Not long after I met Jerry, he convinced me to start selling weed again. He knew I had the customers, plus the car to get around the neighborhood. Between the weed and the Percs, we knew we'd be hustling and making money all day. So, I waited until a busy Friday night at the pizza shop and saved all my tip money. Once I had the money, Jerry introduced me to his weed connect, "Biggie," who was the spitting image of Biggie Smalls.

Even though I worked at the pizza shop and sold weed every day, it still wasn't enough money to support my habit. So, I did what any addict would have done in my situation and started stealing from Penelope. At first, it was just a few dollars here and there, but after a while, I started jacking her ATM card to take money from her savings account. One day, while she was in the shower, I grabbed her card and ran to the ATM. But when I got back, she was already out of the shower, so I couldn't slip the card back into her purse without her noticing. I had no choice but to hold on to it until I could put it back in her bag, but the opportunity never came.

A little while later, Penelope needed to hit the ATM but couldn't find her card, probably because it was still in my pocket. When she asked if I had seen it, I just played dumb and helped her search the house for it. I even flipped the couch cushions and checked her coat pockets to make it seem like she really lost it. But as soon as her back was turned, I pretended like I found it underneath some papers on the dresser.

Penelope never caught me stealing from her, but she probably would've kicked me out if she had. The fighting became so severe that neither of us wanted to be with each other. We probably could've worked things out if we tried, but I didn't want to. I wanted to get high, and living with her was getting in the way of that, so I left.

After Penelope and I split up, Jerry let me stay with him for a while. I got a job down the street from his apartment at Mayfair Pizza. I made much more money there than I did at Papa John's, but it still wasn't enough; a million dollars wouldn't have been enough. I was probably spending at least $70 a day on Percs, if not more.

As I mentioned earlier, Jerry always gave me free Percs to drive him around to different places. One place I always took him to was his Percocet dealer, who lived in the North Philly Badlands. Anyone familiar with Philadelphia knows this is one of the worst sections of the city. The area is well known for its open market drug trade, where you can find any type of drug you could possibly think of. The neighborhood was like candy land for drug addicts like Jerry and me. We were down there almost every day to get different shit, whether it was weed, coke, zannies, wet, or even the occasional E pill. But then, one day, Jerry asked me to drive to Third and

Indiana, a corner I wasn't familiar with. You can imagine how surprised I was when Jerry told me he wanted to go there to pick up some heroin.

I had known Jerry for a good six months and had no clue he was using heroin. I never did heroin before, and I swore I never would, but the desperation of my Perc addiction threw all of my promises out the window. Jerry explained that one bag of dope was equivalent to taking a whole bunch of Percs at once. But instead of spending hundreds of dollars on Percs, a bag of dope only cost $10. I didn't even have to think about it. Why waste money on Percs if I could get a much stronger high for a fraction of the price? Without hesitation, I reached into my pocket and handed Jerry $10.

I'd been to plenty of drug corners in sketchy neighborhoods, but the dope corners were in a league of their own. The houses were literally falling apart, cops were everywhere, and dealers were highly suspicious of us. I got paranoid when Jerry left me alone in the car to get the dope. The dealers and dope fiends looked at me like a piece of meat they wanted to feast their teeth into. I was afraid of getting carjacked or even killed while sitting there waiting for Jerry. When Jerry finally got back in the car, I got out of there as quickly as possible.

It was broad daylight as we approached a red light at Fifth and Allegheny, a busy intersection with plenty of cars and pedestrians. But I didn't care how many people were around. I needed to test this shit as soon as possible. Jerry handed me a rolled-up dollar bill and a CD case with a small line of what looked like cocaine, except it was light brown. I used the dollar bill to snort the dope but didn't feel anything at first. I expected it to be like cocaine, where you feel an instant rush as soon as you snort it. Heroin was a little different, though. The first thing I noticed was the taste in my throat. Jerry hated the taste, which always made him gag, but I actually liked it. Once I could taste it, I cleared my passageways and felt it drip into the back of my throat. That's when it hit me.

If I had to explain the feeling in one word, I wouldn't be able to because there isn't a word in the English language that can describe a sensation of that magnitude. It was the most amazing feeling I'd ever felt in my life. It was like how I felt the first time I took Percs, except this was much better. An instant feeling of euphoria swept over my entire body, and my chest felt like a thousand little kitten claws were kneading all over it. The warm and fuzzy feeling made me forget all of my problems and worries. At that moment, I didn't have a care in the world; I felt like I had died and gone to heaven.

We blasted my Ghostface Killah CD as we cruised down Fifth Street, smiling and laughing like if we were untouchable. I remember feeling like I had discovered the answer to all of my money problems. A $10 bag of heroin was much cheaper than the $70 worth of Percs I was spending every day. I had this crazy notion that I could now afford my own place and move out of Jerry's apartment. Drugs had my mind so clouded that I actually thought I was moving forward in life. But in reality, I was moving backward at a very rapid pace.

At first, I did save some money, at least enough for me to rent a room in someone's basement for $100 a week. Between dealing drugs and delivering pizzas, I had no problem paying my rent every week, so I didn't think heroin was a problem; at least, not yet.

A few weeks after I started doing heroin, I ran into my old head, Adam, who used to hang out with my older brothers. I knew Adam was using dope because he had mentioned it a few years back. So I told him I'd drive him down to the Badlands if he ever needed any because I was driving there every day, anyway. Adam tried to warn me, but it all went in one ear and out the other. He told me to stop before it was too late and that I had no idea what I was getting myself into. I really wish I would've listened to him, but I think we both knew it was already too late. After a few minutes of preaching, Adam asked me which corner I was getting dope from.

"I'm goin' to Third and Indy."

"Nah, Brain, that dope is garbage. I know a much better spot."

Adam jumped in the car and directed me to a spot that wasn't too far from Third and Indiana, but it might as well have been a different world. The block he took us to was the worst of the worst. I thought the other spot was bad; this place looked like a fucking war zone in a third-world country. I couldn't believe how decrepit this block was. Most of the houses were bandos with boarded-up windows. Some of them were missing doors, while others had doors but were missing steps to even get to the door. Dope fiends nodded out on the corner as dealers screamed down the block to one another in Spanish. Everyone moved at a fast pace, too. Customers came and went with the quickness, one after another, scurrying along as soon as they got their shit.

Adam got out of the car to get the dope while I circled the block. Too many cops were driving around, so I didn't want to park and look like a sitting duck. After I swung back around the corner, Adam jumped back in the car, and we got out of the neighborhood as quickly as possible. On our way back, Adam emptied his dope into a water bottle cap and carefully mixed it with some water. He asked me to drive slowly and not hit any bumps as he stuck the needle in his arm. When he pulled the syringe from his arm, he breathed a heavy sigh of relief. A moment later, his eyelids became too heavy for him to hold open, and he slowly drifted away from reality.

The following day, I went with Jerry to the new spot that Adam introduced me to. I parked on the corner and walked up the street as Jerry waited in the car. There must have been about 15 people on the block, and that's when I realized I didn't know who was selling dope and who was just hanging out. Luckily for me, I didn't have to ask. When they see a white guy on the block, they know what he is there for.

"Whatcha need, young buck?"

"Four dope."

"Lemme see ya track marks, white bol."

"Oh nah, I don't shoot. I sniff it, man."

"You a cop! Get da fuck outta here!"

I tried to convince him I wasn't a cop, but he wasn't buying it, so Jerry and I were forced to try somewhere else. I drove around the corner to another spot and walked to the crowd of dealers. One of them walked to the corner to look out for the cops, as another walked to an alley and grabbed the dope from an empty cigarette pack. We did a swift hand-to-hand exchange, and then I got out of there as quickly as possible.

After driving for a couple blocks, I noticed a cop car tailing me. Something told me he was going to pull me over, and a few seconds later, I saw those flashing lights. I pulled over to the side of the road and started sweating bullets. He stepped out of the car, and the closer he got, the faster my heart pounded. By the time he reached my window, I felt like I was going to have a heart attack.

"License, insurance, and registration."

I reached into my glove box, grabbed my paperwork, and handed it to the cop. As he examined my license, I began to get really nervous. I was afraid he would ask me to step out of the vehicle and search it for drugs.

"You down here trying to cop?"

Now, if someone asks if you are trying to "cop" something, they are really asking if you are trying to buy drugs; it's just a slang word. I knew what the officer meant but played stupid as if I didn't know what these drug-related slang words really meant.

"Huh? No, I'm not tryin' to be a cop. I'm a painter."

The cop must've figured that I wasn't a drug user if I didn't know the slang words because he didn't even search the car. He just ran my information and let us go with a warning. When we got back to the neighborhood, I dropped Jerry off at his apartment and paid an unexpected visit to Adam. I wanted Adam to show me how to shoot up, but he refused to teach me. So, I offered him a free bag of dope if he showed me, and he just couldn't resist. He pulled out a small metal cap, known as a cooker, and showed me how to mix the dope and draw it up into the syringe.

"Don't we gotta cook it with a lighter first?"

"Nah, Brain, this ain't Hollywood. You only do that with black tar, like with the dope you find on the West Coast."

When Adam pushed the plunger on the syringe, I felt like an angel had swooped down and brought me to heaven. It was the most incredible rush I had ever experienced. It was as if all my worries, pains, insecurities, and everything else had just slipped away. I felt like I was in a dream state, but eventually, that dream would turn into a nightmare.

Chapter 13

Once I started shooting dope, I could never go back to snorting it; it just wasn't the same. That would be like going back to my ex after finding a prettier, cooler girl who made me 10 times happier. And once I started shooting up, Adam told me I could shoot coke just like I would heroin, although it seemed dangerous to me at first. But since when have I ever let danger stop me from getting high?

The first time I shot cocaine was in the room I was renting on Torresdale Avenue. Within seconds of injecting it, I felt it pumping through my entire system. I heard a unique sound, best described as a bass drum banging inside my ear canal. My heart pounded at a tremendous pace, to the point where I thought I was going to die. So, I ran to my roommate as fast as possible and asked him to bring me to the hospital.

"Wassup, dude? You OK?"

I explained how I had just shot coke for the first time and felt like I was about to have a heart attack. He just laughed and told me the feeling was normal and that I probably just did too much. So the next time, I only shot half of a bag, which allowed me to enjoy the high a lot more. After that, I learned I could mix coke and dope and shoot them at the same time, more commonly known as speedballs. Doing speedballs made me feel like Superman, as if nothing in the world could touch me. Ironically, the same thing that made me feel like Superman was also the kryptonite that would destroy me.

Even though Penelope and I split up, I still hung out with her friends, especially Chris, who loved to get high just as much as I did. When I started doing dope, I didn't hide it from him because I knew he didn't give a fuck and wouldn't tell anyone. But before long, Chris asked if I could get him some dope. I didn't want to get it for him because I didn't want him getting hooked on the shit. But he begged and explained how it wasn't his first time doing it. I looked at it like this: Chris was a grown man and could make his own decisions. Besides, if I didn't get it for him, he would have gotten it one way or another.

Chris began taking rides with me to the Badlands every day, but he would get super paranoid when we got to the neighborhood. He was a straight-up headbanger with long, grungy blonde hair, so he stuck out even more than I did. I understood why he was scared, though, because I felt the same way when I first stepped into that neighborhood, but now it didn't even faze me; part of me felt like I belonged there.

One night, after we copped a couple bags of dope, Chris and I drove to A and Ontario to get a few jars of wet. I parked around the corner and told Chris to wait in the car. It was a cold winter night, so I left the car running with the heat on while he waited for me. When I got to the corner, I had to wait a few minutes for the dealers to get their next bundle. Five minutes later, as I walked back to the car, I saw Chris walking toward me, being his paranoid self. He said he got scared because some guy kept walking up and down the block, staring at him every time he passed.

"It's cool, man. He probably thought you was a cop or sumptin'... Here, lemme get the keys."

"I left them in the car."

"Are you fuckin' serious?"

I ran to the car as quick as possible. The keys were still in the ignition with the engine running and the doors unlocked. We were lucky that nobody had taken the car. Even though Chris and I were polar opposites when it came to things like street smarts, taste in music, and clothing style, we got along great because we both loved to get high.

Every night after work, I would pick Chris up and drive to Kensington Avenue and Somerset Street. This corner was like junkie central. It's where all the addicts sold needles and pills to scrounge up a few dollars and get some dope. You could even pay someone to take you to the spots with the best dope in the neighborhood, but we just went there to buy syringes most of the time.

Our nightly routine was always the same. We went to Kensington and Somerset for our needles, grabbed a few bags of dope from a nearby corner, and then found a dark shady block where we could shoot up. Sometimes we waited until we got back to the neighborhood to shoot up, but that wasn't always an option if we were dope sick.

Now, just in case you've been living under a rock, the term "dope sick" is another name for heroin withdrawal. It can be described as having the flu, times 10. Your muscles become extremely weak, with aches and pains all over your body. The pain is so intense that it penetrates deep into your bones. You get so cold that you feel like you're standing in a subzero freezer, yet you're sweating so much that you'd think you were in a sauna.

Then your nose runs like crazy. It just keeps leaking, and no matter how many times you try to blow it, there is always more that wants to come out.

Next are the stomach aches, followed by explosive diarrhea. And while you're sitting there, shitting your brains out, you begin to vomit, and then you vomit some more. Just when you think you're finished, you vomit again and then dry heave until you feel like you can't breathe. The whole time that this is happening, your anxiety skyrockets. You get restless leg syndrome so bad that you literally can't sit still. This means that you can never sleep because your legs constantly need to move, 24 hours a day. And while all of this is happening, you have a panic attack. Except, this panic attack doesn't go away after a few minutes. This panic attack stays with you until you stick a needle in your arm.

The physical withdrawal is only half the battle. The mental part of it can be just as bad. Your mind is telling you that you can get rid of all these symptoms in an instant; all you need to do is get a bag of dope. So every waking moment is spent obsessing over heroin. Literally, every single thought is spent plotting ways to get money so that you can get your fix. It's not like other addictions. You can't distract yourself or try to turn it off because the physical symptoms are right there to remind you about it.

Whenever I bought dope, I always tried to wait until I got home to shoot up. But sometimes, I would be too dope sick and have to park somewhere to give myself a fix. But shooting up in the car was risky, especially in the Badlands where cops were always swarming around. So, sometimes, instead of waiting 15 minutes until I got home, I would shoot it while driving on the highway. I would have Chris or Jerry mix the dope and put it into the syringe for me. Then I would use my knees to steer the car while I stuck the needle in my vein. Driving 65 mph on I-95 with no hands while shooting a bag of dope probably wasn't the brightest idea I ever had.

My addiction had gotten so bad that I started spending every dime I could on heroin. I wasn't even drinking or smoking weed anymore because I felt like that was wasting money that could've been spent on dope. I even started skipping meals just to buy myself an extra bag. It got to the point where I would only put $2 at a time in the gas tank. Obviously, $2 of gas doesn't get you very far, but it got me to where I needed to be most of the time. However, there were times when I ran out of gas and had to spend my dope money to get back home. This wasn't a once in a while thing either; this happened every week. It was happening so much that, after a while, it just seemed normal to me.

72

After a few months, the guy I rented a room from got hooked on dope too. I gave him rent money every week, but he blew it on heroin instead of paying the rent, so we both got evicted. Luckily, my friend Chuck let me stay with him. Chuck was good friends with Penelope and Chris, so we drank, smoked weed, and even snorted coke together, but he never knew I was using heroin. He definitely wouldn't have approved of that, so I hid it from him pretty well. But after a while, Chuck noticed the insanity being caused by my drug use. The first time he realized it was probably the night he came home and found me hiding in his closet with a baseball bat, dressed in nothing more than my boxer shorts. I told him I was getting ready to play a game where I would get 50 points for every car window I smashed. What can I say? PCP is a hell of a drug.

Not long after that night, Chuck kicked me out of his apartment. I don't know if he just wanted his privacy back, or maybe it was because of how I was acting. Whatever his reasons, I had to find a new place to live. So, I asked my brother Mike if I could stay with him for a while, and he happily agreed. At the time, my brother thought I was only smoking weed and taking pills. He had no clue that I was shooting heroin. He would have never let me stay with him and his family if he had known.

The best part about living with my brother was the free room and board. Instead of paying rent, all I had to do was babysit my niece once a week so he could go to the bar with his girlfriend. It was a really sweet deal, but I couldn't even hold up my end of the bargain like I was supposed to.

As my addiction progressed, I became more prone to being dope sick. It used to be where I could go seven or eight hours before I became sick, but now I could only go three or four hours before feeling it. I couldn't even get through a night of babysitting. So, sometimes I had Chris watch my niece while I drove to Kensington to get some dope. Mike would have been pissed if he came home and found some headbanger junkie, who he didn't know, watching his two-year-old daughter while I was out buying drugs. My only other option was to strap her in a car seat and take her with me, but I could never bring myself to do that.

After a while, my dope habit got so bad that delivering pizzas just wasn't cutting it anymore. So, I got a second delivery job at a dry-cleaning company in North Philly, which was perfect because it wasn't too far from the dope spots. This made it easy for me to grab some dope before or after work every day.

One day after work, I cashed my paycheck and headed to my favorite spot to buy both a bundle of dope and a bundle of coke. I noticed a red pickup truck slowly creeping by as I parked my car. They looked like undercover cops, but I wasn't 100% sure until they pulled over down the block and started looking at me through the rearview mirror. I knew it was risky, but I was dope sick, so I said, "Fuck it," and walked across the street to the dope spot. Once I was out of the cop's line of sight, I did the hand-to-hand with the dealer and got my bundles.

When I got back in the car, I stashed the drugs in my favorite hiding spot. The fabric on the car's interior roof was loose, so I could pull it down just enough to stash a few bundles. After hiding my stash, I saw the undercover cops in the red pickup truck still parked up the block. I knew they would follow and pull me over once I drove past them. So instead of driving past them, I put the car in reverse, backed up into the intersection, and made a left turn at the cross street. But, at the end of the block, I got stuck at a red light. I looked in the rearview and saw the red pickup reversing into the intersection, making the same maneuver I had just made. Now I 100% knew they were cops, and they were coming for me!

I couldn't wait for the light to turn green, so I made a left turn and almost crashed into another car, but he slammed on his brakes just in time. With no time to waste, I pushed the pedal to the floor and made the first left I could, followed by a right, then another quick left. I then drove for a few blocks until I was sure I had lost them. WHEW! That was close.

I wanted to get out of that neighborhood, but I desperately needed a syringe. So I drove to Kensington and Somerset and parked on the corner. As soon as I turned off the engine, the red pickup truck pulled behind me and boxed me in. Two cops, one white and one black, jumped out of the car with guns drawn and told me to stick my hands out of the window. They were fucking pissed as they dragged me out of the car and slammed me onto the ground.

"You thought you lost us, didn't you?"

"I did lose you! You just got lucky."

He didn't like what I said because he knew I was right. The white cop searched my car while the black one politely asked why I stopped at a known drug corner. They were trying to play good cop/bad cop, but I saw right through their bullshit. I told him I thought I saw an old friend on the corner but realized it wasn't him when I got out of the car. The cop knew I was lying, which made him so mad that he forgot he was supposed to be the good cop.

"You think I'm a fucking idiot? Why were you really there? And don't fucking lie to me!"

He knew why I was on that corner, and I knew he knew why I was on that corner. So I told him the truth, but I didn't tell him the whole truth. I told him I had stopped there to buy some dope, but the dealers didn't have any and told me to come back in 10 minutes. As the cop continued to search my car, my heart continued to pound harder and harder. I was afraid he would find the bundles stashed inside my roof, but to my surprise, the only thing he found was $23 and an old, broken syringe. They assumed the $23 was my dope money, so they thought I was telling the truth and just let me go.

After that day, I realized I needed a foolproof plan. Making up stories on the fly wasn't cutting it anymore. I needed a legitimate reason for being in that neighborhood, one that seemed credible enough for the cops to give me the benefit of the doubt when I got pulled over. So I took a paint bucket and some brushes I had found in my brother's basement and threw them in the back seat of my car. Then I got myself a notebook and wrote some random addresses in the area. Next to the addresses, I wrote fake names, phone numbers, and parts of a house that may need painting. It worked like a charm. A week or two later, I got pulled over again and told the cop that I was on my way to give an estimate. I even pretended to be lost and asked the cop for directions. That notebook got me out of trouble so many times, and the cops never thought twice about it. Sometimes I think I was too slick for my own good.

Chapter 14

I didn't have to pay rent at my brother's house. In fact, I didn't even have to pay for food because he fed me every day. Not to mention, I didn't have any personal bills; unless you count my car insurance. But I stopped paying for that after I scanned the card onto my brother's computer and edited the date to make it look valid. Now, even though I worked two jobs and had no bills to pay, it still wasn't enough to support my ever-growing drug habit.

My addiction was becoming an animal, and that animal was getting hungry. The more that animal grew, the more I had to feed it. But it began interfering with my job at the dry cleaners. While out on deliveries, I'd pull the work van over to get high, and if I wasn't out on a delivery, I'd just shoot up in the bathroom. Not to mention, I was constantly running late because I had to get my dope before going to work every day.

It didn't take long to realize that the dry cleaners I worked at didn't have an actual cash register. When customers came in to pay, my boss put the money in this little box he kept behind the counter. It wasn't locked up or hidden away in a secret spot or anything. It was almost like he wanted me to steal it. At first, I would only take $10-20 at a time. But like most addicts, I eventually got greedy and started taking $40-50 at a time. That's when my boss realized somebody was stealing, and I got caught red-handed. My boss was pissed! But after a couple minutes of yelling, he tried to have a serious talk with me. He knew I was on drugs and was worried I would end up dead or in jail. He made me promise to never steal from him again and asked me to at least consider getting help for my drug problem.

After our talk, he decided to give me a second chance. But a few days later, I ran out of gas on my way to work and was an hour late; that was the straw that broke the camel's back. After my shift ended, my boss handed me a canister of gas so I could get home, and then he fired me. I couldn't even be mad at him. I mean, I was surprised he put up with me for as long as he did.

I was kicking myself in the ass for getting fired, but at least I still had my pizza delivery job. And since the pizza shop paid me under the table, I could collect unemployment after losing the dry cleaning job. Besides, when one door closes, another one always opens up. A few days after losing that job, I ran into my second cousin, Billy. Billy was a painter and had customers who needed their houses painted but didn't have a car to get to them. Since I had a car, he asked if I wanted to make some extra money. A few days later, I was standing next to my cousin with a paintbrush in my hand.

I wasn't sure if I would like painting or not, but it wasn't as hard as I thought it would be, and the money wasn't bad either. Plus, I got to work with one of my favorite cousins every day. Billy and I had always been close, ever since we were kids. We even smoked blunts together every year at our family reunion and occasionally sold weed to each other here and there.

One day after work, Billy asked if I knew anyone who sold coke. It threw me off guard because I didn't know Billy did coke. But I told him about a spot in the hood we could go to, and without hesitation, he agreed to take the ride with me. We drove to Fifth and Westmoreland, which at the time had some of the best coke in the city. When we got there, I hopped out of the car to buy two bags, and Billy couldn't believe how I just walked around that neighborhood like it was nothing. I mean, Fifth and Westmoreland didn't even seem that bad of an area compared to some of the dope spots I went to every day. I became so comfortable going to these corners that it just didn't faze me anymore.

Whenever Billy and I did coke together, I always had to snort it because I didn't want him to know I was shooting it. But once in a while, Billy would tell me to take a break from painting so that I could go get some coke for us. I always used this opportunity to shoot the coke before I got back to the worksite. I would pinch a small amount from each bag and shoot it up, and he never knew the difference. Although, sometimes, I got greedy, and he would ask why the bags were so small. I felt bad for stealing from my cousin, but drugs made me do things I didn't want to do. It started getting to the point where I couldn't control myself anymore.

The last job I did with my cousin was at our uncle Denny's house in New Jersey. It took about three days to complete the job altogether. On the last day of the job, our uncle treated us to a few beers at the bar. Even though I didn't really drink anymore, I wasn't about to turn down free beer. But, when we got to the bar, I quickly learned that dope and alcohol don't mix well. I couldn't keep my eyes open. I felt like a narcoleptic, falling asleep and then waking up 20 seconds later, just to fall asleep again. This is the same effect I would get if I shot too much dope. Most people refer to this as "nodding out."

You may have seen dope fiends doing this on the street or in the countless videos you can find on YouTube. Sometimes they lean all the way down and almost touch the ground, but they never actually fall over. They call this the "dope lean." I rarely nodded out unless it was some really potent dope. Even though I loved shooting heroin, I hated the feeling of nodding out. It always made me feel weak and vulnerable. After nodding out at the bar, my cousin and uncle asked if I was OK. I told them I was just really exhausted, so they ordered some coffee to wake me up. I was so embarrassed and thought for sure that they knew I was high, even though they never mentioned it.

After a while, my cousin Billy couldn't get any more side work. Luckily, I still had the pizza job and my bi-weekly unemployment check, but it still wasn't enough; I was constantly dope sick. It felt like I wasn't even getting high. I was only shooting heroin so that I wouldn't feel like shit every day. Doing drugs just wasn't fun anymore, but I kept chasing that thrill I felt when I first started using them.

If there was one thing I couldn't deal with, it was being dope sick. I would always pray and hope to die just so I wouldn't have to deal with it anymore. So, it's no surprise that I would try anything to eliminate the feeling. This includes injecting alcohol directly into my bloodstream. If I couldn't get enough money for a bag, I'd just steal some liquor from my brother and inject it the same way I would heroin. It was a horrible, horrible feeling. The alcohol burned like crazy as it moved through my veins. But as much as I hated it, it helped ease some of the withdrawal symptoms. It made my anxiety and restless leg syndrome go away, but only for five minutes at a time, so I had to shoot it over and over again.

Eventually, I got sick and tired of being sick and tired. I was sick of waking up dope sick every morning in a bed that wasn't even mine. I was tired of never having money and needing to steal from people just to get a bag of dope. It was time for me to fight back and get my life together. I always knew I had a problem, but this was the first time I admitted to myself that I needed help.

Adam and his girlfriend were both trying to get clean and told me about this methadone clinic they were going to. They explained how a daily dose of methadone prevented them from getting dope sick every day. They also explained how methadone blocked other opioids, so if they tried to shoot dope, they would be wasting money because they wouldn't be able to feel it. It sounded too good to be true, but they hadn't used heroin in a few weeks, so I figured I'd give it a shot.

I couldn't go to the same clinic as Adam because they didn't have space for new clients, so I had to go to one on the other side of town. On my first day at the clinic, they assigned me to a counselor and introduced me to my group. It was a small group of about six people, and I could tell that none of them wanted to be there. The counselor tried to teach us how to deal with our emotions and talk about our feelings and childhood; it was a bunch of bullshit. After the group ended, hundreds of people lined up to get their methadone, and I quickly realized why it was so damn popular.

Shortly after receiving my first dose, the withdrawal symptoms I had been feeling all day slowly faded away. It felt like I shot a bag of dope, except it didn't hit me all at once. Instead, it came on gradually and lasted all day long. Even the following day, when I woke up, I barely felt sick. At that moment, I really thought that methadone was going to help me stay clean.

A few days later, Chris started going to the methadone clinic with me. So every day, after getting our methadone, we would meet outside so that he could catch a ride back to the neighborhood with me. One day, Chris and I were walking toward the car when I noticed a big yellow boot on my front tire and a bright orange sticker on my windshield. It was a notice from the Philadelphia Parking Authority stating that I owed them money for unpaid parking tickets. I was furious! It's not like I owed them thousands of dollars; it was three fucking tickets, barely totaling $200. The notice stated that I would have to pay the $200 plus an additional $100 to remove the boot. My only option was to work for a couple of days until I had enough saved up. But here's the kicker: I couldn't deliver pizzas to make money if I didn't have a car.

So with no money and no car to make money, I had to wait until I got my unemployment check. But by the time I got my unemployment check, the parking authority had already towed the car. So now, on top of the $300 I already owed, I had to pay an additional $300 in towing and storage fees. My unemployment check was only $450, which wasn't enough to cover the $600 needed to get my car back. So, I had no choice but to quit my job.

After losing both my car and my job, I did what any addict would have done. I got high so that I wouldn't have to deal with the anger I was feeling. Using my unemployment money, I grabbed a couple bags of dope but quickly forgot that methadone blocks other opioids, making it much harder to feel the desired effects. However, I discovered it didn't stop it completely. It was still possible to experience that rush; I just had to shoot a lot more heroin if I wanted to feel it.

When I lost my car, I also lost my desire to get clean, but now that I was on methadone, my tolerance for heroin was inconceivable. I had to shoot five bags at once just to feel something. So I couldn't afford to do it that much, especially now that my only income was from unemployment. To make matters worse, the methadone clinic had mandatory group therapy; if I missed one of these sessions, they wouldn't give me my dose for that day. So, if I overslept or didn't have enough money for the bus, I would get dope sick and have no choice but to get some heroin. It wasn't much of an issue when I delivered pizzas because I was making money every day. But when I lost my job, it became a real problem.

One day, I missed my group, and they wouldn't let me get my methadone, so I felt dope sick all day. I tried to tough it out as long as possible, but later that night, while trying to sleep, I kept tossing and turning, scheming ways to get money so I wouldn't have to feel like this. By 5:00 a.m., I finally had enough and decided to take action.

I threw on a pair of black sweatpants and a hoodie, and then walked down the street to the Tacony Train Station. After waiting for what seemed like an eternity, I saw a middle-aged man getting out of a taxi. One look at his business suit and the dollar signs flashed before my eyes. The cab pulled away as the man walked toward the train stop, where I was waiting in the shadows. When he got closer, I stepped out of the darkness and asked if he knew what time it was. He looked at his watch, and before he could answer, I had a straight-edge razor aimed at his throat.

"Gimme ya wallet, mother fucker!"

"OK. Calm down. Don't do anything stupid now."

I could see the fear in his eyes as he cautiously handed me his wallet. I felt terrible for doing this, but I also felt like I didn't have a choice. After taking the cash out, I handed the wallet back to him. I didn't want his credit cards; because I knew I would get caught if I tried to use them. I wasn't about to be on the next episode of America's Dumbest Criminals. After stuffing the cash into my pocket, I ran as fast as possible down the street. I was only a block away from my brother's house, so I was home before the guy could even call the police. But my brother Mike was awake now and getting ready for work. So when I rushed into the house, out of breath, at 5:45 a.m., he gave me a puzzled look.

"What the hell are you doing?"

"Oh, I couldn't sleep, so uh, I decided to go for a little run."

It was the perfect alibi since I was sweating and out of breath, so Mike thought nothing of it and left for work a few minutes later. But that night, when he got home, he started questioning me.

"What the fuck did you do this morning?"

"Wh-what? What are you talking about? I didn't do anything."

"When I left for work, cops were looking for someone in a black hoodie."

"Huh?"

"Weren't you wearing a black hoodie?"

I tried to convince him it was just a coincidence, but I don't think he bought it. He knew those cops were looking for me, but he also knew I would never tell him the truth. Robbing and stealing off complete strangers was one thing. However, the guilt really hit me when I started stealing from my brother and his girlfriend. They let me live in their home rent-free and fed me every day. And how do I repay them? By fucking robbing them.

It started small, taking a few dollars from the change jar they kept in their room. I would take just enough so that they wouldn't notice. But, after a while, I got greedy. I started hitting up that change jar every day until all the quarters were gone and had to resort to taking dimes and nickels. After that, I graduated to stealing from my brother's wallet. I would wait for him to jump in the shower and then sneak into his room to see how much cash I could get without him noticing. If he had $60, I would only take $20. I didn't want to take it all because then he would definitely know someone stole it. But it would be harder for him to notice if I just took a little bit.

Sometimes, I even waited for Mike to fall asleep so I could steal his ATM card, take money out of his account, and then put the card back without him noticing. It was only a matter of time before I found his girlfriend's money stash and started stealing from her, too. I didn't enjoy stealing from them. I felt so fucking guilty for doing it, but I just couldn't stop. Heroin had me by the fucking balls, and I would've done anything just to get one more bag.

Being dope sick put me in a state of desperation, and when I was desperate, the Devil would start calling my name. I tried to ignore it, but it always spoke to me in my own voice. It's hard not to listen to what your own voice is telling you, even if that voice tells you to rob a church.

It was a Sunday morning. I sat across the street from Our Lady of Consolation Church, the same church I was once an altar boy at. This was also the same church where I received my sacraments and attended mass with my mom every Sunday when I was a child. So you can imagine how conflicted I was as I sat there plotting to steal from the same church that I practically grew up in. However, my only concern was getting that next fix, and I didn't care what had to be done to get it.

I stood in the back of the church to get a good view of the ushers as they collected the money. They had baskets attached to long poles and went pew to pew, collecting money from the churchgoers. My eyes followed the money baskets as they slowly made their way to the back of the church. The head usher took the money from each basket and stuffed it into a large envelope. I knew his next step would be to bring the cash to the rectory across the street, so I went outside and waited for my opportunity.

I sat on the rectory steps, anxiously waiting for the usher to come out of the church. A few minutes later, the door opened, and the money man came walking out. As the usher got closer, my heart began to race, and I knew my feet would soon be doing the same. I was about to reach for the envelope when the usher's words threw me off guard.

"Good morning, and God bless you."

His words paralyzed me like a deer in headlights. I couldn't move. I couldn't speak. I couldn't do anything. I felt like a little kid who got caught with his hand in the cookie jar. The usher gave me a confused look and asked if I was OK. I lacked the courage to even answer him. Instead, I darted toward my brother's house. When I got home, I splashed water on my face and took a deep look at myself in the mirror. Honestly, I didn't recognize the person staring back at me. I saw evilness in my eyes that I had never seen before.

"Who da fuck are you?" I asked myself.

I might as well have been talking to a stranger because I didn't know who I was anymore.

Chapter 15

Every year for Thanksgiving, my family would have dinner at my sister Kim's house in Warminster, PA. This was something I always looked forward to, not only for extra helpings of stuffing and cranberry sauce but also to spend time with my nieces. The holidays were the only time I ever saw them, so I cherished our time together. I loved tickling them to death and chasing them around the house, but I loved chasing that dope even more.

My daily routine consisted of waking up and heading straight to the methadone clinic. But on that Thanksgiving Day, I didn't make it to the clinic. I can't remember exactly why I didn't go. Maybe they closed early for the holiday, and I woke up too late. Or perhaps, and this is most likely the real reason, I got a case of the "fuck its" and decided to get high instead. Regardless of the reason, I had to get some dope before going to Kim's house. There was no way I could be dope sick in front of my whole family at Thanksgiving dinner.

Since my brother Mike was also going to Kim's for Thanksgiving, he offered me a ride, but I had to get some dope first, so I told him I'd just meet him there. My plan was to get my dope and then take the bus to Warminster. But, for some reason, all the buses were running late that day. By the time I finally got to Kensington, an hour had already passed. Then, on the way back to the bus terminal, the bus was late again. That's when I realized the buses weren't running late. They were running on a holiday schedule; I was screwed.

I had to take three buses to get to Warminster, and because of the holiday schedule, they only came once an hour. I started feeling dope sick before I even got halfway there. So I thought about shooting up on the bus, but I didn't want to risk getting caught and kicked off in the middle of East Bumblefuck.

When I finally arrived at Kim's house, not only was I super dope sick, but I was also super late. I was supposed to be there by 3:00 p.m., and it was now 5:30 p.m. As soon as I walked in the door, I could feel the tension in the air. Instead of the usual cheery smiles and excitement, all I got were half smiles and looks of disappointment. I immediately noticed the empty, dirty dishes sitting on the TV trays in the living room. A normal person would have felt embarrassed, but I was too dope sick to worry about it. I honestly didn't even have an appetite. The only thing I cared about was getting that dope in my arm.

I wasted no time at all. In fact, I didn't even take my coat off. I pretended my bladder was about to explode and rushed straight to the bathroom. I mixed my dope up as fast as I could. But, when I tried to inject it, I couldn't find a decent vein. This is not uncommon for people that have been using heroin for a while. After shooting up for so long, an addict's veins start to collapse, making it difficult to find a suitable one to use. When this happens, they usually start shooting up in different areas of the body, such as the neck or the legs, but I had not reached that point yet. I was still shooting it in my arms, so it took me a while to inject it. I was probably in the bathroom for almost 20 minutes before I finally came out.

I thought I had everyone fooled. I thought that nobody knew I was getting high in that bathroom. But my family is pretty clever. I showed up almost two hours late, over-anxious and sweating like I had just run a marathon. Then, I immediately head to the bathroom and come out 20 minutes later, calm and relaxed. But no one said anything to me that day, probably because they didn't want to ruin the holiday.

A couple of weeks later, I started thinking about what to get everyone for Christmas. Even though I would rather spend every last dime on heroin, I promised myself I would get gifts for everyone. I didn't want my family to know I was on heavy drugs. So, I figured that getting everyone presents would make it seem like I had my shit together; or so I thought. I wasn't working at the time, but my unemployment check was a little over $400. The money came on an electronic debit card every other Wednesday. That year, Christmas Eve landed on one of those Wednesdays. So I waited until the last minute to get all my shopping done.

When Christmas Eve finally came, I went to "the Gallery," a popular mall in Center City, Philadelphia, to grab gifts for everyone on my Christmas list. After I finished shopping, I walked around Center City for a while. I wanted to get into the holiday spirit and check out the Christmas lights. But as I watched all the families walk around, happy and smiling, it made me think about my own family, whom I barely talk to anymore. Then I started thinking about how much I missed Penelope and how I practically had nothing; no car, no job, and living in my brother's basement. Finally, I started thinking about my mom and how I would give anything just to talk to her again.

84

I stood there in the heart of the city, feeling lonely and depressed, as all these families strolled past me, living their happy-go-lucky lives. Why do they get to be happy while I have to suffer in misery? It felt like I was being tortured. Every time I saw someone smiling, I just wanted to punch them in the face. And every time I heard someone laughing, it sounded like nails on a chalkboard. I just couldn't take it anymore! My only solution was to get high. So, on my way home, I stopped to pick up a little Christmas present for myself. Let's face it; I was a bad boy that year, so I knew Santa wouldn't be leaving any dope under the Christmas tree for me.

When I got off the el at Somerset Street, the familiar stench of Kensington Avenue put me at ease. The only thing that sucked was I had to lug all the shopping bags around the neighborhood. I was paranoid about being robbed, leaving me with no gifts for my family on Christmas morning. But getting high was worth the risk, so I bought five bags of the best dope in the neighborhood. Part of me wanted to wait until I got home to shoot it, but the addict inside me said, "Fuck that shit!"

After I got my dope, I walked down Tusculum Street, a quiet, shady block right off Kensington Avenue. I sat down on the steps of the first house I saw. It was late at night, so I figured none of the neighbors would be awake to bother me. When I shot the dope, I felt that rush of relief sweep across my entire body. Damn, I forgot how good this dope was. I closed my heavy eyelids so that I could enjoy the moment.

"Hey buddy, are you OK?" an unfamiliar voice suddenly asked.

I opened my eyes to find a paramedic standing over me. Behind him was a group of firefighters standing near a fire truck with flashing lights. I looked down and saw the needle still sticking out of my arm.

"You OK? Whatcha doin' here?" a firefighter asked.

I had never felt so confused in my life. I didn't know what was happening because they had abruptly awakened me in the middle of a very vivid dream. In that dream, I was lost and trying to find my friend's house. So when the firefighter asked what I was doing there, I must've still been dreaming and thought I was looking for my friend.

"Wh-wh-what do you mean? I'm going to see my friend."

I stood up, walked to the first house on the block, and knocked on the door, thinking it was my friend's house. But when I knocked on the door, a Spanish lady leaned out of the window from above.

"I know you ain't bangin' on my door, you fuckin' fiend."

When I heard the lady screaming from above, I realized she was not my friend. In fact, I had no clue who she was. That's when I slowly started coming back to reality. The last thing I remembered was it being so dark outside that I could barely see my veins to get the needle in. But now it was broad daylight, and that's when I realized it was morning. But not just any morning, it was Christmas morning! I looked around, and all my shopping bags were gone. Somebody stole all the Christmas gifts I had bought for my family. I reached for the phone in my pocket, but it wasn't there. My wallet was missing too! FUCK! They got me for everything.

The paramedics tried to convince me to go to the hospital, but I refused because I was afraid the cops would start asking questions. Then, the firefighters asked if I wanted to make a police report for my stolen gifts, but again, I didn't want to get the cops involved. So I shook my head no, brushed myself off, and walked away.

As I walked down the street, I began thinking about how most people wake up with their family on Christmas morning and open gifts. But I woke up on a sidewalk off of Kensington Avenue. And it's not like I could have rushed home to exchange gifts with everyone because they were all stolen. I couldn't even call anyone to explain what happened, because they had also stolen my phone. Shit, I didn't even have money to get home! Then, to top it all off, I saw my reflection in a car window and noticed a massive bruise on my forehead. When I overdosed the night before, I must've banged my head on the pavement and laid there, frozen, in the cold winter air all night long.

Years later, I realized how lucky I was to be alive, and I still believe it was a Christmas miracle. But back then, I didn't believe in things like "Christmas miracles." Shit, I didn't believe in miracles at all; I barely believed in God. All I knew was that it was Christmas morning, and I felt like a piece of shit. I felt worthless and ashamed of myself. I was an embarrassment to my family and a disgrace to humanity. As I walked down the street with all these thoughts rattling in my mind, I realized I didn't even know where I was walking to. I just walked around aimlessly with no money to get home.

After realizing I was literally walking nowhere, I decided to rest for a bit until I could figure out what to do. I picked a spot on the curb along Kensington Avenue, near Somerset Station. As I sat down, I couldn't help but think of myself as another lost soul stuck under the el with nowhere to go. The more I thought about what had happened, the more worthless I felt. But what really put the icing on the cake was the fact that I couldn't give my little nieces their Christmas gifts. That's when I had to fight back the tears, and eventually, the tears won. They felt warm rolling down my cold cheeks, but by the time they got to my chin, it felt like they were going to turn into icicles. This moment was the lowest I'd ever felt in my life, at least up until this point. But as I sat there in my own self-pity, little did I know that a Christmas angel would come to save the day.

As I sat on the curb, crying my eyes out, at least two dozen people had passed me without even blinking an eye. This made me feel even worse because it proved that nobody gave a fuck about me. But then, I suddenly felt someone standing close to me.

"What's wrong, my brother?"

I looked up to find a tall black man with a bald head, wearing black sunglasses and a black leather coat. I explained what had happened and how I was stuck with no way to get back home. He stood there in silence as he looked at me with sorrow.

"Follow me," the mysterious man said.

I didn't know where he was taking me or what he had planned, but my day couldn't get any worse. So, I followed him up the steps to the Somerset Station, where he handed the cashier a few dollars.

"This is for his fare," the man told the cashier.

I couldn't believe it! This man, whom I had never met before, was willing to help a worthless junkie like me. At that point, I realized there was still hope in the world.

When I got home, I made up some bullshit story to tell my brother. I told him I was visiting a girl the night before and got mugged on my way home. I even used the bruise on my forehead as evidence to convince him that someone had attacked me. But Mike saw right through my bullshit. Nobody could believe a word I said anymore. I felt so alone in the world and slipped into a state of deep depression. No matter how hard I tried, I just couldn't see the point of living anymore.

Chapter 16

This brings us back to the beginning of the story. Hopefully, now you have a better understanding of how I got to such a dark place in my life. I was feeling hopeless and thought I would never be able to get clean. I was angry at myself for even getting hooked on heroin in the first place; how could I let myself get to this point? It felt like my existence on this earth just didn't matter anymore. I tried to stop doing drugs, but it obviously didn't work. The methadone clinic wasn't working either. I was stealing from my family, mugging people on the street, and even came inches away from robbing a church. I felt like a demon had taken control of my body.

I was tired of waking up every morning and trying to figure out how to get $10 for another bag. I knew I had a serious problem, but I thought I was beyond the point of getting help. It even seemed like God had given up on me because I asked him for help more times than I could count, but time after time, my prayers were never answered. I was at the end of my rope and just wanted the pain to end. Honestly, I thought the world would be better off without me, so I planned out the details of my suicide. I figured an overdose would be my best option because it would look like an accident. I was worried about what people thought of me, even after I was dead.

Just like I had explained at the beginning of the story, I bought all the drugs I could afford and took them all at the same time. But, when my plan didn't work, I stumbled onto the train tracks and waited for a train to take my life. My ex-girlfriend, Penelope, called me at just the right moment. If she called 60 seconds later, you wouldn't be reading this story right now.

After I walked off the tracks and the train zoomed past me, I immediately realized how lucky I was. I felt like I had experienced a divine intervention of some sort and began to wonder why God spared my life. I didn't have an answer at the time, but I knew God must've given me a second chance for a reason. Whatever that reason may have been, I decided to take full advantage of it and told myself I was 100% done with drugs, but it wasn't that simple. I knew that if I wanted to get clean, I would have to get off the methadone. But I couldn't stop going to the clinic because then I would get dope sick, leading me right back to heroin. So, I continued going to the clinic but promised myself I was done with getting high.

That first day of staying clean started off as planned. I went to the clinic to get my dose and felt good about doing the right thing. Everything was fine until I got back home. I was so used to running around, scheming, and plotting ways to get high that I didn't know how to just sit down and relax. I tried watching TV but started going stir-crazy after a few hours. A little while later, my brother went out to the bar, and that's when that little voice started to talk to me again. I didn't even try to fight it; I caved in immediately. I snuck into my brother's room, stole some money, and headed to dope town. After grabbing some dope, I went to a bando to shoot it up and then got right back on the el.

As I headed back home, I began to feel guilty for stealing from my brother again. I knew I needed help and wouldn't be able to do it on my own. So, later that night, I wrote Mike a letter that explained how I was hooked on heroin and needed help. The letter also admitted how I had been stealing from him and tried to take my own life.

The following day, my brother found the letter on the kitchen table. He gave me two choices: I could get off the methadone and into rehab or get out of his house. The decision was easy, but there was one problem: I couldn't get into detox because of the methadone clinic. A government program called BHSI, which stands for Behavioral Health Special Initiative, provides funds for drug and alcohol treatment programs. But since I was already on methadone, they were giving me trouble about paying for the detox and rehab. I didn't want to be on methadone anymore, but my only other option was to quit cold turkey. And let's face it, that was never going to happen.

A few days later, I was expressing my frustrations with someone at the methadone clinic when they told me about a loophole in the system. They explained that if I were to attempt suicide or even have suicidal thoughts, then BHSI may be more willing to get me into rehab. So with this new information, I came up with a game plan. I tried to check myself into Friends Hospital, but when I explained how I attempted to kill myself on the train tracks, they wouldn't admit me because I was not suicidal at that moment. Instead, they gave me the number to BHSI and told me to contact them directly. So, I called BHSI and explained my situation. The man on the other end of the phone helped me tremendously and said he would try his best to get me into rehab. We kept in contact over the next few days while he tried to find me a bed at a detox center, but day after day, we had no luck.

Before I could get into detox, I ended up stealing from my brother again. He noticed it the next day and immediately kicked me out of his house. I couldn't blame him. I couldn't even get mad; it's not like he didn't warn me. Deep down, I knew my brother loved me, and in the long run, he helped me hit rock bottom a little faster by kicking me out. It jump-started the motivation I needed to get clean. It put me in a state of mind where I was determined to hurdle any obstacles that got in my way.

I spent the next couple of weeks couch surfing, going house to house with a trash bag full of clothes. One night I would stay at Chris' place, and the next night I might stay at Jerry's. And then there were some nights when I had nowhere to go and had to rest my head on a park bench. But I managed to stay clean even on those cold, lonely nights. I patiently waited two weeks before I finally got into a detox center, and for those two weeks, I did not use any heroin at all.

I had to go to Kensington Hospital for my detox, and when I got there, it was nothing like I expected it to be. The hospital was on a small block in the middle of the ghetto. It was an old, dirty, three-story brick building. If you didn't know any better, you could easily mistake it for a small apartment property. I had to fill out some forms and wait a few hours while they processed my paperwork. Sitting in that waiting room, I couldn't help but think about how much better life would be once I got out of rehab. I was eager to get a record deal, meet the girl of my dreams, and settle down in a big fancy house with a white picket fence. I had it all figured out, that is until I met Tanya.

Tanya checked into detox the day after I did. The first time I laid eyes on her, I thought she looked like a young Juliette Lewis, only a lot cuter. She had a petite body, a pretty smile, and beautiful blue eyes. On her first night there, all the other guys were hawking her. It reminded me of seagulls at the shore surrounding a sunbather eating chips. I wondered if they realized how pathetic they looked. I came here to get clean, not to pick up chicks. I wasn't about to drool over her like a piece of meat that someone threw into a cage full of animals, so I just went to bed.

The following day, I woke up, grabbed my breakfast, and sat down to eat by myself. As I ate my breakfast, Tanya approached and asked if she could sit with me. I wasn't going to be a dick, so I introduced myself and told her to sit down. We got to talking, and somehow the conversation led to us laughing about the guys hitting on her the night before.

90

"So why weren't you hitting on me last night? What, I'm not good enough for you?"

I knew she was only joking, but I didn't know how to answer her. I was attracted to her, and after a few minutes of talking, it was evident that she was also attracted to me. We instantly clicked, laughing and smiling whenever we were near each other.

When we were in detox, different people from AA and NA came and held meetings with us. They explained how we should attend meetings after rehab if we wanted to stay clean. I heard what they were saying, but I definitely wasn't listening. One person suggested how we shouldn't start any new relationships until we had at least one year clean and sober. Tanya and I looked at each other as if we both said, "Fuck that shit," with our eyes, followed by a devious smile. That same guy pointed to us and said we should stay away from each other if we were serious about getting clean. I just laughed it off and threw everything he said right out the window; if only I would have listened.

That year, I had to celebrate my birthday while I was in detox. It wasn't as bad as it sounds, though. One of the nurses brought me a cake so everyone could sing happy birthday to me. After we had cake, Tanya said she had a birthday gift for me and that I should sneak into her room later that night if I wanted to get it. So I waited until everyone was asleep, and when the nurse wasn't looking, I crept down the hallway and into the girl's room. I army crawled over to Tanya's bed so I wouldn't wake the other girls. But when I nudged Tanya to wake up, she became startled and screamed, waking all the other girls up. The lights in the room suddenly came on, and one of the older ladies was staring me down.

"You're not supposed to be in here!"

"Oh, I uh, I had to tell Tanya something very important."

I couldn't think of anything else to say. I knew I was busted, so I just left. A few days later, I got called into the back office. I walked in and met a flamboyant gay black guy who introduced himself and asked me to sit down. I thought I was about to get in trouble for sneaking into the girls' room. But, it turns out he just wanted to discuss which rehab I would go to after detox. He told me about this one place called "Self Help Movement" and then handed me a pamphlet. I looked over the booklet for a minute and noticed it was an all-male facility.

"All-male? So no girls?"

"Brian, you need to leave the girls alone and focus on yourself right now."

He explained how Self Help Movement was the only rehab with a bed for me, so Tanya and I wouldn't be able to go to the same place. I then explained to him that if I couldn't go to rehab with Tanya, I wouldn't be going to rehab at all.

"So tell me, Brian, how are you going to stay clean? What's your plan?"

"I'll get clean with Tanya. We'll keep each other clean."

He shook his head in disbelief and wished me the best of luck. The next day, when I got out of detox, I was still withdrawing a little bit. So, I got myself a bag of weed and rolled a blunt to help calm my nerves. At the time, I didn't see anything wrong with this. After all, my problem was with heroin, not weed. A couple of minutes after I lit that blunt, my sister Kim called to tell me how proud she was of me. Here I was, smoking weed, telling my sister how great it feels to be clean. It was obvious that I hadn't changed at all.

Tanya left detox the next day and met up with me as soon as she got out. We were excited to be with each other without the restriction of being stuck in a detox. Now, neither of us had money, food, or even a place to live. So, I called my boy Chris and asked if we could stay with him until we figured out what to do. He had no problem with it, but it wasn't like he had his own place; he was still living with his parents. Chris hid us in the basement for as long as he could, but his dad figured out what was going on by day three. Chris' dad didn't kick us out, but we could tell that we weren't exactly welcome there. So Tanya called her brother Roy and asked if we could stay with him for a while. He agreed to let us stay there, but on one condition: we had to stay clean!

After Tanya hung up the phone, we packed our bags and jumped on the el. I didn't know where Tanya's brother lived, but it didn't matter; I was just happy to have a place to stay. When the train got to Somerset Station, Tanya grabbed her bags and started to leave. I thought she was playing a joke on me, but once I realized she was serious, I grabbed my stuff and followed her. At first, I thought she was trying to be sneaky and just wanted to get a bag of dope or something. But I quickly learned that her brother lived on Somerset Street, near Frankford Avenue. I got clean to stay out of that neighborhood, yet there I was, moving into it. If that's not irony, I don't know what is.

Tanya and I were still dope sick when we moved into Roy's house. Even though the detox helped wean us off heroin, we still felt the withdrawal effects for that first week or two. Neither of us could deal with the withdrawal, but we didn't want to get high either. So, we drank away the symptoms with a bottle of liquor instead. And since we were going to get drunk, I figured I might as well get a bag of weed, too.

After that night, we started drinking and smoking weed all the time. Eventually, we even started taking zannies again. We saw nothing wrong with this because we thought we would be fine as long as we stayed away from the dope. We even went to meetings because we thought they would help us stay away from it. One night, we popped some zannies and stopped by the liquor store before going to our meeting. There I was, sitting in a meeting, high on Xanax with a bottle of vodka in my bag. I even raised my hand and told everyone I had been clean for three weeks. The truth is, I was only lying to myself.

About two months later, Tanya and I found a room for rent not far from her brother's house on Huntingdon Street. I used my unemployment money to pay for the first two weeks' rent. Everything seemed to be going great after we moved in, but as time passed, drinking, smoking weed, and popping zannies just weren't enough. We both wanted something more, so we started smoking wet again. And then, a few short weeks later, I started doing coke again. I quickly realized that I was following the same pattern that led me to heroin in the first place. The only difference was, this time, it didn't take years for me to graduate to coke.

When we stayed with Tanya's brother, Roy, we had to play it off like we were clean, so we hid our drinking and drugging from him the best we could. But when we moved into our own place, all bets were off. It only took a few short weeks to get evicted because we spent all the rent money on drugs and alcohol. So, Tanya asked her other brother, Joey, if we could stay with him until we found a new place to live. He agreed to let us stay there, but only for one month.

Joey's apartment was on Emerald Street, near Lehigh Avenue, a few blocks from Roy's house. He had a small spare bedroom in the back, which he used as storage, but there was no bed, dressers, or anything like that. It was packed to the ceiling with a bunch of knick-knacks and random stuff. We had to move shit around just to clear a spot on the floor for us to sleep. We slept on that hardwood floor with literally nothing, not even a blanket to cover ourselves with. Despite these conditions, neither of us complained because we knew it was better than sleeping on the streets.

A couple of days after we moved in, we were sitting on Joey's stoop, drinking forties with his neighbors. I went inside to use the bathroom, but when I got back, Tanya was gone. She told everyone she was going to the store, but almost two hours had passed before she finally came back. We fought half the night until she finally admitted how she went and copped some heroin. In my mind, I kept thinking about how unfair that was. It was unfair that she got to do dope and I didn't.

I was mad at Tanya for doing heroin again, and I wanted to get even with her. So, I stormed out of the house and walked around the corner to grab myself a bag. Then I brought it back to her brother's apartment, so I could shoot it up right in front of her. I don't know why, but I thought it would make her jealous or something; she didn't give a fuck.

When we reached our one-month deadline at Joey's apartment, we didn't have enough money to move out because we had been spending all of our money on dope. So, Tanya called her ex-boyfriend, who she'd borrow money from every once in a while. She knew he was still in love with her and took full advantage of him. I wasn't fond of the idea of her meeting up with her ex like that, but she always used his money to buy us dope, so I never argued with her about it. Tanya knew he just got paid and would be walking around with the money in his pocket. So, she called and asked if she could borrow a couple of dollars, and, like always, he happily agreed to meet up with her.

After she left, I quickly dressed in all black clothing, borrowed a ski mask from her brother, and waited down the street from where Tanya was supposed to meet him. A few minutes later, I saw him walking toward her. So I threw the ski mask over my face, crept up from behind, grabbed Tanya's hair, and put a knife to her throat.

"Give me da money, or I'll fuckin' cut her. You too bitch! Give up da money!"

Tanya reached into her pocket and handed me $2, but her ex hesitated.

"Brian, I know that's you!"

I threw Tanya to the ground, pointed the knife at him, and said, "You think this is a fuckin' game? I'll slice da shit outta you!"

94

He reluctantly reached into his pocket and handed me a wad of cash. Once I had the money, I ran down the street, cut through an alleyway, and went straight into Joey's apartment. When I walked in the door, the phone was ringing, so I answered it.

"I just got fuckin' robbed. Some dickhead put a knife to my throat," Tanya screamed into the phone.

She sounded so convincing that she could've won an Academy Award for her performance. She was clever for calling me because it made him think I was at the apartment the whole time and had nothing to do with it. When Tanya returned to Joey's apartment, we laughed about it as we counted his money. We got about $300 from him, which was more than enough to rent a room. So we looked in the paper and tried to find one for rent, but the only place available on such short notice was near 26th and York Street. It was a few miles away, but our only other option was to be homeless, so we had no choice but to take it.

Even though we moved, our dope habit still forced us to walk back and forth to Kensington every day. It was a rough walk, not only because of the distance but also because we were the only white people in the neighborhood. Now don't get me wrong, our new neighbors showed us mad love and made us feel welcomed from day one. But people from the other blocks, who didn't know we lived in the area, always gave us trouble. They usually just talked some shit and left it at that, though. I only had one incident that turned violent while walking that route every day. And it wasn't even in that neighborhood; it was in West Kensington. It was late at night, and I had just bought a few bags of dope. I was walking up Lehigh Avenue when a young, stocky Spanish guy approached me.

"Qué pasa, papi? Whatcha lookin' for? I can get whatever you need."

"Nah, I'm cool, papi."

He asked again if I needed anything, so I again told him no. This dude just wouldn't give it up. He kept telling me about this new spot that was giving away free samples. It didn't seem that farfetched because the dope corners sometimes did this to attract new customers. So, I asked him where this corner was, and he told me to follow him. He took me down a very shady block with no houses. I never heard of anybody selling dope on this block, but I continued to follow him anyway. I thought maybe it was a new spot I didn't know about yet. Halfway down the block, he took me into a parking lot of an abandoned building, where he quickly changed his demeanor.

"Give up your shit, white boy. I got a gun. Don't make me use it."

I knew he didn't have a gun. If he did, he would have shown me instead of just telling me he had one. But I played along and pretended to be scared.

"I ain't even got nuttin' man. C'mon, don't shoot me."

"Empty your fuckin' pockets, white boy!"

I reached into my pocket, grabbed my blade, and pressed it against his throat. That straight razor was like my American Express; I never left home without it.

"Why don't you empty yours first?"

He stood frozen, as if he had just seen a ghost. He didn't know what to do. A second ago, he was trying to rob me, but now, he was the one being robbed. I made his pockets look like bunny ears by turning them inside out. He didn't have much, just a crack pipe and some cigarettes. So I took the pack of smokes and let him keep his pipe. As I pulled the knife away from his throat, he swung and landed a nice, clean punch to my mouth. My natural reaction was to punch him back, but I forgot I was holding the blade. I think I might have sliced his cheek a little, but I didn't stick around to find out. Instead, I took off and escaped into the darkness.

Chapter 17

I think it's safe to say that, by this point, my drug addiction was really getting out of hand. Even though I was collecting unemployment every other week, it just wasn't enough to support my habit. Whenever I got my unemployment money, I put half of it aside for the rent and usually had about $200 leftover. That $200 was supposed to last us two weeks, but it was usually gone after a day or two. One day, we were really dope sick, so Tanya tried to borrow cash from her ex, but he just wasn't budging. So in order to get money for us to get high, Tanya started prostituting.

In Philadelphia, prostitutes line up and down Kensington Avenue, all day and night. And Tanya was a pretty girl, so she had no problem getting customers. I hated the idea of her sleeping with strangers for money. I'd always been a jealous guy, so at first, it killed me inside. But after a while, I didn't even think twice about it. She always came back with enough money for us to get high, and that's all I really cared about. I guess I loved drugs more than I loved her.

Whenever Tanya worked the corner, I always stood close by in case any assholes gave her trouble. And after she got into each car, I would jot down the license plate number just in case she went missing. I was always afraid that something terrible was going to happen to her. Sometimes, waiting for her to get back felt like an eternity; it was like time stood still while she was gone.

One day, while waiting for Tanya to get back from turning a trick, this guy slowly drove by and smiled at me. He obviously mistook me for a gay prostitute, so I just ignored him and continued waiting for Tanya. But the guy circled the block and tried to get my attention again. I was dope sick, so I was already aggravated, and he just kept adding fuel to the fire. But again, I decided to let it go. I just wanted Tanya to get back with the money so we could get high. Would you believe this mother fucker circled the block a third time? Except for this time, he didn't just drive by and smile. No, this time, he pulled over, rolled down his window, and called me over to his car.

"Oh, you're cute. Are you working?"

"Yeah, 40 bucks, and I'll do anything you want."

I got in the car, and we drove around the corner to a secluded spot, where he parked the car and turned off the engine. But as he pulled out his wallet, I pulled out my knife. I saw the fear in his eyes as he handed me his wallet, and when I opened it up, there was exactly $40. I was disappointed he didn't have more money, but I guess beggars can't be choosers. After stuffing the cash in my pocket, I got out of the car and calmly walked away. I knew he wouldn't call the cops because then he would have to explain how he was trying to pick up a prostitute.

Eventually, our habits started growing bigger and bigger. Even with Tanya prostituting and me collecting unemployment, it still wasn't enough to keep us from getting dope sick every day. There were nights we didn't eat because we would rather starve ourselves than be dope sick. So, we got creative and figured out ways to conserve money. Sometimes we would steal sugar packets from McDonald's and buy a loaf of bread to make sugar sandwiches. And to save money at the laundromat, we wore the same clothes at least twice before washing them. And if it came down to it, we would scrub our clothes in the bathtub with a bar of soap.

This lifestyle continued for a while until Tanya met up with a friend one night and disappeared for five days. I was worried that something had happened to her, but my primary concern was how I had no money to get any dope. Tanya was the one who brought home money every day, so when she was gone, I was stuck like Chuck. I tried waiting for her to come back, but I started getting really sick after the second day. By the third day, I had to do something. So I got some free needles from the needle exchange and sold them at Kensington and Somerset for a buck a piece. I couldn't believe I turned into one of the junkies who sold works on Kensington Avenue. Before that point, I thought I was better than them or something, as if my addiction wasn't as bad as theirs; who was I kidding?

It was tough trying to sell works on that corner. You had to really hustle to make a dollar down there. Imagine 10 people trying to sell syringes to the same person, all at the same time, just to get $1. We were a bunch of vultures stalking our prey. On an average day, I could spend 12 hours on that corner and only make $30. That was barely enough to keep me going. I needed at least $70 worth of dope a day. And that wouldn't even get me high; it just made me feel normal and not be sick.

After a few rough days of hustling works on the corner, Tanya finally came back home. I was mad at her for letting me suffer like that, but I couldn't stay angry for too long, especially when she surprised me with two bags of dope. As soon as I saw those little blue bags, I instantly forgave her. I should've realized it, but she only came back because I was getting my unemployment money the next day. How could I be so naive?

98

The next day, I went to the bodega to hit the ATM. When I came back from the store, I tucked $200 for the rent in the top drawer of my dresser. Then I kissed Tanya goodbye and ventured out to get some more dope. I took the bus to Kensington, grabbed a couple of bags, and came straight back home. But when I got back, Tanya was gone; again. Only this time, she had taken all of her belongings with her. I was upset that she left, but I had a pocketful of dope, so I didn't really need her. I was actually happy because it meant I had more dope for myself.

I sat down on the bed and threw the bags of dope on the dresser. That's when I noticed that the top drawer was opened a crack. I thought about it for a minute, and I knew for a fact that I had shut that drawer before I left. Then I got that sinking feeling you get in your chest when you know something isn't right. So, I opened the dresser's top drawer and saw that the $200 was gone. I rummaged through the drawer, hoping it was hiding under a t-shirt or something, but it was nowhere to be found.

"Fuckin' bitch!" I shouted to myself.

I couldn't believe she stole the rent money. I didn't know what to do. Rent was due in a few days, and I had just spent my last dollar on dope. How could I explain this to the landlord? It's not like I've been living there for years, and this was the first time I missed rent; I had only been there for a few months, so I started thinking of ways to make some quick cash. I thought about going to Kensington Avenue to sell some works, but there was no way in hell I'd make $200 that fast; I was screwed.

I explained to the landlord what had happened, but he had no sympathy for me and told me I had to go. So, I packed all my clothes in a trash bag and headed out the door. I didn't know what to do or where to go. I had already burned bridges with my brother and didn't talk to any of my old friends anymore. So once again, I was all alone in the world. It was just me, myself, and I.

I spent the next couple of weeks roaming the streets. I moved from place to place, sleeping in bandos, park benches, or anywhere else I could rest my eyes. Hanging around with other homeless addicts, I quickly learned the secrets of living on the streets. One of the most important things I learned was how to eat for free every day. The soup kitchen on Kensington Avenue was a good spot for breakfast and lunch, but we had to find other sources for dinner. The trick was to hang out back of the restaurants as they were closing for the night so that we could scoop up the leftovers as they threw them away.

It's not like we had to dig food out of the dumpster like you see in the movies. The restaurant workers knew we were waiting for it and would leave the pans of food on top of the dumpsters for us. The only problem was that there would be 10 people trying to eat all at once. And like the scavengers we were, we always fought over who got the most food.

I hated living on the streets. I mean, nobody likes living on the streets, but some people I've met had grown so accustomed to it that it didn't even bother them. But not me; I was not one of those people. I hated how I had to watch my back and sleep with one eye open to make sure nobody stole my stuff. Sometimes, if I caught somebody else sleeping, I would slice their pocket open with my razor blade to get the dope out without waking them. It was every person for themselves, and I did whatever I had to do to survive.

After a few weeks, I felt like a zombie, just roaming the streets of Philly. But unlike zombies, who were constantly searching for brains, I ran around all day looking for dope. It didn't even feel like I was living anymore; I just existed. To tell you the truth, I didn't even care if I lived or died. In fact, every time I shot a bag of dope, I prayed it would be the last one, the one that would finally bring me to my fate. I often got disappointed if I felt high after shooting up because if I could feel it, then I knew I was still alive.

I always had it in the back of my mind that things would eventually get better. I kept telling myself that one day I would get clean. But every day, I woke up and kept doing the same shit, over and over again. Sometimes I thought I was just stuck in a bad dream, but I was brought back to reality when I woke up every morning and realized I was still trapped in hell. Do you know what the ironic part is? Those who get stuck in a living hell usually end up there because they were trying to find a little piece of heaven. And for people like me, that piece of heaven came in a little blue bag.

One day, while selling works, an old man named Lenny approached me out of the blue. He asked a few harmless questions and then invited me to his house for something to eat. I thought it was a little weird, but maybe he felt bad because I was homeless or something. Lenny could've been a serial killer for all I knew, but I didn't care whether I lived or died anymore, so I would've been OK with it either way. Besides, my stomach was growling at the time, so it was hard for me to pass up a free meal.

100

On the way to Lenny's house, I decided to rob him. My plan was to eat whatever food he gave me and then force him to give up the cash and any other valuables he might have had in his house. He was older, so I knew he wouldn't put up a fight. When we got to his house, we sat at his kitchen table and ate peanut butter and jelly sandwiches. While eating, Lenny told me I could stay at his place if I wanted to. He said I didn't even have to pay rent, but there was a catch: I had to let him suck my dick every once in a while. I told him there was no way that was ever going to happen, and then I quickly gobbled down my sandwich. I wanted to hurry up and rob him so I could get the fuck out of there. But, as I reached for my knife, Lenny made me another offer.

"Listen, if you really need a place to stay, you can still stay here, but it'll cost you. Let's say $25 a week."

I decided to take him up on his offer because I was so sick of living in dirty bandos with no heat or running water. And for $25 a week, I would've been stupid not to take it. After I moved in, the first thing I did was I took a steaming hot shower. I hadn't had a real shower in weeks, so it felt like I had died and gone to heaven. Later on, I relaxed on the couch and watched some TV. It all felt surreal to me. It was like a load of bricks had been lifted off my shoulder. That night I slept like a baby. I didn't have to sleep with one eye open or worry about someone getting into the bando and taking my shit. I also didn't have to sleep on an old, beat-up couch with no cushions. I had actually forgotten what it felt like to sleep in a real bed.

A few days later, I ran into Tanya on the avenue. She said she was worried about me because she found out I got evicted. She apologized for stealing the rent money and told me how much she missed me. Deep down inside, I didn't want to get back with her, but I knew she had dope on her, and I was dope sick. So how could I not forgive her? I mean, yes, OK, she stole $200, got me evicted, and left me homeless on the streets with a broken heart... But c'mon, she had a bag of dope for me.

After we got back together, I wasn't dope sick as much as I used to be. This was mainly because Tanya could make money a lot easier than I could. For the next couple of weeks, everything seemed to be going OK. But then, one night, Tanya sat me down to talk about something very important.

"Please don't be mad, but I found out that I got HIV."

I was speechless. I didn't know how to respond. What was I supposed to say? I felt sorry for her but scared for both of us. I honestly didn't want to stay with her because I was afraid I would catch it, too. Even though we always used condoms and never shared needles, I was still terrified. As much as I wanted to leave her, I knew that if I did, I would have to go back to being dope sick all the time. I didn't want that, so I stayed with her. That's how powerful addiction is; I put myself at risk of catching HIV just so I could keep getting high. Tanya and the heroin both had me by the balls, and they refused to let me go.

The day after Tanya told me about her HIV status, I went to get tested. I sat in that room and waited for what felt like an eternity, but in reality, it was only 10 minutes. When the results came back, I was afraid to know the outcome. So you can imagine the relief I felt when they told me I was HIV negative. But they also explained how I wasn't in the clear yet. It could take three to six months for HIV to appear in my system, so I had to return and get tested again. I wanted to be 100% sure, so I followed their instructions and went back every three months to get tested.

I tried to convince Tanya to go to the free clinic to get the medication and take care of herself, but she never listened. She was too worried about getting high to give a fuck about staying healthy. I guess I had the same mentality, though, because I was right there with her. When Tanya started prostituting, I always watched her back to make sure she was OK. But after a while, I realized we could make more money if I sold works while she was out doing her thing. Even though I didn't make a lot of money selling works, it was better than nothing. And over time, people got to know me on that corner, which opened up opportunities to make more money.

A young black guy, Dave, hung out at Kensington and Somerset every day. He was well known for hustling Suboxone, but he didn't do hand-to-hand transactions. Instead, he would just get other people to sell for him. He must have been watching and liked the way I hustled because he approached me out of the blue one day and asked if I wanted to sell Subs for him. Suboxone, also known as "Subs," is a pill similar to methadone. The difference is that you don't have to go to a clinic every day to get it, so you can easily buy it on the streets. After I agreed to work for Dave, he told me I would earn $1 for every pill I sold. It doesn't sound like much, but Suboxone sold much quicker and easier than the needles did. So, for a dope fiend like me, it felt like I struck a gold mine.

Dave gave me 10 Subs to start with, and I sold them all in less than five minutes. He couldn't believe it when I came back with the money that quick.

"Damn white bol, you flipped them things quicker than a motha fucka!"

It really wasn't that hard. The Subs practically sold themselves; I just had to hustle a little more than the competition did. Whenever the train stopped and let the customers off, I would run up the steps to meet them before the other dealers got there. In between trains, I kept my eyes open to see if anybody was coming down the street. Sometimes I saw customers from a block away and would walk toward them before they reached the corner. This eliminated the competition from even having a chance.

Between selling works and flipping Subs, I made enough money to keep myself from getting sick every day. Add that to what Tanya gave me, and I was making well over $100 a day. But just like any other addict would have done, I used that extra money to buy extra dope, and with the extra dope came a bigger habit. The bigger my habit got, the more I had to feed it. And the more I fed it, the more money I needed. It was a vicious cycle. I felt like a hamster running on a wheel, and no matter how fast I ran, I was still stuck in the same place. And even though I knew I wasn't going anywhere, I kept running and running and running...

Chapter 18

I was selling works at Kensington and Somerset one day when I noticed two Dominican guys standing off to the side, looking around at everyone. They looked familiar, but I couldn't figure out where I knew them from. The only reason I noticed them was because they stuck out from all the other addicts on the corner. They were clean-shaven, with clean clothes, and one of them even had a silver chain around his neck. I didn't know what they were up to, but I noticed how they kept looking over at me. I thought that maybe they were stickup boys who were plotting to rob me, so I cautiously watched them out the corner of my eye. And sure enough, a few moments later, they approached me.

"Yo white bol, you wanna make some real money?"

"Fuck yeah, what's up?"

"Think you can flip dope like you be flippin' them Subs?"

I suddenly realized where I knew them from. These guys sold dope around the corner on Boudinot Street. I figured I'd make way more money selling dope than I would from selling Suboxone, so I told them to count me in. They introduced themselves as Manny and Josh and then walked me around the corner to the dope spot. When we got to the corner of Boudinot and Auburn Streets, they explained how I'd make $30 for every bundle that I sold. A bundle was only 15 bags, and in that neighborhood, 15 bags sold pretty quickly. I might as well have been selling candy to school kids.

They gave me my first bundle and told me to keep it in a nearby trashcan. After I stashed the bundle, Manny and Josh sat down on the stoop across the street. They didn't go that far; they made sure to keep a close eye on me so that I wouldn't dart off with the bundle, but I wasn't that stupid. My first customer was a regular from around the corner who sold works at Kensington and Somerset. When I told him I had dope for sale, he didn't take me seriously; he thought I was trying to scam him. In fact, he walked across the street to try to buy from Manny and Josh, but they sent him right back to me. After he realized I wasn't trying to scam him, he came back and bought two bags of dope off of me. A few minutes after I made that first sale, a Puerto Rican with tattoos covering his face approached me.

"Ay papi, lemme get three."

104

I quickly grabbed three bags from the stash that I had hidden in the trashcan. But when I put my hand out to collect the money, he hesitated.

"Damn, I left my money in the car."

"Aight, go get it. I ain't goin' nowhere."

"Well here, just gimme da dope. I'll come right back wit da money."

"Ay yo, get da fuck outta here, man!"

This guy must've taken me for a fool. It might've been my first day working on that corner, but it definitely wasn't my first-day selling drugs. When he realized I wasn't going to budge, he just quietly walked away. But a few seconds later, I heard laughter coming from across the street. I looked over to find the tattooed man joking around with Manny and Josh. It turns out they were just testing me. They had to make sure I really knew how to hustle on the streets. Apparently, I passed the test with flying colors.

I met some of the other dealers who worked on the block throughout the next couple of days. They all gave me tips on where to hide the bundles and how I should switch up the hiding spots every day. They explained that if I kept the bundles in the same place, the cops would quickly catch on and find the stash. So, we switched it up every day to keep the cops on their toes. The next day, I flattened an empty beer can, tucked the bundle inside, and placed it in the gutter. Later that day, I got stopped by the cops, and guess what? They searched the same trashcan I kept my stash in the day before. Thank God I moved it. Here's the kicker, they didn't stop me because they thought I was selling dope. They stopped me because they thought I was buying it. I was about to sell it to a Puerto Rican guy, and they thought he was the one selling it to me.

Most of the white people in the neighborhood were addicts, so every time I got stopped, cops just assumed I was an addict looking to buy some dope. It was both an advantage and a disadvantage at the same time. It was a disadvantage because every time cops drove by the corner and saw me, a white person, they thought a drug transaction was taking place. But it was an advantage because nine out of 10 times, they'd give me a quick pat-down and then tell me to leave.

After I started working on that corner, the other dealers noticed how we began to get a lot of new customers. Most of the new customers were white, and some of them were racist as fuck. A few of them even told me that the only reason why they came to our corner was because they rather hand their money to a white person. Look, I'm not a racist, but I wanted their money, so I would always just nod and agree with them. I actually hated the fact that some of the customers acted like that. But, at the end of the day, the only color I really cared about was those green dollar bills.

The first week I worked there, I could tell that most of the other dealers didn't trust me, and I couldn't blame them. I mean, how could anyone trust a junkie, right? But, after a few days, an opportunity presented itself which allowed me to earn their trust. An old, dirty white van pulled up on the block and parked across the street. A middle-aged white guy with long, headbanger-type hair, who wore grungy-looking clothes and a bandana as a headband, stepped out of the van. He looked like the poster child for a failed rock star who turned dope fiend.

"Dope dope dope! How many? How many?"

"Dude, lemme get two."

I ran across the street, grabbed two bags from the stash, and did a quick hand-to-hand. He headed back to his van very quickly, a little too quickly if you ask me. I knew something was up. So I looked in my hand and saw the green paper, but it wasn't money; it just looked like money from a distance. He was only a couple feet away when I noticed, so I quickly grabbed him before he could get into his van.

"Dude, I'm sorry, I'm dope sick."

I kind of felt sorry for him because I knew he must've been really desperate to try and pull some shit like that. But at the same time, I couldn't just go around giving free drugs to everyone in the neighborhood, so I told him to give me back my shit. He handed one of the bags back to me and tried to walk away as if I had forgotten that I had given him two bags. I would've let him go with a warning if he would've just given me both bags back, but I couldn't do that now because the other dealers were watching from across the street. I tried to pry the other bag from his hand, but he held on so tight that I couldn't get it. However, you'd be surprised how fast a punch to the face can change someone's attitude. He stopped dead in his tracks, and when he saw the other dealers running toward us, he handed me the other bag and made a break for it. He got halfway down the block before I caught up and threw him against the wall. The other dealers were right behind me, swarming toward him.

"Yo yo yo, fall back. This pussy is mine!" I shouted.

106

They all backed up and let me do my thing. I beat this dude's ass in the middle of the block as my new friends cheered me on. I didn't beat him that bad, but enough for him to never show his face on that corner ever again. Afterward, P-rock walked to the head banger's van and opened up the back doors. It must've been his work van because he had a whole bunch of tools in the back. So we grabbed whatever tools we could carry, threw them in the stash house, and then sold them later that day. After this incident, everyone on the block started to treat me differently. It was obvious that I had earned their respect, and they knew I wasn't just another punk.

A few weeks later, this dude named Black started hanging around at the spot. He wasn't a hand-to-hand dealer, though. He was a caseworker. For those that don't know, a caseworker is basically the guy who distributes the bundles to the workers. When you are done selling your bundle, you give the caseworker the money, and he gives you the next bundle. Black, Manny, and P-rock were the three main caseworkers on the block.

Shortly after Black started coming around, we began to sell coke on the block. The dope we had wasn't that good, but we were so close to the Somerset Station that people bought from us just because it was convenient. But the coke we got? Man, it was some good shit! It drew a lot of customers in, which meant we were making a lot more money. It took no time at all for everyone to realize that we had the best coke in the neighborhood.

The first customer who bought coke from me went to a bando down the street to shoot it up. A few minutes later, he jumped out the second-floor window. I don't mean that he hang-jumped or climbed out the window and then jumped down. No, he took a running start from inside the house and barreled through the window like he was some sort of stunt double in an action movie. I don't know how, but he managed to land on his feet with no injuries whatsoever.

"Yo man, you cool?"

"There's three guys in there with guns!"

There was nobody in that house. I had been out there all day, and he was the only person I saw go in. So he was obviously high as shit.

"Nah, man, that coke gotcha paranoid."

"Yeah. That's some really good shit. Let me get six more."

Even though the extra customers brought in extra money, it also brought extra attention from the cops. There were days when cops would park on the block just to be assholes. They did it so that we couldn't sell anything, but luckily I could still go make money with Tanya and not have to worry about being dope sick.

Besides Tanya, I also got to know a few other prostitutes in the neighborhood. I watched their backs while they picked up their dates, the same way I did with Tanya. They gave me $10 for every date that they picked up. So if I stayed out there long enough, I was able to make enough money to support my habit. It still wasn't as good as hustling on the block, but it was a lot safer. But honestly, I didn't care about being safe at that point. I just wanted to go wherever I could make the most money.

Chapter 19

The cops always fucked with us while we were hustling on the block. They knew we sold drugs, but they could never find anything on us because, like I mentioned earlier, we always switched up the stash spot to throw them off. They would get so mad because even though they knew we were hustling, they couldn't do anything about it unless they found the drugs on us.

On September 9th, 2009, I sold the last bundles of coke and dope and had to wait to get a new pack. The boss told Black that the bundles were on their way and would be there in five minutes. Anyone who has ever waited for a drug dealer knows that five minutes can easily turn into an hour. Even though we ran out of dope and coke, it didn't stop the customers from coming. Whenever this happened, we had no choice but to tell them to come back. One after another, customers kept coming to the block, and we kept telling them to come back in five minutes.

"Yo, I need one dope," a customer requested.

Before I even had a chance to tell him that we were sold out, someone tackled me from behind. When I hit the ground, the customer put a gun to my head and pulled a badge out from around his neck.

"Don't you fucking move dickhead!"

They were obviously undercover cops, but I wasn't even sweating it. I knew they couldn't do anything because I had nothing on me; there wasn't even anything in the stash spots. I figured they would just search around for a while, and once they realized nothing was there, they would let me go. I even tried to play it off and told the cops I wasn't a dealer and was just a customer trying to buy some dope, but they knew I was full of shit.

"We been watching all day. Where'd you hide the dope at?"

"I ain't even got nuttin'!"

Even though I was telling the truth, they didn't believe me, so they threw me in the back of the cop car and searched the area. They literally searched every single hiding spot that we had ever used. One of our customers must've snitched and given up all of our stash spots. After about 20 minutes, the cop who tackled me to the ground walked to the car and opened the back door.

"Oh, look at what we just found in your pocket!"

He opened his palm to show me four bags of dope and three bags of coke, but the bags didn't come from our block. They had a different stamp on them, so it must have been from another corner. For those who don't know, every dope spot has its own stamp, similar to a brand name. The bags are stamped with a name, design, or sometimes both. The bags that we sold were stamped with the word "Scorpion," but the bags the cops supposedly found on me were stamped with the name "Two Shot." Look, I know I was wrong for selling drugs, and I totally understand why they did what they did. But at the time that it happened, I was fucking pissed! I hated them for what they did, and it was at that point that I lost all respect for cops.

I only had to spend one night in jail, but it was worse than it sounds. Being locked in a jail cell is horrible, but being locked in a jail cell while dope sick could be considered a form of torture. At first, it was just a runny nose and some sweaty skin, so it wasn't really that bad. But then, I started getting really weak, and my muscles got awfully sore. Next, it was the stomach aches, followed by diarrhea and vomiting. But even all these symptoms combined couldn't compare to the restless leg syndrome and level of anxiety that I felt.

Don't get me wrong, I've been dope sick plenty of times in the past, so none of this was new to me. But this time, there was absolutely nothing in the world I could do about it. I was stuck in a jail cell, so I couldn't go out and sell some dope. I couldn't go and find Tanya to get some money off of her. I couldn't go sell a couple of works on the corner or go rob somebody. I couldn't even steal something and sell it for a few dollars. I was forced to deal with it until someone let me out of my cage.

I was released on my own recognizance the next day, which meant I didn't have to pay bail. All I had to do was show up for a court date a few months later, but I didn't care about that at the time. I was just happy that I was getting out. I was so dope sick that all I could think about was getting a bag of dope.

After being released, I went directly back to the spot. I didn't even go home to eat or change my clothes or anything. When I got to the block, Black and J-Rock, P-Rock's little brother, were the only two there. J-Rock had a bundle he had to finish hustling before I could start working, but they took one look at me and could tell that I was dope sick. So Black gave me a bag of dope and told me to pay him back on my next bundle.

It was at this point that I knew they trusted me. Under normal circumstances, a dealer would never give a bag of dope to a fiend and let him pay him back later. However, I had been there for a few months and never once came up short or tried to steal anything. They also knew that I didn't snitch when I got booked. I could have easily snitched to avoid going to jail and being dope sick all night long, but there was a code of honor in the streets, and they knew I followed that code.

A couple weeks later, cops started to come down hard on the entire neighborhood. They figured out all of our stash spots, and a couple of the other dealers got booked. With no stash spots left, I started to tuck the bundles in my sock. I don't remember where I heard it, but I knew that cops couldn't search my shoes and socks because it was considered an illegal search. And sure enough, every time I got stopped, they never once made me take off my shoes.

I knew that stashing drugs in my sock wasn't going to completely stop me from going to jail, especially if a cop ever saw me make a hand-to-hand transaction. So when a cop saw me making a deal one day, I made a break for it. The lights on the cop car lit up the block like a Christmas tree as he chased me down the street. I hopped a fence, dashed through a yard, ran across the street, and then cut through an alley. When I came out the other side of the alley, I didn't see any cops, but I knew it was only a matter of time before they found me, so I came up with a plan.

I wanted to go back to the block to make some more money, but I knew that the cops would recognize me, so I decided to change my clothes. Instead of going all the way home and risking getting caught, I ran into the thrift shop on Kensington Avenue. I bought myself a different colored shirt from the one that I was wearing and a ball cap to hide my face a little bit. After paying the cashier, I put on my new shirt and hat and threw the old shirt in the trash.

I walked back to the block in my new clothes and borrowed a broom from one of the neighbors so that I could sweep the block and make it look like I wasn't selling drugs. I did this every once in a while so that the cops wouldn't fuck with me. But every now and again, a cop would stop and ask me why I was sweeping the block, and I would just tell them that a neighbor gave me $5 to clean the front of their house. I guess it seemed pretty believable because cops never gave me trouble as long as I had that broom in my hand.

Even though I only used the broom to make it look like I wasn't hustling, a few neighbors really did appreciate how I tried to keep the block clean. It also made me feel good about myself, as if I was making a difference or something. I figured that if I was out there selling drugs, the least I could do was give back to the community a little bit. That kind of sounds stupid now that I think about it, but it made perfect sense to me at the time.

Chapter 20

On the morning of my hearing, I woke up dope sick with no money to buy myself a bag. There was no way in hell I could go to court if I was dope sick, so I went to the block to make a couple dollars before I left. But that day, business was unusually slow. The corner was like a ghost town with no customers in sight.

I was so desperate to make a sale that I broke one of my cardinal rules. A young mom pushing a baby stroller came to the block to buy a couple of bags. Now, normally I would never sell drugs to someone who had a kid with them, but an hour and a half had passed, and I hadn't sold a single bag yet. I needed to flip the bundle as quick as possible if I wanted to get to court on time, so I went against my own rule and sold her dope in front of her child. To justify it, I told myself that if I didn't sell it to her, then someone else would have.

It took over two hours just to sell that first bundle. By then, I was already late for court, so I said fuck it and decided not to go at all. I planned to turn myself in the next day, but when the next day came, I was dope sick again and had to hit the block to make some more money. This continued for a few weeks until I realized I had missed a second court date for a shoplifting case that I caught a while back. I had completely forgotten about it until I cleaned my room one day and came across my release papers.

I knew I had to turn myself in as soon as possible, so I called the courthouse, and they advised me to come in at 7:00 a.m. the following morning. The timing was perfect because I had just gotten my unemployment check. So I bought a few extra bags and set them aside for the following day. Now I had no excuses; I could go straight to the courthouse without being dope sick.

The next morning, I turned on the radio and listened to music as I enjoyed my heroin breakfast. I was barely listening when the DJ announced that SEPTA had gone on strike. For those who don't know, SEPTA is the public transportation system here in Philadelphia. So, since SEPTA went on strike, there were no buses or trains running, which meant I had no way to get to the courthouse to turn myself in. Why did these types of things always happen to me? I was trying to do the right thing by turning myself in, but it seemed like every time I took a step forward, I would get pushed two steps back.

My plan was to turn myself in as soon as the strike was over, so until then, I just continued on with my life as usual. That Friday night, I was on the corner playing wall ball as I waited my turn to hustle. When J-rock sold his last bag, Black handed me two bundles of coke, and I immediately stashed them in my sock.

A couple of minutes later, I made a quick hand-to-hand transaction with a customer. After the customer left, one of the other dealers asked me why I kept the bundles in my sock. So, I explained to him how it was illegal for cops to search my socks on the street and how they could only search them at the police station if I got arrested. But if they don't find anything on me, then there's no reason to arrest me.

A few moments later, a paddy wagon pulled up on the corner. Two cops stepped out from the wagon: a white one who looked like he had just graduated from the academy and a Spanish one who looked to be in his mid-30s. They started asking questions, but they were pretty cool about it, not your typical asshole cops. They didn't make us get against the wall or empty our pockets or anything like that. In fact, they even started joking around and asked if they could play wall ball with us. But for some reason, the Spanish cop picked me out of the crowd and asked me for ID. So, I handed the younger cop my ID, and he walked back to the wagon to run my name in the system. I started sweating bullets. It had only been a few days since I missed my court date, so I wasn't even sure if I would have any warrants yet. But a few moments later, the young cop threw me against the wall and put me in handcuffs.

"Should've told me you had warrants before I ran your name," the young cop said.

"Got any drugs or anything sharp that's going to poke me?" the Spanish cop asked.

I shook my head no as he patted me down and searched my pockets. I was afraid he would find the coke in my socks, but he didn't even search them.

The cops gave me another chance before they arrested me and again asked if I was holding any drugs. I thought about coming clean with them for a minute, but I had 22 bags of coke on me. There was no way in hell that they were going to let that slide. So I took my chances and told them I didn't have anything. After they closed the doors to the paddy wagon, I tried to grab the bundles of coke from my sock and tuck them somewhere. But, with my hands cuffed behind my back, it was impossible.

I twisted myself like a pretzel to try and reach those bundles, but it just wasn't happening. A few minutes later, we pulled up to the 25th district, and the doors to the paddy wagon opened up.

"You sure you don't have any drugs? This is your last chance," the young cop warned.

Part of me wanted to tell them the truth, but another part of me thought that I could somehow pull it off. So, I just shook my head no. They brought me into the search room, where a third officer was waiting to give me a more thorough search. When it came time to search my socks, the officer told me to take them off and flip them inside out. As I took my sock off, I tried to hide the bundles in my palm, but the officer immediately noticed and snatched the coke out of my hands.

"You stupid fucking prick! We gave you two chances to get rid of that shit, asshole!" the Spanish cop furiously stated.

I started getting dope sick a couple of hours after they put me in my cell, so needless to say, I had trouble sleeping that night. The following day they transferred me to the Curran-Fromhold Correctional Facility, also known as CFCF. They served breakfast shortly after I arrived, but I was way too sick to eat. Prison food was hard enough to eat on its own, but being dope sick made it nearly impossible.

By Sunday afternoon, my withdrawal symptoms began to get worse. My anxiety was through the roof, every muscle in my body ached, and I felt like I was standing in a subzero freezer. A couple hours later came the stomach aches, followed by diarrhea. I had to puke, but there was nothing in my stomach, so I just kept dry heaving all night long. I tried my best to get some sleep, but my restless leg syndrome wasn't letting that happen. I slept in five-minute increments here and there, but I got no real rest at all that weekend.

Monday morning finally came, and they took me to see the judge. He asked me why I missed my court dates, so I just told him the truth. I told him how SEPTA went on strike, and I couldn't get to the courthouse. He immediately lifted the warrant and gave me a new court date. As luck would have it, the SEPTA strike ended a few hours before they released me. So when I got released, I was able to walk across the street and wait for the 84 bus. While waiting for the bus, I found a cigarette butt on the ground, picked it up, and smoked it. I mean, this wasn't anything out of the norm for me. I used to do it all of the time while hustling works on

Kensington Avenue. Why spend money on cigarettes when I could pick up a few cigarette butts and smoke them for free?

I only had to wait 10 minutes for the bus, but it felt more like 10 hours. Time seemed to move in slow motion whenever I was dope sick. The ride itself seemed like the longest bus ride in all of history. No matter how fast the driver went, it wouldn't have been quick enough for me. All I wanted was to get back to the block and put some dope in my veins.

I finally made it to the block only to find out that nobody was there. So, I walked around the corner to Kensington and Somerset and asked one of our customers where everyone was. He told me that the cops raided the block earlier that day, so they shut down the spot for a while. I thought about looking for Tanya, but I wasn't even sure if she was working or not. I was too dope sick and just didn't have the patience to find out, so I resorted to other means of making money.

I stepped into the bando and grabbed an empty coke bag that I found on the ground. Then, I chipped off a piece of sheetrock from the wall, crushed it into a powder, and poured it into the empty bag. After making my dummy bag, I sat on the stoop and waited for a customer to come. A couple of minutes later, one of our regulars, Ashley, came to buy a bag of coke. She was one of the prostitutes who gave me money to watch her back sometimes, but I didn't have time for that today. So, I sold her the fake coke and used the money to buy a bag of dope. I felt bad about ripping Ashley off because she didn't deserve that. She was a good customer, and I worried about what would happen if the other dealers found out what I did. But as soon as I put that dope in my vein, all those worries faded away.

The next day I got to the block early in the morning, and we were up and running again. It felt good to be out of jail and back to the regular routine. Later that day, Ashley stopped by to grab some more coke, but before she had a chance to say anything, I apologized and gave her the $10 back. Everything just seemed to be going perfect that day. Tanya was even on the block hanging out with me for a change. And to top it all off, we didn't see any cops drive past the block all day.

"Yo, did the cops take the day off or something?" I jokingly said.

I must have jinxed us because as soon as we stopped laughing, a cop car pulled up on the block, and guess who stepped out of the car? That's right, the two cops who arrested me a few days earlier.

"How you out already! Get against the wall, asshole!"

Thank God I didn't hide the drugs in my shoe this time. Instead, I had them hidden across the street underneath a loose slab of concrete.

"Why don't you strip for your girlfriend here? You can start with the shoes and socks."

I thought the cops were joking, but they weren't. They wanted me to really strip down to my boxers. When I refused, the Spanish cop pointed his Taser gun at me and threatened to use it if I didn't take my clothes off. I didn't have much of a choice. I was so embarrassed standing there on the corner wearing nothing but my boxers, but that's exactly what the cops wanted. They wanted to embarrass me in front of my girl. I guess it was revenge for me making them look stupid at the police station.

A few weeks later, I had another court date, but this time I saved myself a few bags for the morning so that I wouldn't trip myself up again. There was no way in hell I was going to get another warrant. On my way to the courthouse, I started to get worried. I was afraid the judge was going to throw the book at me for skipping out on my last court date, not to mention the new drug charges I got when I was arrested for my warrants. But to my surprise, the DA offered me six months of probation, so I happily took the offer.

After leaving the courthouse, I walked around the corner to the probation office to meet my new probation officer. She was nothing like I expected. I always thought probation officers were supposed to be assholes, but the one I had seemed pretty laid back. Since it was my first time on probation, she put me on something called "non-reporting probation," which meant I only had to go and see her every once in a while. She gave me an appointment to see her in two months, but before I could even make it to that first appointment, I got arrested; again.

I was on the block trying to flip the last bundle of the night when a customer pulled up in his car and asked for a bag. I told him to step out of the car and walk across the street with me, but he refused to get out and wanted me to sell it to him through the car window. He was trying to pull an old scam that had been around forever. I'll hand him the bag of coke as he hands me a dollar wrapped around a wad of fake bills, and then he'll speed off in his car before I could count even it. I knew what he was trying to pull, but I wasn't falling for it.

Eventually, he gave up and pulled away without buying anything. But just as he pulled away, a cop car slowly cruised through the intersection down the street. From the cop's point of view, it looked like I had just made a sale. I was afraid he was going to circle the block and bust me. So I grabbed the coke from the stash spot, tucked it in my shoe, and tried to get out of there as quick as possible.

I hurried off the block and turned the corner, only to find the cop car speeding toward me. I thought I'd try to play it cool, but my plans quickly changed when I saw who was driving. It was the same cops who arrested me for the warrant. The same ones who made me strip on the corner in front of my girlfriend. As soon as I saw them, I knew they would check my shoes and find the coke, so I made a break for it.

I dashed up the street, hopped a fence, and then cut through an alley. When I came out the other side and sprinted across the street, a car slammed on the brakes and nearly hit me, but I didn't let it slow me down one bit. I continued down the block and quickly turned the corner, where I was met by two random foot cops who tackled me to the ground. Now, the foot cops didn't know me, so they didn't check my socks and find the coke when they searched me. I actually thought they were going to cut me loose until I saw a cop car pull up; at that moment, I knew I was fucked. The car doors opened and out stepped the cops who were chasing me, and they were PISSED.

"Make sure you check his shoes! This sneaky prick likes to hide shit in his shoes."

The cops ripped the shoes off my feet, and bags of coke flew everywhere. They didn't even say anything. They just hauled me right off to jail. I sat in the cell for a few hours until it was time for me to get my fingerprints and mugshots. When they finally took me to the processing room, the officer who took my fingerprints immediately recognized me.

"You again? We're going to have to start charging you rent."

After they took me back to my cell, I started to think about what the officer had said. He was absolutely right. When was I going to learn? I needed to make some serious changes in my life. I needed to stop getting high, but I just didn't know how to do that.

The next morning at my bail hearing, the judge set my bail at $1000. This meant I had to pay 10% in order to be released. The only problem was that I couldn't call anyone to post my bail because all my phone numbers were saved on my cell phone. And, of course, the cops wouldn't let me have my cell phone while I was in jail, so once again, I was stuck.

A few hours later, I was transferred to CFCF, where my withdrawal symptoms began to get worse as time went on. By the fourth day, I couldn't bear the pain anymore. I was ready to rip the hairs out of my head. At one point, I even contemplated suicide, but I just couldn't figure out a way to do it. I kept thinking of ways to get out, and my only option was to post bail. But I needed to get in touch with someone on the outside if I wanted to do that, and the only number I had memorized was my brother Mike's. However, the last time I saw Mike, he kicked me out of his house for stealing from him. I knew it was a long shot, but it was at least worth a try.

I called my brother and told him how I was stuck in jail and needed $100 to get out. I expected a lecture about drugs, followed by him telling me to go fuck myself, but to my surprise, he told me he would put up the money as long as I paid him back when I got my unemployment check. I had the best brother in the world. Even after all the bullshit I put him through, he was still willing to help me out. He loved me, even when I didn't love myself.

My brother posted my bail the next day, and I was released a few hours later. I went directly to his house to thank him. He only lived about a mile away from the jail, so it wasn't exactly out of my way. When I got there, he offered me something to eat and a ride back home, which I happily accepted. On the drive back home, I told Mike that I was done using drugs. I told him how heroin took three days to get out of my system, and since it had been five days since I'd used, I didn't need it anymore. I had convinced myself that I was never going to shoot dope ever again. I was tired of all the bullshit, but the truth is, I was really just bullshitting myself.

My brother dropped me off at old man Lenny's house, where I took a quick shower and then headed to the block. But, I didn't go to the block to get high. I seriously just wanted to make some money to buy a pack of smokes and food for the rest of the week. But once I got to the block, my addiction started to call my name. I did good, though. I didn't get high when I was on the block. I flipped a few bundles, made a few dollars, and then headed back home. I was so proud of myself for not getting high that day. But, on my way home, I thought about how I hadn't had a good night's sleep for the past five days because of the withdrawal symptoms. I figured that just one bag wouldn't hurt. Plus, it would really help me sleep so that the next day I would be nice and refreshed, and then

I could quit again. So, I stopped by a spot on my way home and grabbed myself exactly one bag.

I got home that night, shot the bag of dope, and passed out in my bed. It felt great to finally be able to sleep after a week of no rest. The next morning, however, I felt like absolute shit. I took some ibuprofen and drank a cup of coffee, but it didn't help. It felt like I got hit by a truck, and I knew that there was only one cure. So, I walked around the corner and grabbed myself another bag of dope. I didn't even want to shoot it, but I knew that I had to if I wanted to feel better. I felt like a puppet, and heroin was like the puppet master pulling my strings.

For the next couple of months, I kept on doing the same old shit. I kept selling drugs, running from the cops, getting in fights, etc. None of it even bothered me anymore; it all just became normal to me. But as the holiday season approached, I realized that I hadn't spoken to my family, except for Mike when he bailed me out of jail. Thanksgiving Day came, and I didn't even receive an invite to my sister Kim's house. I understood why, but I still felt hurt by it. That Thanksgiving Day was the loneliest I had felt in a very long time. While all the other dealers left to go eat with their families, I sat there and sold drugs by myself. As I sat on the corner in my own self-pity, one of the neighbors from the block brought me out a plate of their Thanksgiving dinner. It made me realize that even though there were a lot of scum bags in the ghetto, there were some good-hearted people too.

As I ate my Thanksgiving meal on the corner by myself, the loneliness didn't even seem to bother me anymore; I was just happy to be eating. And you can say whatever you want about Puerto Ricans, but they know how to cook a turkey! It was the best damn turkey I ever had in my life. They say a way to man's heart is through his stomach, and I definitely felt the love that day.

As Christmas approached, I knew I wasn't going to be invited to celebrate the holiday with my family. But I still wanted to buy them gifts to make up for the previous year when I OD'd and had all their gifts stolen. So when I got my unemployment check, I bought a bunch of gift cards and mailed them out to everyone. Gift cards were much cheaper to ship than actual gifts, and the less money I spent on Christmas, the more money I could spend on dope. When Christmas Day came, I didn't even call anyone to wish them a Merry Christmas. I was still mad that no one invited me to Thanksgiving dinner, so as far as I was concerned, sending the gift cards

120

was more than enough. In my mind, it didn't even matter because nobody called me either.

A few weeks later, I received a letter from my sister Kim, and inside the envelope was the gift card I had sent to her. The letter said that she didn't want any gifts from me and how I needed the gift card more than she did. But the real message in the letter was much deeper. It told me what she wanted for Christmas next year. The only thing she wanted was to have her little brother back in her life, the little brother she used to know before I started doing drugs. When I read that, it felt like someone punched me in the chest. My heart ached with a heavy pain as I tried to fight back the tears in my eyes.

In the letter, Kim also told me that I couldn't see my nieces until I straightened my life out. The letter continued with how my nieces were growing up fast, and soon they would no longer remember me. By this point, I could barely read because my vision was distorted from all the tears. I tried, but I couldn't stop them from leaking down my cheek and dripping onto the paper.

That letter was a real wake-up call for me. I never realized what I had been putting my family through. I should have known better because my brother Shawn had been doing the same thing for years. Shawn started using drugs as a teenager, and his addiction grew to the point where it caused him to become homeless. With him living on the streets, we always worried about him and were afraid that he was going to end up dead. The only time we ever saw him was when he was pushing his shopping cart of empty cans down the street. My nieces grew up not knowing who he was, and I didn't want the same thing to happen to me. So I decided to do something about it!

As much as I loved my brother Shawn, I didn't want to follow in his footsteps. So, the next day I told old man Lenny that I wanted to go to rehab. Lenny suggested that I go to the public defender's office because they could get me into rehab through the court system. It sounded like a good idea because I was already on probation and had two open cases, so it would probably help me the next time I had to see the judge. I took Lenny's advice and saw my public defender. I was surprised at how quickly he was able to get me the help that I needed. He told me to report to Mercy Hospital the following day to start my detox.

When the next day came, I woke up feeling sick as shit. I thought I was just dope sick, so I walked around the corner and grabbed some dope.

But even after shooting my dope, I still felt like shit. When I got to the hospital for detox, the nurse took my vitals and told me I had a fever of 103 degrees. It turned out that I had the flu, so they gave me some medicine and then sent me into the detox section of the hospital.

The next five days felt like I had died and gone to hell. Having the flu, on top of heroin withdrawal, was one of the worst experiences of my life. I couldn't even get out of bed some days, but still, I was just glad that I was there. If I didn't have to go to the hospital for detox, I would not have went to the hospital at all. I would have just continued to get high, weakening my immune system even more, which probably would've killed me.

When my detox was finally over, they recommended that I go to Self Help Movement for a 30-day rehab. This was the same all-male facility they suggested to me the last time I went to detox, except this time, I didn't have Tanya holding me back. Technically speaking, we were still together, but I just wanted to get clean, so I didn't care where they sent me. At that point in my life, I was willing to try anything.

When I arrived at Self Help that Monday afternoon, I was still withdrawing a little bit, or maybe I was just still sick from the flu. But from the moment I walked in, I didn't like the place. They made us sit on these hard wooden church-style pews while people from AA and NA came and gave us advice on how to stay clean. I also attended group therapy that day, where I was encouraged to open up about my feelings. I didn't even talk about my feelings with my own family, so why would I talk about them with a group of strangers. I just didn't want to be there, but I stuck with it anyway and hoped it would get better.

The next day, after we ate breakfast, one of the employees told me how everybody gets assigned to do a specific chore each week. My assignment for that week was to clean the cafeteria. They wanted me, along with three other guys, to move all the tables and then sweep and mop the entire floor. I tried to tell the employee that I was too weak from the withdrawal symptoms, but he didn't seem to care. That was the straw that broke the camel's back. I felt like they were trying to save money by forcing us to clean instead of hiring a janitor. I just wanted to get out of that place as soon as possible.

I didn't talk to anyone for the rest of the day. I just kept quiet and plotted ways that I could escape. Deep down inside, I wanted to stay clean, so I could see my nieces, but I wanted to get high even more. I could have easily walked right out the front door if I wanted to. It's not like I was being kept prisoner. In fact, the doors weren't even locked. But I stopped myself because I was afraid that someone would try to convince me to stay. I didn't want anybody to talk me out of getting high, so I decided to not even chance it.

My unemployment money always became available on my card on Wednesdays at 12:00 a.m. So at 12:01 a.m., I climbed out the window of my room to make my escape. I knew there were cameras in front of the building, so I had to be slick about it. I placed my back against the wall to avoid the cameras' detection and then slowly inched my way toward the front gate. I felt like I was in a James Bond movie, sidestepping along the wall of the building, trying not to be seen by the cameras.

When I reached the edge of the building, I speed-walked right out the front gate. I thought I was in the clear until I heard a door swing open.

"Yo, where you going?" a voice screamed from across the parking lot.

I didn't respond. I didn't even look back. I completely ignored the voice and began to walk even faster.

"Yo! Where you going? What's your name?" the voice yelled again, but this time it sounded closer.

I turned around and saw one of the employees running toward me. So, I picked up the pace and began to jog.

"Just hold up! I need your name!"

"Don't worry about it. I ain't coming back!" I yelled.

I couldn't understand why he was chasing me because they told me the doors were unlocked and I could leave anytime I wanted to. When I got to the corner, I turned around, and again he was right on my tail, so I had no choice but to put the speed boosters on. I felt like the white Jesse Owens as I bolted down Roosevelt Boulevard. I ran as fast and as far as I could until I had to stop to catch my breath. I looked behind me, and nobody was in sight; He must've given up.

I was relieved that nobody was chasing me anymore, but I had to find an ATM to get some cash to hop on the bus. I walked about a mile down the road before I finally found one. I took $60 out, bought a pack of smokes, and then walked to a bus stop to catch the 14 bus. At that time of night, the 14 bus only ran once an hour, and that hour seemed like an eternity. But for the moment, I was glad to be out of that place. I felt free.

But even though I was free from the rehab, I was still trapped in my addiction. It was almost as if the drugs had sentenced me to a life imprisonment, a sentence I had to serve inside of my own mind.

Chapter 21

I finally got back to Kensington at 2:30 a.m. and had to find a dope corner that was open all night long, which was rare because the stickup boys were out robbing dealers during those hours. But I knew of one spot near Clearfield Street that was open all night. So when I got off the bus, I hiked over there as fast as I could and approached a small group of dealers on the block.

"How many, papi?"

"I need four."

One of the dealers pulled a gun from behind the step and stuck it in my face. I could tell these guys were serious. They had that look of desperation in their eyes. I had no choice but to reach in my pocket and hand them my money. To be honest, I wasn't even shaken up over the incident; I was more concerned with getting high. Luckily, I still had money in my unemployment account, so I found an ATM and took out another $40.

This time I headed closer to the block that I worked. All of the dealers on that side of the neighborhood knew me, so I figured I wouldn't have any issues over there. However, it was the middle of the night, so most of these spots were closed. But, I didn't let that stop me from trying. I walked around for a few minutes but couldn't find any dope, so I walked to Kensington and Somerset to ask the other addicts if they knew any spots that were still open. On my way there, I happened to pass by Celli's house. Celli was the only female dealer who hustled on the block with us. When I passed by her house, I saw her drinking on the stoop with P-rock and J-rock.

"Ar--Aren't you supposed to be in rehab?" J-rock drunkenly slurred.

"Rehab's for quitters," I jokingly replied.

After they were finished laughing and busting my chops, I asked if any of them had any dope on them. Celli had a few bundles stashed, but they weren't exactly open for business. However, after seeing how desperate I was, she ran inside and grabbed me four bags. After Celli sold me the bags, I snuck into a bando down the street. The bando was so dark I could barely see anything, making it extremely difficult to mix the dope up. Luckily, a street lamp was shining through the window, giving me just enough light to see what I was doing. But just as I was about to put the needle in my arm, I heard a voice come from the shadows.

"Yo, gimme that shit before I fuck you up."

The voice sounded familiar, but it was so dark that I couldn't tell who it was. It didn't matter anyway because there was no way in hell I was going to give up my dope.

"You want this shit? You gonna have to shoot me in the motha fucking head."

"Is that Brain?"

As the shadow came closer, I immediately recognized who it was.

"Oh shit! Wassup Jerry?"

It's been a while since I had last seen Jerry, and to be honest, he looked like fucking shit! I could tell he was dope sick, so I gave him some of my dope to make him feel better. It didn't take long for me to figure out that Jerry's addiction had gotten just as bad as mine did over the years. He told me how he was homeless and had been going around robbing people to support his habit.

I felt bad because I used to be in the same situation that Jerry was in. I just lucked out when Manny asked me to hustle on the block and make money every day. So, the next day I asked Black if he could hook Jerry up with a job. Black was reluctant at first, but he agreed to let Jerry work with me since I vouched for him. It actually worked out to Black's benefit because the block was so hot that nobody wanted to hustle anymore. Most of the time, Black and I were the only ones who wanted to work. But since Jerry would be working with me, Black wouldn't have to risk being out there anymore. So, we came to an agreement where I would make a couple extra dollars. Black would drop off a few bundles at a time, and once we sold them all, I'd call him, and he'd swing by to drop off a couple more.

I totally understood why the other dealers didn't want to work anymore. Over the weekend, there had been a lot of raids in the neighborhood. We also began to notice a lot of extra squad cars, along with foot cops and bike cops, flooding the area. The recent influx of cops had the entire neighborhood on its toes. But even though cops were crawling all over the place, it didn't faze me. I needed money for dope, and at the end of the day, that was the only thing that really mattered to me.

126

On the second day that Jerry worked with me, we waited all morning for Black to drop the bundles off. He finally came around lunchtime and gave us five bundles to start out with. By this point, we weren't selling dope anymore. The boss man didn't want to leave a bunch of dope with two dope fiends and no one to watch over us. It didn't really make a difference to me because the dope we had was garbage, and nobody was buying it anyway. On the other hand, the coke that we had was the second-best in the neighborhood, so it sold like hotcakes. When Black dropped off the five bundles, I stashed four of them in the bando and handed one to Jerry while I looked out for the cops.

Jerry made a sale or two with no signs of cops anywhere, which was unusual, but we weren't about to complain about it. When the third customer of the day came, Jerry walked across the street and made a quick hand-to-hand transaction. Just as he collected the money, a cop car quickly cut the corner.

"Eighty-Eight! Eighty-Eight!" I yelled from across the street.

"Eighty-Eight" was the street code that we used to let everyone know that cops were coming. When Jerry heard me yell this, he darted down the side street where the cops couldn't see him. I didn't have anything on me, so I just stayed on the stoop and played it cool. I expected them to jump out of the car and throw me against the wall, but they just flew by and continued onto the next block.

I assumed that Jerry ran around the corner and was waiting for the dust to settle, but he never came back. Did another cop see him running down the street and grab him? Maybe he was just hiding somewhere and afraid to come back? Customers kept coming to buy coke, and I kept telling them to come back in five minutes. After a while, I walked around the corner to Kensington and Somerset to see if I could find him. A huge sense of relief swept over me when I walked into the Chinese store and saw Jerry leaning against the wall.

"Yo, Jer! I thought they gotcha, man."

"Nah, I just came here to hide for a minute."

"Aight, well, c'mon, we got customers waiting."

"Aight, I'm waitin' on my eggroll. I'll be around in two minutes."

I walked back around the corner and told the customers to hang tight for two more minutes, but those two minutes turned into five minutes. Then five minutes turned into 15. That's when I said "Fuck it"

127

and grabbed another bundle to make the sales myself. An hour had passed, and still no sign of Jerry. I couldn't understand it. Even with that entire bundle, it would only last him a day or two at the most. And once it was gone, he'll go back to being dope sick again. Whereas he could've kept working on the block and never been dope sick again.

I sold the other four bundles and then called Black to explain what had happened. Black dropped off five more bundles and told me that since I vouched for Jerry, I had to pay back the money for the bundle he stole. I ended up paying it back in no time because I was literally the only dealer on the block now, which meant I was making a lot more money. But with the extra money came additional risks. For one, I didn't have a lookout, so I had to be extra careful to make sure cops didn't catch me hustling. Plus, with nobody to watch my back, I was an easy target for anyone who wanted to rob me. But I played it smart and stopped hustling when the sun went down. There was no way in hell I was going to be a sitting duck for the stickup boys.

After a few weeks, Black started to drop off 10 bundles at a time instead of the usual five. But sometimes, I couldn't sell all 10 bundles, and I'd be stuck with one or two of them at the end of the day. I couldn't stash the bundles in the bando overnight because then somebody would just sneak in and steal them. But I also didn't want to bring them home with me because sometimes the cops would stop me while walking through the hood. My only solution was to sleep in the bando every night so that I could protect the bundles.

Even though I rarely stayed there, I continued to pay rent to old man Lenny. I liked having a place to shower and change clothes every couple of days. Besides, I needed a day off to relax and just watch TV every once in a while. I even went to the pawnshop and bought myself a PlayStation Three so that I could play video games on my day off. Three days after I purchased that PlayStation, I came home to find that it was gone! Mother fucker! I immediately knew who it was. Lenny had this other addict, Anthony, who was staying at the house at the time.

"Yo, where's Anthony at?"

"Anthony? Oh, he said he was going to Wildwood to visit his mother."

He must've packed my PlayStation in a bag and acted like he was going on a trip. I ran to Kensington and Somerset as fast as I could to see if I could find him. I figured someone from the corner might know where he was. If not, then I knew it was only a matter of time before he showed his face again. He was an addict just like me, so he couldn't stay away from that corner for too long. When I finally got to the corner, I saw that he wasn't there, so I got everyone's attention and made an announcement.

"I got a free bag of coke for anyone that knows where Anthony is. If you see him, come around Boudinot Street and grab me. I'll give you a free bag!"

I didn't expect anybody to tell me right then and there because then they would be labeled as a snitch. But I knew that a free bag would encourage someone to come and tell me in private if they knew where I could find him. Sure enough, the very next day, one of my customers came to the block to see me.

"Yo, Anthony's 'round da corner right now!"

I stashed my bundle in the bando and hurried around the block. I saw Anthony on the corner and quickly approached him.

"Brain, listen, I'm sorry I stole --"

CRACK! I didn't come to talk. CRACK! I landed another punch to his nose that would've knocked him on his ass, but there was a fence behind him that saved him from falling. He bounced back from the fence and swung at me but missed. This gave him a split second to make a run for it, but I wasn't about to let him get away. I chased after him on the busy avenue, and after about a block, I got close enough to grab the back of his shirt. He spun around and landed a nice shot to my eye. But I stomped on his foot so he couldn't get away and then hit him with a three-shot combo that dropped him to the ground.

I was about to climb on top and pummel him some more, but then he pulled a knife out of his pocket. I thought about grabbing my knife and slicing him first, but there was a crowd of people on the street watching by this point. There were too many witnesses to do some crazy shit like that, so I decided to leave him alone. Fuck it, I got my point across.

I walked back to the block and saw the guy who told me where to find Anthony. So I grabbed my bundle and handed him his free bag of coke, as promised.

"Thanks, dude. Hey, listen, don't tell anyone that I told you, OK?"

He didn't want anyone to know that he was a snitch. Plus, there was always the possibility that Anthony would try to come after him. But he needed his fix, so he did what he had to do to get it. It just goes to show that people will do anything when it comes to getting their drugs.

Chapter 22

When it came time for my next court date, I wasn't sure what the outcome was going to be. But I remember thinking that I could end up going to jail. I thought about not showing up at all, but I knew that would only make things worse, so I faced my fears and headed to the courthouse. The public defender told me that the DA's office offered me a plea deal, in which I would serve no time but would have to enter into something called "Treatment Court." She explained that I would first have to go to rehab. Then, after completing rehab, I would have to attend IOP (intensive outpatient program) and get drug tested every week. On top of that, I would have to come back to court every month for 12 months to meet the judge and make sure I was staying on the right track. It sounded like a lot at the time, but I literally had nothing to lose. My only other option was to plead not guilty. But if I did that, I probably would've lost the case and had to serve time. So my choices were literally jail or rehab; I chose the latter.

I thought I was going to have to go rehab right away. But the public defender told me that it would be a few more months before I was officially sworn into treatment court. I was glad that I didn't have to go right away because I just wasn't ready yet. I still wanted to get high, so waiting a little longer was perfectly OK with me. I mean, I lasted this long, so what's a few more months, right? Besides, what's the worst that could happen?

For the next few weeks, I continued to live my life as usual, by getting high and hustling on the block every day by myself. I'd be lying if I said I wasn't scared to work on the block by myself. I was like a sitting duck for cops and stickup boys and knew it was only a matter of time before one of them got to me. But, I had a vicious dope habit, and if I wanted to continue to support that habit, I had no choice but to keep flipping those bundles.

The cops busted my balls every day because they knew I was selling drugs, but no matter how hard they tried, they could never find my stash. It didn't take long for me to learn that standing on the corner all alone was an open invitation for cops to fuck with me. So, I came up with a plan to throw them off a little bit. I stayed on the block and hustled every day, but I would never stay in one spot. I constantly walked up and down the street all day long. Whenever I saw a cop car, I would just stagger to make it look like I was another junkie walking down the block. I figured it was better to look like a drug addict rather than a drug dealer.

After a few weeks, one of the neighborhood cops started to catch on to me, though. As I walked down the street, acting as if I wasn't selling drugs, he jumped out and threw me against the hood of the cop car. He searched my pockets but couldn't find anything because I had it tucked inside of a wooden fence across the street.

"You walk up and down this street all day, pretending like you're not selling drugs. It's only a matter of time before I catch you."

I swore to him that I wasn't selling drugs, but the money in my pocket told a different story. However, without any evidence, he had no choice but to let me go. After he left, I just laughed it off. I thought I was too slick and would never get caught.

February 19th, 2010, is a date that I will never forget. The day started off like any other day. I woke up at seven in the morning, flipped my first bundle of coke, grabbed myself a bag of dope, and then went back to the bando to shoot it up. When I was done getting high, I walked outside and saw a large group of addicts briskly walking up the street. There must've been at least 15 of them, which could only mean one thing: free samples! When a new dope spot opens up or an existing one gets a new product, they give out free bags to let everyone test that new product. It's a very effective way to attract new customers. There's not an addict in the world that would turn down a free bag of dope, and if the dope is good, all those addicts will become returning customers.

The biggest problem with free samples is getting there before all the other addicts do. They only give out a limited amount of bags, and if you get there late, you're shit out of luck. Luckily, I had a bike that I had bought from one of my customers a few days earlier. So when I saw all the addicts walking up the street, I hopped on my bike and headed to the new spot.

When I got there, the dealer handed me a bag of dope and a bag of coke. I was surprised that they were giving out samples of both, but I wasn't about to argue with them. When I got back to the block, I stashed the sample bag of dope in the bando and saved it for later. I had just shot some dope a few minutes earlier, so I didn't really need it yet. But, I was curious to see if the coke was any good. Honestly, I was hoping that it wasn't because that would mean less business for me.

132

When I shot the sample bag of coke, I immediately felt the rush, followed by that "WOM! WOM! WOM!" sound that you hear when you shoot some really good shit. Even though the coke was good, it still wasn't as good as the coke that I sold, so I wasn't worried about losing customers over it. After I shot the coke, I realized that I had no cigarettes left, so I walked to the store to get a new pack. I only had two bags left in my bundle, but I didn't want to risk leaving it in the stash spot where anybody could've grabbed it. So I hid the two bags in my coat sleeve and then walked to the store to get the smokes. I got halfway up the block when I realized that there were two foot cops following me.

Normally I wouldn't even worry about the cops because I never kept my stash on me. Even though the bags were hidden very well, inside a small hole that I had strategically sliced on the inside of my coat sleeve, I didn't want to take the chance, so I planned to make a break for it. The plan was to hurry up to the end of the block and turn the corner. Then, as soon as I was out of the cops' line of sight, I'd dart off and duck into a bando around the block. I picked up my pace a little bit and hurried to the corner. But when I got there, I was surprised by a group of foot cops walking up the street, coming right toward me. I turned around to run the other way, but three more cops were coming from the other direction. There was no point in running; I was screwed either way.

One of the regular cops from the neighborhood was there. This particular cop busted my balls constantly. Every single day he would stop me, throw me against the wall, and search my pockets. And every single day, my pockets would be empty. He would get so mad because he could never find anything on me and swore up and down that he was going to catch me one day. When I saw that I had nowhere to run to, I just shook my head and gave up. The cop threw me against the fence and searched my pockets while all the other cops stood around and watched.

"Where's it at? I know you got it on you."

I don't know what made me do it, but something inside told me to be honest and give up the coke. I had a feeling that they were going to find it anyway, so maybe if I was honest with them, they'd give me a pass and let me go. After all, it was only two bags. It wasn't like I had an entire bundle or anything.

"Aight, aight, look, it's in my coat sleeve, OK?"

They took off my coat and searched the sleeves but still couldn't find it. I guess my hiding spot was better than I thought. Eventually, the cop got frustrated and handed me the coat.

"Here, get it out for me."

I was kicking myself in the ass for even saying anything. They would have never found it if I had just kept my mouth shut. But it was too late now, so I stuck my fingers inside the hole in my sleeve, and two bags of coke fell to the ground. As soon as they saw the coke, they put me in handcuffs. That's when I knew I wasn't getting a free pass for being honest.

"Just tell us who gave it to you, and we'll let you go," one of the other cops asked.

I'm not a snitch, but even if I was, I knew they weren't going to let me go. I was going to jail either way, so I decided to have a little fun with them.

"Aight, aight, man, look… his name is Sumguy."

"Sumguy? Sumguy who? What's his last name?"

"I dunno, man, it was just some guy."

I chuckled at my little joke, but the cops didn't find it as funny as I did. When they took me to the 25th district, it was the same routine as always. They strip-searched me and threw me in the cell with a stale cheese sandwich and a bottle of water. A few hours later, it was time for my mug shots and fingerprints. While waiting for my mug shots, one of the cops recognized me from the past few times I've been there.

"You again? You're like VIP around here. We're going to have to get you your own special cell."

Early the next morning, I had to talk to the bail commissioner. He told me that I was on probation, had two open cases, and was now being charged with another case of possession with intent to deliver. So without hesitation, he set my bail at $7500. To be released, I would have to come up with 10% of that, or $750. I knew it was a long shot, but I tried to call Black anyway. Sure, $750 was a lot of money, but I also made a lot of money for the block. I was out there hustling every day by myself; they owed me! However, when I called Black, it was 4:00 a.m., so he didn't pick up his phone. I thought about calling my brother Mike, but I knew he wasn't going to help me again.

134

A few hours later, I was transferred to CFCF, and once I got there, they gave me a "cold pack," which is basically a Styrofoam tray that contains a lunchmeat sandwich, an orange, and a small carton of iced tea. I tried to eat the sandwich, but my stomach just couldn't handle it. After only two bites, I was ready to vomit. It was probably because I was dope sick, but then again, it's not like this was a premium sandwich from an actual deli or anything.

I forced myself to eat the orange, which actually did make me feel better for a couple of minutes. There's something about sugar that helps with the withdrawal symptoms of heroin. There's some sort of scientific reason behind it, but I never really understood it. I just remembered hearing about it when I was in detox a few months earlier, so I tried to eat as much fruit as possible. It was the only thing that made me feel better.

After eating, they took all of my personal belongings, strip-searched me, and then threw me in a holding cell with a group of other prisoners. We were herded around like sheep, moving from cell to cell. They took us from one cell, gave us a change of clothes, and then put us back into a different cell. Then they moved us from that cell, took our mug shots, and then put us back into another cell. It felt like we were playing musical cells, minus the music.

At one point, the guards took us to see a nurse. When I walked into the office, I was drenched in sweat, and my restless leg syndrome just wouldn't let me sit still.

"Let me guess, you're dope sick?" the nurse sarcastically asked.

While talking to the nurse, I asked if there was any type of detox or medication she could give me to relieve my symptoms. She just laughed and told me the only thing she could give me was aspirin. Aspirin? By this point, I was shooting $150-200 worth of heroin every day. What did she expect me to do with some aspirin?

So after taking the aspirin, she started to ask me a bunch of questions about my mental health. One of the questions she asked was if I felt suicidal, and honestly, I did. I would've rather died than go through another minute of withdrawal. The last time I was in CFCF, I hung on by a thread only because I had hopes of posting bail. But my bail was too high this time, and I knew I was stuck in there. I tried to manipulate her by telling her I was suicidal in hopes of being sent to a psych ward or to get better meds. But instead, she put me on suicide watch, which only made my situation worse.

Suicide watch was horrible. I had to be in a cell by myself with a guard standing outside my door at all times. They wouldn't even let me keep my blanket for fear that I would hang myself with it. Usually, I wouldn't care too much about a blanket, but it was the middle of February, and that jail cell was cold as fuck. On top of the frigid temperatures, the withdrawal became worse with every minute that passed. Once the stomach aches began, I knew it was just a matter of time before the nausea kicked in. Sure enough, 20 minutes later, I was hovering over the toilet to vomit. I didn't have much food in my stomach, so the little I did have came up immediately. I kept dry heaving over and over again until I was physically defeated. Eventually, I dry heaved so much that I started puking yellow bile from my stomach. To make things worse, I began to lose control of my bowels. I was literally vomiting in the toilet while diarrhea exploded out of my ass; it was not a pretty picture.

I thought my stomach had settled down a bit, but I was wrong. I found myself running right back to the toilet. I puked stomach acid until my throat was so sore that I could barely swallow. The stomach bile tasted so disgusting and was extremely thick. So thick, in fact, that at one point, it got stuck in my throat, and I couldn't breathe. I tried to cough it up, but it wouldn't move. I attempted to swallow it back down, but again, it just wouldn't budge. I literally could not breathe. It only lasted for a couple seconds, but it felt like an eternity. I seriously thought I was going to die. And to be honest, death seemed like a better option at the time.

I hadn't slept in over 48 hours. I was freezing cold with no blankets. My pants had shit stains that leaked to the outside where everyone could see. I was drenched with sweat, and my shirt was covered with vomit. All I wanted was a nice hot shower and a bed to sleep in, but there wasn't even a bed in this cell, just four walls and a toilet. I thought I died and went to hell. That was the only logical explanation. Since I was already in hell, I figured it wouldn't hurt to say a little foxhole prayer. So I prayed and asked God to forgive me for the way that I've been living. I promised that I would never touch another drug again as long as God got me out of jail. But, that long dreadful night continued, and I began to think that God just didn't care about me anymore.

The next morning I saw another nurse. I told her I felt a little better, mentally speaking, but was still very dope sick. She asked if I still had suicidal thoughts. I told her no, even though I was lying. I just didn't want to be on suicide watch anymore. I wanted to go to a regular cell where I could get some sleep.

136

When I was sent to general population, I met my new cellmates, and ironically one of them was another dealer/addict that I knew from the neighborhood. We always bought dope and coke off one another, and now we were both dope sick in the same prison cell.

Later that day, we ate lunch or at least tried to. Anything I ate usually came right back up. An hour later, my face was in the toilet again. My vomit must have triggered my cellmate because a few seconds later, he knelt down right beside me and started puking too. We were both vomiting at the same time, in the same toilet. The third cellmate just shook his head at us.

"Why you do drug that make you feel bad for?" he asked in broken English.

It was a damn good question, but I didn't have an answer for him. I couldn't tell you why I continued to torture myself like this. Heroin made me feel like shit, took all my money, and made me do things I really didn't want to. It was like I was in an abusive relationship, and no matter what happened, I kept on going back to it.

After a few days of being tortured by heroin's withdrawal, I was finally able to fall asleep for 15 minutes at a time. It doesn't sound like much, but it was better than not sleeping at all. A big part of not being able to sleep was due to my restless leg syndrome. No matter what I tried to do, I just couldn't sit still. I had no control over my legs. It felt like an involuntary muscle was causing them to shake constantly. Sometimes it would settle down for a few minutes, and I could finally relax. But every time I closed my eyes, 15 minutes later, I'd be awakened with the sudden urge to move my legs again.

Whenever I fell asleep for a few minutes, I would always dream about getting high. The obsessive thoughts I had about heroin were unreal. I am not exaggerating when I say that every single waking moment was spent thinking about heroin. But I guess every waking moment just wasn't enough because it was also the only thing I dreamt about when I fell asleep. I thought about that bag of dope that I stashed in the bando on the day that I got locked up. It was the free sample that I got, so I knew it was probably some good shit. For the next few weeks, it was the ONLY thing I could think about. When it got quiet, I swear I could hear that bag calling my name. I plotted ways to escape from jail, not because I wanted my freedom, but because I wanted that bag. I even thought about breaking out of prison, shooting that bag of dope, and then breaking back into prison before anyone noticed I was gone. That bag of dope was literally the only thing that I wanted.

I may have been locked behind bars, but it was nothing compared to being trapped inside of my own head. Drugs had me locked inside a mental cage for the past 17 years of my life. I never knew that the prison inside of my mind was the only prison I needed to escape from.

Chapter 23

After I was transferred to CFCF, I kept trying to call Black so that I could ask him to post bail. But every time I called, it went straight to his voicemail. After a few days, I finally got a hold of him, and I convinced him to post bail for me. I was excited because I knew I'd be getting released soon. I just couldn't wait to get out of that place. All I wanted to do was shoot a bag of dope so I could get a good night's rest. But four long days after I talked to Black, I was still sitting in a jail cell, so I knew I wasn't going anywhere. I thought Black was my boy, but I guess I didn't have any real friends, only acquaintances.

While incarcerated, I was still collecting unemployment. But to file and receive my money, I needed to call an automated line every week. This was impossible to do on the payphones in jail because they couldn't be used to make regular phone calls like that. So, I called old man Lenny and gave him my information to file my unemployment for me every week. I also had him request a new ATM card to be sent to the house so that once I had enough money in my account, he could withdraw the cash and post bail for me. I was collecting $450 every two weeks from unemployment, but my bail was $750, so that meant I had to wait at least two more weeks before I had enough saved up to post bail. But I didn't even care; at least I could see the light at the end of the tunnel.

After spending a little more than a week in CFCF, I was transferred to the House of Corrections, which is basically just an older-style prison that is located right next to CFCF. Once I got there, I met my two new cellmates, Spot and Domey, who both turned out to be pretty cool. I explained to them how I was dope sick and hadn't slept in days. So, Spot offered to give me his medicine that night, which was Thorazine, to help me sleep. I don't know how he smuggled it back to the cell because they make you open your mouth and lift your tongue to check and see if you actually took it. But he somehow slipped it past them and gave it to me when he got back to the cell. A couple of minutes after I took it, I began to zone out until I finally fell asleep. It was the first time I slept in over a week.

Even though I had a good night's sleep, I felt like shit the following day. My legs were shaking, and my anxiety was out of control. However, I woke up feeling something that I hadn't felt in over a week: hunger! I was surprised I had an appetite. I was even more surprised when I ate an entire meal without vomiting. I mean, I couldn't really afford to miss any more meals. At six feet tall and only 120 pounds, I was so skinny that you could literally see my rib cage.

My cellmates made these meals called "chi-chi" every night. Compared to regular prison food, chi-chi tasted like it came from a five-star restaurant. Spot and Domey also hooked me up with cigarettes every day, but cigarettes were expensive in jail, so they rolled up tobacco in rolling papers and passed it around like a joint. It doesn't sound like much, but those simple gestures made time in jail seem a little less stressful. I couldn't thank them enough. Spot even gave me a pencil and some paper to write letters to my siblings.

I sat on the top bunk with a pencil in my hand, but I just couldn't find the words I wanted to write to my sister. The only thing I could come up with was "Dear Kim…." All of a sudden, I heard banging coming from the next cell over. That banging quickly turned into a familiar sound: a hip-hop drum beat. I bopped my head to the beat as I stared at the blank sheet of paper in my hands. I hadn't written a rhyme in years, but at that moment, it felt like the hip-hop Gods were trying to tell me something.

I felt like a soda bottle that was shaken up and ready to explode. All of the anger, stress, sadness, pain, and loneliness that I had built up over the years had suddenly hit me all at once. I could feel all of these emotions trapped inside me being released as they flowed down my arm and out through my pen. Tears leaked out of my eyes as my feelings spilled out of my heart and onto the paper, but I didn't even care; I was in my zone. I didn't even feel dope sick anymore. I distracted myself from even thinking about it. But as soon as I was done writing, I felt sick again. So I wrote another rhyme, and then I wrote another one after that.

I wrote rhyme after rhyme after rhyme until I ran out of paper. It got to a point where my cellmates wouldn't even give me any more paper, so I had to start writing rhymes on napkins. When I ran out of napkins, I started writing on the walls. I felt like a mad scientist, but as long as I was thinking about rhyming, I wasn't thinking about dope. It made me fall in love with hip-hop all over again, allowing me to escape the walls in which I was mentally trapped. Writing rhymes was the only thing that kept me sane. It was the one thing that nobody could take away from me. Even without my pencil and paper, I could create rhymes in my head, one line at a time, until I had them memorized.

After Spot and Domey found out that I was a rapper, they told everyone on the block. So every time I left the cell, people asked me to spit some rhymes. It earned me a little respect on the block, which felt good to have, but nobody really gave me trouble anyway. After the word got out, people started talking about how dope my rhymes were. Spot even joked around about opening up a record label and calling it "Dope Sick Entertainment." But then, one day, Spot and Domey were suddenly transferred to another cell block. They packed up their belongings, and just like that, I never saw them again.

I got two new cellmates, but I don't even remember their names. One of the guys was annoying as shit and just wouldn't shut up. He walked around like he was the coolest guy in the world and thought his shit didn't stink. This dude bragged about all the drugs he sold, how many girls he fucked, and how many people he beat up. But I saw right through his bullshit; he was just starving for attention. The attention seeker was also a rapper, who thought that he was the best in the city, but his rhymes were horrible. Listening to him spit verses made me not want to rap at all because I was afraid it would encourage him to rap even more. Instead, I just ignored him, hoping that he would eventually get the hint, but he never did. It was rare that I would get any sleep since I was still withdrawing, but whenever I could fall asleep, he kept me awake by trying to talk to me or spit some rhymes. He was the most annoying person I've ever met in my life, and he started to get under my skin like a TB shot.

I needed to get out of there ASAP, so I continued to call Lenny to see if my unemployment card had come in the mail yet. When he finally got the card, he didn't understand how to activate it. So, he had another guy named Pat (another addict who lived in the house) help him out with it. When they activated the card, they said my balance was $450. He also told me that they filed my unemployment for that week, so I knew that the other $450 would be deposited on that Wednesday, totaling $900. I instantly felt a sense of relief because I knew I would finally be getting out, and I kept thinking about the bag that was waiting for me in the bando.

A few days later, I called Lenny again to see if he had withdrawn the money from my account yet, and he told me that there was only $20 left in my account when he went to the ATM. At first, I thought that Lenny may have stolen it, which confused me because I really thought that I could trust him. He wasn't on drugs or anything, and he had no reason to screw me over. Lenny just wasn't that type of person – but Pat was! I realized that Pat must have stolen my money! He had all of my information because he helped Lenny activate the ATM card, so he would have known the PIN number and everything. He probably stole the card while Lenny was asleep, withdrew the money, and then put the card back without Lenny even noticing. I wouldn't put it past him. After all, he was a heroin addict, just like me.

I was so furious! Not only because he stole $900, but because now I was stuck with no way to post bail. It caused me to fall into a deep state of depression. All I wanted to do was go home and get high. There were times when I literally cried myself to sleep. It was hard to hide my tears when my cellmates were only a few feet away. I didn't want anyone to see me crying because that would make me look weak, and jail was not the place to appear weak. So once again, I felt like I was in hell.

A few days later, I had my court date, so they threw me on the prison bus with everyone else who had court that day. It was nice to be on that bus and actually see the outside world for a few minutes. We drove past my brother's house, the same house I grew up in as a child. I saw the park across the street from my house and began reminiscing about my childhood. I thought about the fun times I had with my friends - playing manhunt, building treehouses, getting soaked under the fire hydrant, etc.

"LISTEN UP, EVERYBODY!" the sheriff screamed.

I instantly snapped back to reality. I was too busy daydreaming and hadn't even realized that we were at the courthouse already. It was time to face the music. We were escorted off the bus and given two sandwiches and an iced tea as they piled us into the holding cells.

After waiting five hours in a small holding cell with 10 other people, they finally called my name. The bailiff escorted me to the 10th floor of the courthouse on an old shaky elevator. We stepped off the elevator, and he placed me into another holding cell by myself. About a half-hour later, the same bailiff unlocked the cell and brought me into the courtroom, where I met with the judge. The judge told me that I was officially entered into Treatment Court and would be transferred into a rehab facility within the next couple of weeks. This was great news because it meant that I was finally getting out of jail. But even though I knew I was getting out, the struggle was far from over.

Chapter 24

A few days after my court appearance, I received a discharge notice which stated I would be released to a drug and alcohol rehab facility in two weeks. Even though I knew I was getting out soon, it didn't make the next two weeks any easier. It was still a horrible experience. I was still locked in a cell with an asshole who wouldn't stop talking, still constantly hungry, and still couldn't sleep. But by this point, most of the withdrawal symptoms were over. The one symptom that stuck with me, however, was the restless leg syndrome. It kept me awake every night, so I barely got any sleep. Whatever sleep I did get came in 15-minute increments. This lack of sleep caused me to be so exhausted the next day that I barely had any energy to get up and move around. I would literally lie in bed all day long. The only time I got up was to eat or use the bathroom.

I lay in bed so much that when I did get up to walk, I could barely lift my legs off the ground. It was a combination of not using my muscles and the slippers that they gave me. The slippers were way too big and always slipped off of my feet. I probably looked like a real-life zombie because I had to drag my feet across the floor while walking around. If I lifted my feet up off the ground, the slippers would just slide right off.

Two days before I left for rehab, I had an epiphany. I guess you could call it a moment of sanity. Something just clicked in my head, as if somebody had suddenly turned a light switch on, and I started thinking logically again. I was staring at the ceiling when all of a sudden, this crazy thought popped into my head. But it was more than a thought; it was more like a decision. And it was probably the best decision I had ever made in my life. I told myself that I was done getting high. I had never been more sincere about anything in my entire life. In the past, I always told myself, "I'm done getting high, blah blah blah," a thousand times, but this time it felt different. Every time in the past when I told myself that I was done, I really did mean it. I honestly wanted to stop every time, but in the back of my mind, I knew that I wouldn't be able to do it. But this time, I knew I could. I don't know how, but I just knew!

The day I got out of prison, the guards woke me up super early to eat breakfast and complete my processing. I sat in a holding cell for a couple hours until the sheriff's department came to get me. I didn't mind waiting because I knew it would be the last time I ever had to wait in a jail cell. When it came time to leave, a guard handed me a bag with the clothes that I wore when I got arrested. When I opened the bag, I smelled that stale, moldy scent that every prison has. I put on the clothes and realized that my sneakers, cell phone, and wallet weren't in the bag. I was told that personal items like that were stored in a different department, which was closed at the time, so I would have to come back later to get them. Five minutes later, they put me in the back of the sheriff's van, and I started my journey to rehab. I had no idea where they were taking me, so I decided to ask the driver.

"Yo, so what rehab you takin' me to?"

"Self Help, on Southampton Road."

Self Help! That was the same rehab that the detox tried to convince me to go to, but I refused because I wanted to be with Tanya. It was also the same rehab that I stayed at for two days and then escaped from in the middle of the night. They say the third time is the charm, right? The truth is that I didn't even care where they sent me because anyplace would have been better than jail. They could have shipped me to Alaska for all I cared. I was OK with it as long as I didn't have to spend 20 hours a day stuck inside a dirty jail cell.

When I walked in the doors of Self Help, I literally had nothing but the clothes on my back and the prison slippers on my feet. The muscles in my legs were so weak that I could barely walk. I smelled like a dirty prison cell and hadn't shaved in over a month. I had a sad look in my eyes like the world had robbed me of all my dignity. I was just another lost soul trying to find his way home, and I felt like I finally found it.

The sheriff took me into the building, where a short man with a caterpillar mustache introduced himself as Ron. The sheriff handed Ron some paperwork and then took my handcuffs off. It felt like the weight of the world had been lifted off of my shoulders.

"Hey man, you hungry?" Ron asked.

"Yo, I'm starving!"

Ron told me to walk down a flight of steps to get to the kitchen. When I got there, I was greeted by a flamboyant man named Timmy. He seemed pretty cool, especially since he hooked me up with a plate of eggs benedict and some hash browns. It felt like I was eating at a fancy restaurant compared to the prison food I had been eating. I ate the entire plate in record-breaking time. One of the other kitchen workers saw how quickly I ate it and asked if I wanted another serving.

After finishing my second meal, another guy asked if I wanted his plate because he wasn't that hungry. You damn right I took it! The kitchen workers were amazed at how much I ate. They couldn't believe their eyes when they saw me and my skinny toothpick of a body gobbling down three plates of food in five minutes flat. Timmy asked me where I kept all the food because my stomach wasn't big enough to hold it all. All I knew was that I felt like I hadn't eaten in weeks, and I had to make up for a lot of lost meals.

After I was done eating, I wanted a cigarette so bad. So I walked back up the stairs to the main floor and outside to the smoke yard to see if I could bum a cigarette from someone. I saw a guy smoking a cigarette, and before I could even ask him, he handed me one.

"Here, you need a smoke? My name's Mike. You just got here, right?"

Without hesitation, I took the cigarette and lit it up. As I smoked the cigarette and talked to my new friend Mike, I realized that I recognized him from somewhere. He looked so familiar. A few seconds later, it hit me! He was one of my best customers. I sold him coke every single day. I was about to mention it to him, but he beat me to the punch.

"Didn't you use to sell coke on Boudinot Street?"

You have to appreciate the irony here. I go to rehab, and the first person I meet is one of my old customers. We couldn't help but to laugh. We sat there for about 20 minutes, having a deep conversation about getting clean. I told him how I needed to stay clean and didn't want to go back to using drugs again, so he gave me some excellent advice. He told me to open up my ears and listen to what the counselors had to say. I had always been a stubborn person, so listening to others was something I had never really done before. But, I decided right then and there to let my guard down and start taking advice.

I went to my first therapy group later that morning. I wasn't assigned a counselor yet, so they just threw me in a random group as a temporary solution. We discussed the most important thing about staying clean and sober, which is staying away from people, places, and things. This meant that I couldn't hang out with my old friends who still got high. This also meant I couldn't go back to Kensington anymore. And if I wanted to stay sober, I would have to avoid bars at all costs.

This made me realize that my girlfriend, Tanya, was one of those people who I had to stay away from. So, I called her later that day on the payphone, but her roommate picked up and said that she wasn't home.

"Just tell that I'm done getting high, so I just can't be with her no more."

I felt proud of myself after I hung up the phone. It made me realize just how serious I was about staying clean and sober. I was so sick and tired of having that black cloud follow me around everywhere I went. I knew that if I wanted to get rid of that black cloud, I would have to make some crucial changes in my life, and breaking up with Tanya was a good start.

Later that night, they gave me the key to my room, so I lay down on the mattress just to test it out; it felt so comfortable. It was nothing like the old worn-out mattress I had to sleep on in jail. I felt like my body was resting on a cloud. I closed my eyes just for a minute, and the next thing I knew, it was morning. I couldn't believe that I had actually slept through the entire night, something I hadn't been able to do in over a month. I was so rested the following day I began to think that maybe this rehab thing was the answer I'd been looking for.

The next day, people from NA came to Self Help to hold a meeting. I noticed something similar about every person that came in from the NA and AA meetings. I noticed how every single one of them had a smile on their face. I had never seen people so happy before. There's no way that was just a coincidence. Obviously, they were doing something right, and I was determined to find out what it was. So, for the first time in my life, I listened to what these people had to say. The one guy was a heroin addict and had over a year clean. So, I figured I should probably listen to him if I wanted to learn how to get a year clean.

As I listened to this NA guy speak, he suggested that we help another person at least once a day. But he explained that when we help someone, we can't do it for selfish reasons. For example, we can't help someone just so that they owe us a favor later on down the line. Instead, we have to help someone and expect nothing at all in return. I swear to this day that God must have been speaking to me through that man because later that day, I looked out the window and saw a new guy who had just arrived at the rehab. He was sitting all by himself out in the smoke yard. One look at him, and I knew he was withdrawing from heroin. He was drenched in sweat, clutching his stomach and shaking his leg nonstop. I knew that feeling all too well. As I sat there, watching him suffer, that voice from the NA meeting spoke to me.

"Go and help someone," the voice told me.

So, that's precisely what I did.

I went outside and introduced myself to the newcomer. His name was Gary, and sure enough, he was withdrawing from heroin. I sat there and talked to him for a while to try and distract him from the dope sickness. I just got to rehab the day before, so I didn't have the answers on how to stay clean, but I knew I could at least try and make him feel welcome in a place where he didn't know anyone. Look, I'd used a lot of drugs in my life, and they made me feel good every time I used them. But not one of those drugs could compare to the high I felt when I helped Gary that day. Helping him, and not expecting anything in return, gave me the feeling I had been looking for my entire life.

Later that day, I introduced Gary to a couple people that I had met the day before. I introduced him to one guy named Joe. Joe helped Gary just as much as I did, if not more. Joe was the type of person who would talk nonstop. But he wasn't annoying like my old cellmate was because Joe was funny as hell. The more Joe talked, the more we laughed, and the more we laughed, the more it helped us. Joe talked so much that it completely distracted Gary from even thinking about the withdrawal. For that first week or so, Gary didn't have much of an appetite, so he gave me his plate of food at every meal. It worked out perfectly because I was always starving! In exchange, I gave Gary any fruit that came with the meal because I knew that the sugars in the fruit would help him with the withdrawal.

On weekends we were allowed to have visitors. That first weekend I convinced Lenny to visit me so that he could bring me some money, a radio, and my ATM card. I did the right thing and gave the ATM card to the front desk because that was one of the rules of Self Help. Besides, I didn't want to be tempted by having access to all that extra money. I figured $40 would be enough to get me a few packs of cigarettes and some snacks.

That following Monday, I met my permanent counselor. Her name was Marlene, and she played an essential part in my recovery. There was something about her that made us instantly click. I viewed her as a motherly figure who didn't take shit from anyone. She wasn't afraid to tell someone exactly how it was, whether they wanted to hear it or not. She truly helped me on so many levels that you couldn't even fathom.

She taught me about the disease of addiction and opened my eyes to the behaviors of an addict. Just because I stopped doing drugs didn't mean that I would automatically start thinking and acting differently. Marlene explained that if I continued to behave like an addict (even without the drugs), then those same behaviors would lead me right back to getting high. I had to change my behaviors, and Marlene gave me the motivation to actually do it.

Marlene found out that I liked to write hip-hop songs, so she bought me a notebook and a pen. It was the greatest gift I could have ever received; it was exactly what I needed! She encouraged me to write as much as I could and explained how it would be therapeutic and help my recovery process. Marlene didn't have to twist my arm to write. It was something I loved to do anyway, so it worked out perfectly.

For the next couple of weeks, I walked around with that notebook everywhere I went; it never left my sight. I never knew when a rhyme would pop into my head, so I had to keep it close by at all times. I took it with me to every meeting that I attended. I took it to the kitchen when it was time to eat. I even took it to the bathroom when I had to take a shit. Having that notebook with me all the time helped me to express my emotions. When you are new to recovery, your emotions can go up and down and left and right, so it's good to have an outlet to let those emotions out.

The one emotion that got to me the most was anger. I was so angry at myself for allowing the drugs to destroy my life, so I started writing rhymes about it. I wrote about the pain and the struggle of my addiction. For the first time ever, my verses began to make sense. My mind was clear now. My head had been lifted out of the fog, and I was able to focus. I started to spit these rhymes that I wrote about recovery to other patients in the rehab. Word quickly got around, and every couple of hours, someone was asking me to spit a rhyme. My old rhymes would usually impress people, so I wasn't fazed by the positive reactions, but these new rhymes brought reactions that I had never seen before.

I knew my rhymes had a real purpose now: to help other addicts get through the tough times. When I saw how much other addicts could relate, it made me feel good inside. This was the real reason why God gave me this talent. I no longer cared about getting a record deal or becoming famous. I just wanted to use my skills for a good cause. I wrote rhymes to help other addicts get through what I have already been through. If I could help just one person with my hip-hop, then every line I had ever written in my life would be worth it. From this point on, I had two new addictions. I was addicted to helping people and addicted to writing rhymes. So when I wrote a rhyme that could help someone, I got a feeling that no drug in the world could have ever given me.

Chapter 25

I never really believed in karma until I got clean and sober, but I quickly realized that karma was, in fact, very real. Luckily, I was doing all the right things, so karma worked in my favor. I already explained how I started helping people when I first got to rehab, but it didn't stop there. I continued to help people whenever I could. If I saw someone who looked depressed, I would try to talk to them and cheer them up. If someone shared something in a meeting that was bothering them, I would speak to them afterward and see if I could help them somehow. Shortly after I started to help people, I noticed other people helped me when I needed it. It reminded me of that song "Lean on Me." I never fully understood the lyrics in that song until I started helping others.

When I first arrived at Self Help, I didn't have any sneakers because they were still at the House of Corrections, and I wasn't allowed to leave rehab to go and get them. So, I had no choice but to wear those oversized jailhouse slippers, which I hated because I had to drag my feet across the floor in order to walk; otherwise, the slippers would fall right off. One day, as I struggled to walk down the hallway, another client named Snook stopped to ask me a question.

"Ay young buck, what size sneaker you wearin'?"

"They my size!"

I didn't even think about what I said. It was just a natural reaction. See, on the streets, if someone likes your sneakers, then they might ask what size you wear. And if you wear the same size as them, they might try to rob you, so it's best not to tell anybody your shoe size if they ask. When I refused to tell Snook what size sneakers I wore, he tilted his head sideways and gave me this look. That's when I looked down at my old, dirty, oversized prison slippers and knew that there was no way he was trying to rob me for these things. Nobody in their right mind would want these slippers; I didn't even want them. We both started laughing at the same time. It was the hardest that I had laughed in a long time. After we were done laughing, Snook gave me a pair of fresh Nikes that looked barely worn, and they fit me perfectly. It felt weird at first because I wasn't used to wearing regular sneakers anymore. But, my toes were actually warm, and the cushions inside made it feel like I was walking on pillows.

I thought about how Snook barely knew me, yet he gave me a free pair of sneakers. I couldn't stop thinking about how nice of a gesture it was. After that day, I had a whole new outlook on life. I realized that it was the little things in life that mattered. I started to feel gratitude toward things that most people took for granted, like sneakers.

Snook was one of the many good people I met at Self Help. I'm not talking just about other patients but also the staff members who went above and beyond to help me. I will never forget this one guy who worked there, Bobby. Bobby was in recovery and had a few years clean at the time. The first time I met him, he blocked my path as I walked down the hallway so that I couldn't pass him.

"Hey, what's your name?"

"I'm Brian, wassup?"

He extended his arm to shake my hand, so I did the same. As we shook hands, Bobby asked me another question.

"Brian, did you drink or get high today?"

"What? No!"

"Good! You know why? Because you're a fucking winner!"

I walked away with a smile on my face and pride in my heart. For the first time in my life, I actually did feel like a winner instead of the loser junkie that I always thought myself to be. Bobby didn't even know me, yet he believed in me. That gave me the confidence that I needed to believe in myself. Sometimes, all an addict needs is a little push in the right direction.

There was another employee, Greg, who also worked at Self Help and was constantly helping others. Every time I saw him, he had a huge smile on his face. It was almost as if his smile was a permanent tattoo that he could never get rid of. Greg had a very welcoming presence about him. He always encouraged us to talk to him if we needed to, so I took him up on his offer on multiple occasions. There were a few times when I felt like getting high, and Greg was always the one I would go and talk to. He was quick to open my eyes to the reality that my addiction wouldn't let me see on my own.

There was another Self Help employee named Will, who also had a smile permanently glued to his face. Shortly after meeting him, I found out that he was also a rapper, so we started spitting rhymes back and forth to each other. Will and I also had some deep talks about addiction and recovery. He was a very wise man who offered me a lot of good advice. One day, I told him about my previous visit to Self Help and how I climbed out the window as one of the employees chased me down the block. When I told Will this story, his jaw dropped.

"Young bul, that was me! I was that employee."

Will explained how it was his first day on the job, and he didn't want to lose a client on his first day, so that's why he chased me. He joked about how I was the fastest white boy he had ever met and how I should join the Olympic track team.

There were countless employees at Self Help who helped me early in recovery, but there are not enough pages in this book to mention them all. So I'm going to tell you about one last employee who made an impact on my life. His name was Ricky, and when I first met him, I thought he was a miserable prick. Ricky was a former client who graduated from rehab. After graduating, he moved to the transitional living unit, commonly known as "the third floor." On the third floor, you have a lot more freedom, but you also have to pay rent. Some of the third floor residents, like Ricky, worked at Self Help for 16 hours a week, which covered the cost of their rent.

The way I met Ricky was not like the others. Ricky didn't always have a smile on his face, so he wasn't easily approachable. I saw him walking around the building a lot, but we never interacted with one another. Ricky's job was to accompany and transport clients to different places. Clients obviously couldn't leave whenever they wanted, but sometimes they needed to. For example, if someone had to go to the doctors or had a court case or something, Ricky would go with them. He made sure they didn't go and get high or do something they weren't supposed to be doing. He was basically a glorified babysitter.

When I first got to Self Help, I didn't have any real clothes. All I had was the outfit I came in and two other shirts that someone lent to me. So I kept wearing the same clothes over and over again. I requested several times to go to my house to get some of my clothes, and after two weeks of begging, they finally let me go. In the back of my mind, I thought this would be my chance to go get high one last time. I'm not sure why, but addicts always want to get high one last time. The problem is that one more time could turn into a lifetime. I wasn't aware that Self Help would send somebody to go with me, though. I thought I was going on my own, so my plans got all fucked up.

When it was finally time to pick up my clothes, I was called into the office and introduced to Ricky. He seemed irate at first, but he actually

152

turned out to be pretty cool. Once I got to know him, I realized that he was the type of person who would give you the shirt off his back if you needed it. Ricky and I got on the bus and headed to my old house. On our way there, I was thinking of a way to get high without him knowing about it. I had this crazy idea to walk into my house and climb out the back window without him noticing. There was a dope spot right around the corner, so I could quickly grab a bag and make it back within five minutes. He would have never even known.

On the bus ride to the house, Ricky and I started to talk. He told how much better his life has gotten ever since he stopped doing heroin. He didn't have to eat out of dumpsters or steal from people anymore. He no longer had to wake up dope sick or have to go through withdrawal in a cell ever again. Damn! He was right. I didn't miss any of that shit. I was 45 days clean and sober. I was no longer dope sick. I was actually sleeping at night. I was eating healthy and even started to smile every once in a while. So I asked myself if it was worth losing that peace of mind over one bag of dope. Did I really need to get high one last time?

God must have put Ricky in my life that day because Ricky talked me out of getting high without even knowing it. I never told Ricky I wanted to get high. Maybe he saw it in my eyes, or perhaps it was just a coincidence. Or, as I like to believe, everything happens for a reason. I think I was supposed to meet Ricky that day. Even though he always looked angry, I could tell how happy he was on the inside.

When we finally got to the house, Ricky insisted on waiting outside on the porch for me. He wasn't sure if people would be getting high inside the house and didn't want to risk being around it. I understood, but I needed to get my clothes. Once I was inside the house, I had that crazy thought again. I thought about how easy it would be to sneak out the back, buy a bag of dope, and then come right back. But then I thought about everything Ricky and I had just talked about. I knew it wasn't worth it. Instead, I walked upstairs and packed a bag with some of my clothes.

I had an old pair of sneakers in my room that I wanted to grab, but when I picked them up, a syringe fell out and onto the floor. The needle was half full with heroin. I must have hidden it there in case of an emergency. I just sat there for a minute and stared at it. My mind went blank. I felt my hand reaching for it, but I couldn't stop myself. What I did next was inconceivable at the time. Without even thinking about it, I squirted the dope onto the floor and tossed the syringe in the trashcan. It was like an automatic reaction. I couldn't believe that I did it; I had never been more proud of myself in my entire life.

Ricky was on the porch looking up the street when I got back outside. He told me this was the same neighborhood that he used to get high in. He was getting uncomfortable and wanted to leave as soon as possible. As we walked to the bus stop, I told him what had happened inside the house. I wanted recognition for doing the right thing because, well, doing the right thing was something I had never really done before. Ricky looked at me like a proud father would look at his son. I think my story distracted him from his thoughts of getting high. It's funny how helping others really just opens the door to allow others to help you. Ricky helped me to throw that needle away, and by throwing that needle away, I helped him resist the urge to use again.

On the bus ride back, I thought about how this whole sobriety thing was a real possibility for me. I never thought in a million years that I would have thrown away a needle full of dope. I didn't even know who I was anymore, but for the first time in my life, I actually liked the person I was becoming.

Chapter 26

Whenever people from AA and NA came to hold meetings at Self Help, they would always talk about how a "Higher Power" helped them stay clean and sober. Different people have different understandings of what a Higher Power actually is. Basically, it's a power that is greater than yourself. It can literally be anything that you want it to be. Some people believe their Higher Power to be Jesus, while others believe in Mohammad or maybe Buddha. But a Higher Power doesn't have to come from a religion. Some people choose their Higher Power to be aliens. There are even atheists in recovery who use the 12 step program itself as a Higher Power.

I like to keep things simple, so I just refer to my Higher Power as "God." Even though I was raised Catholic, I don't consider myself to be one nowadays. Instead, I like to think of myself as spiritual. The way I see it, every religion has one thing in common: the belief in God. So I take that belief in God and leave the rest behind.

When I first got to rehab, I believed in God, but I honestly thought God had abandoned me. I repeatedly prayed for help throughout the years, but it never came. I spent so many drunken nights on the front steps of that church, crying, praying, pleading, and begging God to help me stop drinking and using drugs. But, my prayers were never answered. The next day I would go back to the bar and drown in my sorrows all over again.

Once I started doing heroin, I pretty much gave up on praying. The only time I did pray was when I was begging God to kill me. I used to pray for a bad bag of dope that would cause me to overdose and die in my sleep. So every morning when I woke up, I would get mad at God for torturing me with another day of living. Over time, this created a huge resentment toward God. The very thought of religion made me cringe. Ironically, it was my hatred toward God that allowed me to continue to believe in him. However, a lifetime of hatred can be wiped away in a heartbeat, and it usually happens when you least expect it.

Self Help had a small chapel, where they held non-denominational services every morning. They made announcements about these services every day, but I thought I was too cool for God, so I just ignored them. I actually laughed at the people who went to those services every morning. So, you can imagine how surprised I was when I convinced myself to go to the chapel one day. But I didn't go to get in touch with God or anything like that. I went for my own selfish reasons.

I overheard two clients talking to each other about the chapel. I tried my best to tune them out, but one of them mentioned something about a movie. Even though I loved watching movies, at the time, I didn't care about watching a religious one, so I paid them no mind. But then the other client mentioned the padded chairs that they had in the chapel. Apparently, these chairs were so comfortable that you could easily fall asleep in them; well, now that sparked my interest. I was tired of sitting on the hard wooden benches in the TV room. So I decided to break free of the regular routine and check out the movie in the chapel. My plan was to sit in the comfortable chair, doze off, and take a nap.

I got to the chapel, and they started talking about God, but all I heard was "blah blah blah." OK. Cool. Whatever. Just turn the movie on so I can go to sleep. After a few minutes of praying, the spiritual advisors, Mr. Blue and Ms. Evelyn, finally turned the movie on. We watched a movie called "The Passion of Christ." Now, I'm not going to lie. The film reeled me in before I even had a chance to doze off. I went to Catholic school my entire life, so I had heard the story of Jesus' crucifixion a million times before. This movie, however, portrayed it in a way that I could have never imagined. It showed the reality of the pain and torture Jesus endured before he was executed. I literally had tears running down my cheek by the end of the movie. But for the first time in my life, I didn't try to hide or wipe the tears away. I didn't care who saw them. I felt God in my presence, and from that day on, my life has never been the same.

I understand that everyone is raised differently with different religious experiences, so I would never bash any religion out there. I was raised Catholic and questioned many things about the religion as I was growing up. I realized at an early age that different faiths have different stories that contradict each other. However, the one thing they all have in common is that there is a God. So, to keep things simple, I believe in God and leave the rest behind. I just try my best to do the right thing. In fact, it took no time at all to realize that if I did the right thing, my Higher Power would always take care of me in the end. Look, I'm not here to try to turn atheists into believers or anything like that. If you don't believe in God, then that's OK. I just know that God was with me every step of the way, even when I thought he wasn't.

On the wall at Self Help, there was a sign that read "Five Things to Guarantee a Day Sober." They are as follows:

1. Ask God to help you stay sober.

2. Make a meeting.

3. Stay away from people, places, and things.

4. Help another alcoholic/addict.

5. Thank God at night.

Since I had already been doing three of these things every day, I figured I might as well do the other two. At first, I kept it simple. I prayed every morning and asked God to keep me clean and sober for that day. And then, at night, I thanked him for keeping me clean and sober. I had never prayed like that before. In the past, I only prayed for things I wanted, like a new car, a million dollars, or for God to wave a magic wand and make me stop drinking. But after my spiritual awakening, I learned that I had been praying wrong my entire life. So, instead of asking for the things that I wanted, I began to thank God for the things I already had.

I started to notice a change in myself. For starters, I had a smile on my face that I couldn't get rid of. I also became grateful for all the little things I had in my life. I was thankful for the things that many people would take for granted, like food on my plate, clothes on my back, the bed I slept in, and the fact that I wasn't dope sick anymore. But even though I constantly had a smile on my face, I felt like something was missing. That something was my family, and I needed them back in my life.

I wrote letters to my sister Kim and my brother Mike, letting them know that I was in rehab. I knew my brother Shawn was homeless, so there was no way for me to send him a letter. And I couldn't write to my dad either, because he had moved to Florida and I didn't have his address yet. To be honest, I had doubts that my dad would want to hear from me anyway, after all the bullshit I put him through. But in my letters to Mike and Kim, I told them how I was trying to turn my life around. I told them how much I missed them and apologized for everything I had done. I wasn't expecting them to write back, but I got letters from them two weeks later.

In Kim's letter, she expressed how disappointed and angry she was at me for allowing myself to become addicted to drugs. I don't think she fully understood how addiction worked. It's not like I "allowed" myself to become addicted. I do take full responsibility for my actions, but I only partly believe that addiction is a choice. Yes, addicts choose to get high that first time, but who hasn't made a mistake in their life? Who hasn't drunk a beer out of peer pressure or curiosity? The problem with addicts and alcoholics is that once they pick it up that first time, they can't put it down, no matter how hard they try.

My sister's letter also explained how my nieces were always asking about me and how she had no choice but to tell them the truth. She used it as a life lesson to teach them what happens when you do drugs. I'm glad she told them the truth because I would never want them to get caught up in the lifestyle I lived.

Kim's letter also stated that, in order to protect her girls, I was not allowed to see them until I had at least six months clean. She wanted to make sure I was serious about my recovery this time. I couldn't blame her. Even I had doubts about how long I would last. After I finished reading the letter, I noticed another piece of paper inside the envelope. When I pulled it out, I realized it was a second letter, but this one was written in crayon.

The letter read, "Dear Uncle Brian, I hope you get better soon. Stay strong. I miss you! Love, Caitlyn."

This broke my heart when I read it, and once again, I felt tears leaking from my eyes. I knew what I needed to do. I was determined to reach that 6-month milestone and get them back in my life again.

Chapter 27

You wouldn't believe the amount of food I ate in rehab. No matter how much I shoved in my mouth, it still wasn't enough to fill my stomach. My counselor, Marlene, gave me snacks every day and sometimes even half of her lunch. This was on top of the lunch that Self Help served me. She also got me a volunteer job in the kitchen at Self Help. I was so grateful for that job because it helped pass the time and kept me out of my own head. Sometimes when I was bored, I would sit around and think about getting high, but if I stayed busy, those thoughts came around less frequently. Working in that kitchen was pretty easy too. All I had to do was wash a few dishes and wipe down a few tables. It was well worth it for all the extra food that I got.

One day, as I was washing the dishes, a staff member from the front desk tapped me on the shoulder.

"Yo, some new guy is upstairs asking for you,"

"What? Who? What new guy?"

"I dunno. He just got here. I think his name is Jerry."

I couldn't believe it! I only knew one person named Jerry, so it had to be my boy! I immediately dropped the dirty pot and ran up the stairs. When I got to the front desk, I saw a red-headed guy standing by the door, but I had to do a double-take because the red hair was the only thing I recognized about him. Jerry looked horrible! His scruffy face was sunken in from losing so much weight, and his dirty, torn-up clothes made him look like an old homeless person.

I wondered if Jerry had always looked that bad, and maybe I only noticed it now because my perception changed after I got clean. Either way, I was just glad he was trying to get some help. We talked for a while, and I told him the same thing Ricky told me when I first met him. I told him how I didn't have to eat out of dumpsters, rob and steal, or sleep in abandoned buildings anymore. I explained how great it felt to wake up in the morning and not be dope sick or have to worry about getting $10 to start my day.

Jerry and I also talked about the last time we saw each other. I was honest and told him how pissed I was at him for stealing that bundle because I had to pay it back out of my own pocket. He immediately apologized, and I didn't hesitate for one second to forgive him. For the longest time, I told myself that I would beat his ass when I saw him, but now that I was clean, that shit didn't matter anymore. I told him not to even worry about the money; I was happy to see him getting the help he needed.

About an hour later, we sat down to eat dinner, but Jerry didn't even try to touch his food. Add that to the sweat-covered forehead and restless legs, and it was obvious that he was dope sick. Jerry told me he couldn't get into detox, so he came straight to rehab instead. Usually, if you have an opioid addiction, you have to detox before you come to rehab. But Jerry didn't tell Self Help that he had an opioid addiction. He lied and said he only used cocaine so that they would let him into rehab right away. In hindsight, I wish I would've told one of the employees so that they could have gotten him into detox, but the thought didn't even cross my mind. Instead, I was trying to focus on what I could do for him at that moment because I could tell that he was really suffering.

I felt sorry for Jerry, but there wasn't much I could do other than get him some fruit from the kitchen to try and alleviate his symptoms. He ate one of the oranges I brought him, but it didn't seem to help. So, I figured a cigarette might help calm his nerves a little. After we finished smoking, Jerry said he had to use the bathroom and would be right back. But instead of going to the bathroom, he walked right out the front door without even saying goodbye.

That was the last time I ever saw Jerry. I didn't understand why he came to rehab only to leave an hour later. They say that this disease is cunning, baffling, and powerful, and it definitely proved to be true that day. Part of me wanted to try to find him so that I could convince him to come back to rehab. But, part of me also knew that he could've just as easily convinced me to get high. Thankfully I had a clear mind and was able to see the reality of the situation. I soon realized that the only thing I could do was pray for him.

Over the next couple of weeks, a few people I knew from the streets checked themselves into Self Help. At first, it was just one or two people from the neighborhood. But then, I started seeing some of my old customers. At one point, even J-rock came to Self Help on a court stipulation, but he didn't stay for too long. A week later, he said "Fuck it" and ended up leaving.

The day J-rock left, I saw a new guy who looked familiar, smoking a cigarette in the smoke yard. I noticed how he kept looking in my

160

direction, which worried me because he could've easily been someone I had robbed or ripped off somehow. I was afraid that my past had finally caught up with me, and sure enough, he began his approach.

"Now I know where you been hiding at!"

I realized who he was when I heard his voice and instantly felt relieved. He was one of my old customers from Boudinot Street. He told me how the block was completely shut down after I got locked up, and nobody was hustling there anymore. Apparently, it was the only corner he liked to buy from, mainly because I was white, which somehow made him feel safe. Honestly, his logic didn't make sense because addiction is color blind. I would've robbed him in a heartbeat if I needed to, and it wouldn't have mattered if he was white, black, brown, or green with yellow fucking polka dots. I didn't discriminate; I was an equal opportunity criminal.

After talking for a few minutes, he told me how he decided to come to rehab once he saw the block wasn't opening back up. At that moment, I realized how much I had contributed to other people's addictions. This guy only came to rehab because he couldn't buy drugs from me anymore. It never occurred to me how much of an impact I made on other people's lives by selling drugs. I know I never forced anybody to buy drugs from me, but I still felt guilty for supplying them with what they needed to feed their addictions. I wanted to make up for it, so I started helping everybody I could. I mean, by this point, I was already helping people, but now I kicked it into high gear and helped anyone and everyone that I could.

Whenever a newcomer came to Self Help, I tried to make them feel welcome. If I saw that they were still withdrawing, I would try to get them some extra fruit from the kitchen. If they looked depressed, I would try to talk to them. If they looked stressed, I would hook them up with cigarettes or do anything else I could to help them out. Even though I tried my best, I quickly realized that it was impossible to help everyone. Sometimes, no matter how much I tried, it just wasn't enough, and they would leave to go get high again.

Some addicts who left rehab probably told themselves, "I'm just gonna get high one last time." Well, one last time was exactly what they got because some of them never made it back. Many of them failed to realize that their tolerance levels were not what they used to be. If they used to shoot heroin every day, they think they can go right back to shooting it. But, their tolerance is not the same when they had been clean for a few weeks. It's like starting all over again. Nobody picks up a bag of heroin the first time they get high. Opioid addicts usually start with pills and slowly build a tolerance until they reach the level where they can handle heroin. So, when they relapse, they can't handle it and end up overdosing. Many people don't realize that it only takes one bag to end a life, sometimes even less than that. It's a sad reality that I had to witness way too often.

I was supposed to stay in rehab for 120 days, but the situation changed after only being there for one month. When I first got to Self Help, they made me apply for welfare insurance to cover the cost of my 120 days. But a couple weeks later, I got a letter stating I was ineligible because I was collecting unemployment. Thankfully, my first 30 days at Self Help were covered by BHSI. Under normal circumstances, Self Help would have discharged me once my BHSI funding ran out. However, since I was court-stipulated, nobody knew what the hell I was supposed to do.

When Marlene found out I had been denied welfare insurance, she brought me into her office and called my case manager for treatment court, Mary Santangelo. She put Mary on speakerphone and explained how I couldn't get insurance to stay in the rehab. Mary put us on a brief hold, and when she picked the phone back up, she told me I could be discharged from Self Help and go back home.

"What? No, no, no, no, no! I can't go back there!"

"Why? What's the problem, Brian?"

"You don't understand – that neighborhood..."

"I do understand, Brian, but –"

"Nah, but it's not just the neighborhood, though; it's the house too. Like, people be getting high in there and shit. I can't. I just can't go back there."

There was a brief moment of silence before Marlene lifted up the receiver to disconnect the speakerphone.

"Mary, let me call you right back," Marlene spoke into the phone.

Marlene told me to hang tight for a few minutes while she went to go talk to someone. She came back five minutes later, trying to conceal a smile that even Stevie Wonder could have seen. When Marlene sat back in her chair, I thought she would tell me that I could stay in rehab even though I didn't have insurance. But instead, she threw me a curveball question that I wasn't expecting.

"How much money do you get from unemployment?"

162

"Like $450 every two weeks. Why?"

"And when's the next time you get paid?"

"Actually, I got paid today. Why? What's up?"

Marlene told me that a room was available in Self Help's transitional living unit. The transitional living unit was more commonly referred to as "the third floor" because, well, it was located on the third floor. So, I would technically still be in the building, except it would sort of be like renting an apartment. I could come and go as I please, but I would have to pay rent and be home every night by 11:00 p.m., except on weekends when I could stay out overnight if I wanted to. Marlene told me in order to move to the third floor, I needed to pay one month's rent in advance, which was $420. Maybe it was just a coincidence, but I found it funny how everything seemed to fall into place at the right time. I genuinely believe that my Higher Power made it all work out the way it did.

When I first got to the third floor, I felt excited, nervous, and scared, all at the same time. I was excited because I finally had freedom and could leave the building on my own now, but this was also what frightened me. I didn't fully trust myself yet and was afraid I would get high. But honestly, I was more fearful of going back to jail than anything else. I promised myself I would never go back, and I was determined to keep that promise!

When I moved to the third floor, Self Help gave me all my personal belongings back, so I plugged my cell phone into the charger and searched through my contacts to see who I could call. I wanted to reach out to people to let them know that I graduated from rehab and was doing well. But, as I scrolled through my contacts, the only phone numbers I had were either drug dealers or drug addicts. These were the "people, places, and things" I was told to stay away from if I wanted to stay clean and sober. So, I did the smartest thing I could have done at the time and deleted every phone number I had.

Even though I deleted all of my contacts, deep down inside, I knew it wasn't enough. I mean, just because I deleted their numbers doesn't mean that they all deleted mine. So what would have happened if someone from my past tried to call me? Without hesitation, I took the battery out of the phone, walked downstairs, and asked the employee at the front desk to throw the phone away for me. I could've easily thrown it into the trashcan in my room, but I know that wouldn't have been enough to stop me. If I changed my mind and wanted that phone back, I would've just picked it up out of the trash. But by throwing it into the employee's trashcan, I wouldn't be able to get to it.

After I got rid of my old phone, I went to MetroPCS to get a new one, along with a new number. At the time, they had some type of deal, and I only had to pay $25 for a month of service and a brand new phone. After I got that new phone, I felt so much better. I no longer had my old friend's phone numbers, and they no longer had a way to get in touch with me, either.

My friend Gary from rehab moved to the third floor the day after I did. And a week later, our friend Joe followed suit. It was nice having my friends up there because I didn't really know anybody on the third floor and felt like I was going crazy from being bored every night. In fact, I will forever be grateful for Gary because, without him, I don't think I would have gone to as many meetings as I did. I had nothing against meetings or anything, but I don't think I would've gone to one by myself, so it was good that I had someone to go with.

One of the employees from Self Help, Greg, who I mentioned a few chapters back, was also in recovery and helped me tremendously when I moved to the third floor. Gary and I only knew of a few meetings in the area, but Greg knew where all the meetings were. He took us to a different meeting every night until we found a few that we really liked. Not only did it help us to branch out to other meetings, but it got us into the routine of going to a meeting every single day. He really gave me the motivation I needed to jump-start my recovery.

The first meeting that Greg took us to was an AA meeting called "Auctus" on Woodhaven Road. I told Greg I felt weird going to AA because I had a problem with drugs, not alcohol. That's when Greg explained to me that he, too, was an addict but just felt more comfortable going to AA as opposed to NA. I didn't really understand what he meant by that. Why would an addict, who had a problem with drugs, go to a meeting for alcoholics? Greg saw the confused look on my face and explained how addiction and alcoholism were the same diseases with the same solution. He then told me that it didn't matter what type of meeting I went to, as long as I went to a meeting. Since we were already in the car and on the way to AA, I figured I would at least give it a shot; besides, it's not like I had anything to lose. I'm so glad I took Greg's advice because, before that night, I really thought that I could still drink every once in a while, as long as I stayed away from drugs, but boy was I wrong.

The speaker at the meeting talked about how he was both an addict and an alcoholic. He explained how there were many times when he wanted to stop getting high, so he would just stick to drinking instead. But as he continued his story, he explained how he could never go out and drink just one or two beers like a normal person. Once he started drinking, he couldn't stop. And, every time he got drunk, it led him right back to the drugs.

I felt like this man was sharing my life story. Until that night, I never realized that I was an alcoholic. In fact, it made me realize that I was an alcoholic long before I was ever an addict. There were plenty of times when I tried to stop doing drugs, only to replace them with alcohol. But, every time I started drinking, I just couldn't stop and wound up getting high by the end of the night. Alcohol always caused a chain reaction in my brain that led me to use other drugs. So, if I wanted to stay clean, I would also have to stay sober.

Even though I liked the AA meetings that Greg and Gary took me to, I still wanted to check out the NA meetings in the area. But when I went to my first NA meeting, this big-bearded, muscular manly man walked up and gave me this huge hug. I was freaked out when he hugged me because I didn't know what to do. It made me super uncomfortable, but after being introduced to a couple of other people, I quickly learned that hugging people was the standard greeting in NA.

Some people may argue that drug addiction is different from alcoholism, but to me, it's all the same. Some drugs are smoked, while others are snorted, injected, or swallowed in a liquid form. Alcohol altered my mind the same way any other drug did. But, this is just my opinion. You don't have to agree with it; I'm not here to argue because, at the end of the day, it doesn't really matter.

Even though AA and NA follow the same 12 steps, the vibes I got from their meetings were completely different. I know NA works for many people, but I didn't really like it that much. At first, I thought it was just that one particular meeting I went to, so I checked out other meetings in the area but got the same vibe from all of them. Well, all of them except for one. There was this one NA meeting that was held on Tuesday nights in a church on Ashton Road. I don't know what it was about that meeting, but I really seemed to like it, so I started going every Tuesday, while the rest of the week, I attended my AA meetings.

When I first started attending meetings, Gary told me that I should raise my hand and let everyone know how I had just gotten out of rehab and was new to AA. Gary used to be in AA before, so he knew more about this stuff than I did. In fact, he raised his hand at almost every meeting and told me that raising my hand would help people to get to know me better. When Gary explained this to me, I was hesitant to agree with him. I was under the impression that I should only raise my hand if I had a bad day or felt like drinking or using. But Gary explained how it didn't matter if I had a bad day or not. If I raised my hand at every meeting, even if I had a good day, then when I had a bad day or felt like drinking, my hand would go up automatically, out of habit. That made a lot of sense to me, so I faced my fears and started to raise my hand at every single meeting. I was nervous at first, but after a few weeks, I got so used to it that it didn't even bother me anymore. And Gary was right; if I felt like drinking or using, my hand went up automatically. There was no hesitation in talking about it.

I was worried that my first sober weekend with freedom would be tough. I was so used to getting drunk and high on the weekends that I wasn't sure what I would do with myself. Thank God I had Gary and Joe as friends. We went to a meeting on Friday night, and afterward, they asked me if I wanted to hang out at some coffee shop on Frankford Avenue. At first, I thought hanging out at a coffee shop would be kind of boring. I pictured a bunch of old rich people sipping espressos and reading books. Not that there is anything wrong with that, but it just wasn't my type of crowd. However, I was in for a big surprise when we arrived at the coffee shop.

As we got off the 66 bus and crossed Frankford Avenue, I noticed about 30 people standing on the sidewalk, smoking cigarettes as they listened to music blasting from the building. I assumed this was a bar or club located next to the coffee shop, but as we got closer, I realized that this was the coffee shop. And the people hanging outside were all young, sober people like us. When we walked in, the first thing I noticed was how everyone was smiling and having a really fun time. Then, I noticed how all of their eyes were glued to the front of the room. So, I turned my head and saw someone on a stage, trying not to laugh as they sang karaoke. I just couldn't believe that this was a coffee shop!

166

Once I started to mingle with the crowd, I began to recognize a lot of faces from the meetings we went to. I quickly learned that most people who hung out at the coffee shop were in recovery, making me feel right at home. I even ran into a few people I grew up with from the old neighborhood who were also clean and sober now. I had an amazing night and even sang karaoke a few times. I never knew that being clean and sober could be so much fun. I always thought I needed drugs and alcohol to have a good time, maybe because that's all I had ever known. Who knew that there was a whole world of people having fun and staying sober on Friday nights?

Chapter 28

After I moved to the third floor of Self Help, I began to hear everyone talk about this thing called "Facebook." Apparently, the rest of the world knew what it was, but I was too busy getting high to stay up on the latest trends, so I didn't hear about it until after I got clean and sober. Even though I kept hearing people talk about it, I didn't know exactly what it was until my sister asked me to create an account. She told me I could use it to reconnect with our extended family and people I hadn't seen in years.

I took the plunge and downloaded the app to my new phone. After setting up my account, I sent friend requests to my sister Kim, my brother Mike, and my dad. I searched for my other brother, Shawn, but couldn't find him on the app. He was probably in the same boat I was in not too long ago; too busy getting high to worry about this new Facebook stuff. After sending my initial friend requests, I saw some people I knew pop up on a suggestion list. First, it was just my cousins, aunts, and uncles. But then it started showing me names of people I hadn't seen in years, even people I went to grade school with. I was amazed at how this app worked. Like, how the hell did it figure out that I knew all these people?

I sent friend requests to everyone on my suggestion list that I knew, and after doing so, the reality of my drug abuse hit me. I started getting messages from people I hadn't seen in ages. Most of them were concerned with my well-being because they had heard that I went off the deep end with the drugs. But, some of them were surprised to get a friend request from me because they thought I had died. They heard rumors about how bad I had gotten, and when they hadn't seen me in years, they assumed the worst. That shit hit me hard and got me thinking about how lucky I was to still be alive.

Reconnecting with my extended family made me realize that just because I was disconnected from the rest of the world doesn't mean that the rest of the world didn't continue on without me. While I was out fighting my addiction, my cousin Charlene was battling cancer. Sadly, she passed away about a year before I got clean. I learned about her death through Facebook when some of my other cousins posted about it on her birthday. I felt horrible when I found out because I should've been there for her and the rest of my family, but instead, I was stuck in Kensington, living $10 at a time. My addiction stole a huge chunk of my life, which I can never get back, and I have no choice but to live with the guilt.

A week after I created my Facebook account, a girl named Michelle sent me a friend request. She looked familiar, but to be honest, I wasn't 100% sure who she was. I only accepted the friend request because I thought she was cute, and after chatting with her for a bit, she said we knew each other from the bus stop back in our high school days.

In high school, I hung at the Cottman and Torresdale bus terminal, where my friends and I would get high and spit rhymes every day after school. It was right across the street from Saint Hubert's, an all-girl high school, so there were always girls hanging out with us, and Michelle must've been one of them. I smoked so much weed back then that I barely remembered anyone who hung out there, but somehow she remembered me after all these years.

Michelle and I exchanged phone numbers and started talking almost every day. She was really down-to-earth and easy to talk to, plus she made me feel really good about myself. It didn't take long for me to ask her out on a date, which she happily agreed to. And since we both shared a love for breakfast food, it was only natural that our first date took place at IHOP. We met each other Saturday morning at the IHOP on Roosevelt Blvd and hit it off almost immediately. We had each other laughing the entire time, and neither of us could wipe the smiles off our faces. The date went so well that we didn't want it to end. So, after we finished eating, we decided to watch a movie. And after the movie was over, we hung out for a little longer. A little while later, we got dinner at a nearby restaurant. By the time I finally got home, it was almost 9:00 p.m. We hung out for nearly 12 hours straight, and every minute of our time together seemed perfect.

For the next couple of weeks, things between Michelle and I seemed to be going great. We only saw each other on the weekends, but it was perfect because it allowed me plenty of time to attend meetings during the week. And even though we only hung out on weekends, I still made sure to hit at least one meeting before meeting up with her for the night. Relationships are said to be a downfall for many newcomers in AA, so I vowed to never let our relationship get in the way of my recovery. In fact, some people in AA suggested not getting into a relationship at all until I had at least one year clean and sober. But I was too hardheaded at the time to listen to them. Looking back in hindsight, I now understand why they suggested that, and I'll get to that later, but at the time, it was the one suggestion that I just didn't listen to.

My friend Greg was one of those people who advised me not to get into a relationship for the first year, but he never tried to force it down my throat. I looked up to Greg and respected him for his knowledge of the 12 step program and for the fact he never tried to push anything on me like some people in AA tried to do. He never said things like "You HAVE to do this" or "You NEED to do that." Instead, he would just offer advice or suggestions. However, the one thing that Greg did try to force on me was the importance of getting a sponsor. But, to be fair, getting a sponsor is a huge part of the AA program. It really is one of those things that you need to do if you expect to stay sober. You literally can't do the 12 steps without a sponsor, and the whole point of AA is to do the 12 steps.

At first, I was a little hesitant to get a sponsor. It's not that I didn't want one, but it was more or less because I didn't know how to ask. Many people describe it as asking another man on a date, and let me tell you, they are not wrong. When it came to picking a sponsor, I had a couple different people in mind, but I wasn't sure which one I wanted to ask. I was most comfortable with Greg because we hung out the most, but Greg didn't have much clean time compared to the other people I was thinking about asking. He just got clean six months before I did, so I wasn't even sure if he was allowed to sponsor people yet. I also had another guy in mind, Frank, who was actually Greg's sponsor. I waited until after a meeting one night to ask him, but just as I was about to approach him, someone else beat me to the punch.

"Yo Frank, I uh, I been thinking. You, uh, you think you'll be able to sponsor me?"

"Yeah, look, I would love to, but the truth is I'm sponsoring too many people right now. It's just that, you know, it just wouldn't be fair to you. But hey, hey, why not ask Greg? He needs to start sponsoring people."

Boom! I had my answer. I felt like God gave me a sign and pointed me in the direction I needed to go. Now, all I had to do was wait for the right moment to ask him. A few days later, Greg asked me to chair a meeting with him at our home group. For those of you who don't know, a home group is like your main meeting that you go to every week. It's a group you are dedicated to, one you never miss. And by consistently attending the same meeting, everyone there gets to know you. Getting to know everyone is essential because if you ever start slipping up, your home group members will immediately notice and call you out on it. It's a great way to keep yourself in check.

When I first started going to AA, I was told I should never say no when someone asks me to chair or speak at a meeting. So, when Greg asked me to chair the meeting for him, I immediately agreed. It was the first meeting I had ever chaired, so I was pretty nervous, but I wasn't about to let that stop me. By this point, I knew I had to do things that made me uncomfortable if I wanted to stay clean and sober. Chairing that meeting wasn't that hard at all. In fact, the anxiety that came before the meeting was 10 times worse than the actual meeting itself. Basically, all I had to do was read a few paragraphs from a sheet of paper and then introduce the speaker, who just happened to be my good friend Greg. By the time I introduced him, all of my anxiety and jittery feelings were long gone. I honestly don't know why I let it build up that much. It wasn't half as bad as I thought it would be.

After the meeting ended, Greg gave me a ride back to Self Help. It was the perfect time to ask him to be my sponsor, but I didn't know how to get the words out. It was only a five-minute drive, but that ride felt like an eternity. The closer we got to our destination, the faster my heart started to pump. I honestly thought I would chicken out and not ask him at all. But then I began to think about how I would feel if I missed this opportunity. I knew I would feel defeated and regret not asking him. Then I thought about how this moment would rattle around in my head for the next 30 years or so. So, instead of torturing myself, I just came right out and asked.

"Yo, Greg, can you be my sponsor?"

"Well, that depends."

"Depends on what?"

"What are ya willing to do to stay sober?"

I couldn't help but crack a smile. Greg already knew I was willing to do just about anything to stay clean and sober. So when I reassured him of this, he agreed to be my sponsor. Then he handed me a copy of the "Big Book" and told me to go home and read a section called "The Doctor's Opinion." The Big Book is basically AA's equivalent of the bible. It has all the instructions you need to work the 12 steps, but it can be hard to understand because it was written using fancy words from the 1930s when

AA was first founded. This is why having a sponsor, who can help you decipher the Big Book and walk you through the 12 steps, is so crucial.

I went home that night and read the Doctor's Opinion, just like Greg had asked me to, but the language used in the Big Book made it difficult to comprehend what I was reading. So the next day, I met with Greg, and we reread the Doctor's Opinion together. As we made our way through the chapter, Greg stopped after every paragraph to discuss what we had just read. By doing this, I was able to get a much better understanding of it.

Once we were finished with the Doctor's Opinion, we moved on to a section called "How it Works." This chapter lists the 12 steps, and Greg gave me a quick rundown of each step in layman's terms before we dove into the first step. I'm glad he did this because even though we recited the 12 steps at every meeting, I really didn't know what half of them meant. But once he explained them, it made a lot more sense to me, and I was officially able to start the first step.

"Step 1. We admitted we were powerless over alcohol—that our lives had become unmanageable."

This step was self-explanatory, but I remember asking Greg if being both an alcoholic and addict would be a problem, considering the step only mentioned alcohol. Greg assured me that these are the same steps I would see in NA meetings, except the word "alcohol" would be changed to "drugs." He explained that there may be some differences between AA and NA, but the steps will work for both. He told me to replace the word "alcohol" with "drugs" as it applies, and I would be fine.

Once we cleared up the whole drug and alcohol dilemma, I was ready to get started. Now, for me, the first step was a no-brainer. All I had to do was admit I was an alcoholic and addict. Well, shit, I didn't need anyone to convince me. One look at how I was living, and anyone with half of a brain cell could tell I was an alcoholic and addict.

"Yeah, man, absolutely. I'm definitely powerless. No question about it."

"OK, but what about the second part?"

"Huh? What second part?"

It's funny how the mind works sometimes. I had been reading this step every single day for the past two months, and I never even noticed that there were two parts to it. The first part was obvious – "We admitted we were powerless over alcohol." But I never even thought about the second part – "our lives had become unmanageable." Like, I knew it was there. I read it a million times. I wasn't blind. I wasn't illiterate. But it's like I never seemed to even notice it before.

So again, Greg asked me if my life had become unmanageable, and it didn't take long at all for me to figure it out. I mean, I was a homeless heroin addict who got arrested for selling drugs because I needed to support my habit. Life doesn't get much more unmanageable than that. So, without hesitation, I admitted that I was powerless over drugs and alcohol and that my life had become unmanageable. After that, we wasted no time and moved right on to the second step.

"Step 2. Came to believe that a Power greater than ourselves could restore us to sanity."

This step wasn't very hard for me to understand either, and Greg explained that this step also had two parts. The first part was coming to believe in a Higher Power, which was easy for me because I believed in God long before I ever came to AA. However, I was ashamed to admit it in public because I thought I was too cool for God. I honestly thought people would judge and make fun of me for it. Besides, it's not like I went to church or prayed every day when I was getting drunk and high. In fact, the only time I ever prayed was when I needed something or when I wanted to get myself out of a jam. So, for the most part, I just acted like I didn't care about God, at least up until I had my spiritual awakening.

The second part of this step was pretty simple to understand too. There was no doubt in my mind that I was living in insanity. Just thinking back, I still can't believe some of the stuff I did. But after I got a little clean time, I felt like I was slowly turning back into a normal person. So I asked myself, "Is God the one responsible for restoring me to sanity?" Without a doubt, I knew the answer was yes. After Greg learned that I agreed with the second step, we moved on to the third step.

"Step 3. Made a decision to turn our will and our lives over to the care of God as we understood Him."

After we read the third step, Greg asked me to say the third step prayer with him. I agreed and recited the prayer, but it included outdated words like "thee," "thy," and "thou wilt," which had always confused me. Words like these are part of the reason why I hated going to Catholic Church and reciting prayers because I never knew exactly what I was praying for. When I pray, I like to talk to God in my own words; it just makes it easier for me. I speak to God the same way I talk to any of my other friends.

This step didn't come as easy to me as the first two did. Greg made me take note of a critical word in this step: "decision." Greg explained that I had to make a decision to stop living the way I wanted to live and start living the way God wanted me to live. I learned that God had a plan for me, and God's plan was better than any plan I ever came up with. Greg told me that sometimes God's will, or God's plan, may not make any sense, and we may not always agree with it, but God knew what was best for us.

"For example, part of God's will for you might have been for you to get arrested when you did."

"What? C'mon, why would God want me to go to jail, man?"

"Bri, are you happy with your life right now?"

"Yeah, kinda. I mean, it's a lot better than it was a couple months ago. Ya feel me?"

"Well, why's it better? What's different?"

"I'm clean and sober now. I don't have to worry 'bout being dope sick no more."

"OK. And how did you get clean?"

"Because I went to rehab."

"OK. But, how did you get to rehab?"

The cat had my tongue. I suddenly had an epiphany. I knew where Greg was going with this, and he was right. Getting arrested was part of God's plan for me; because that was the only way I would ever get clean. Greg explained that even though it's not something I would have chosen myself, it worked because God knew what was best for me. Furthermore, he told me that I probably would have never gotten sober if God had left it up to me. Because whenever people like us make plans, they never work out the way we want them to.

This made me think back to all of my failed sobriety attempts. I thought about how I tried to stop on my own but just didn't have enough willpower. So, I ran away to the Navy to get clean, only to get kicked out a few months later. Then I thought about how I tried the methadone clinic, which only made my tolerance for opioids 10 times worse than it already was. These were all MY plans, not God's, and that's why I failed at every single one of them; because I never asked God what his plan was for me.

Once I understood the difference between God's will and my own, Greg moved on to the part that read, "God as we understood Him." I'm glad Greg talked to me about this because being raised Catholic left me with many doubts about organized religions. I explained to Greg how I definitely believed in God but was unsure of all the other stuff the church tried to teach me. Greg pointed out the part of the second step that mentions the words "Higher Power" instead of the word "God." Then in the third step, it continues with "as we understood Him."

The point Greg was trying to make is that my Higher Power could be anything that I wanted it to be. I could call it God, Jesus, Muhammad, Buddha, Zeus, or anything else I wanted to. But, the best part was when Greg explained that my Higher Power didn't even have to come from religion. It could just be a spiritual presence if I wanted it to be, or even the word GOD as an abbreviation for Good Orderly Direction. Greg explained how even atheists are a part of AA, and sometimes they would believe in the power of AA itself. There were so many different options, and I could literally believe in anything I wanted to. It was my Higher Power; nobody else's.

Once I began to understand all these terms and phrases, Greg taught me what the third step was really all about. I knew I had to make a decision to turn my will and life over to God, but it went a lot deeper than that. Greg told me that once I make this decision, I have to live up to it every day. I can't just say, "Yeah, OK, I'll do God's will," but then go out tomorrow and rob a bank because I need money; it doesn't work like that. But even though I had a better understanding of it, I was still left with one question.

"How do I know what God's will is for me?"

"Just don't be an asshole."

Greg told me I should pray every morning and ask God to let me know what his will is for me. And then, he explained how I won't always recognize God's will, but I will always understand the difference between right and wrong, and I should always try to do the right thing. Greg went on to tell me that I should try to help as many people as I can and to become an open vessel so that my Higher Power can work through me to reach others. In simple terms, God's will was for me to be a good person, and in order to be a good person, I had to remain clean and sober.

After I did the first three steps with Greg, I prayed every morning and asked God to show me what his will was for me that day, so I could carry it out. I really tried my best to do God's will instead of my own. But, it's a lot easier said than done, and sometimes it felt like God was testing me, especially when life started throwing curveballs.

The struggle of my recovery really began when my unemployment money ran out. I used my last check to pay two weeks' rent for the third floor, which meant I only had two weeks left to find a job. I literally went out every single day to apply for jobs but always heard the same thing.

"Sorry, we're not hiring right now."

Eventually, I figured out that I could reach many more businesses through email and employment websites. So I used the computer at the public library every day to search for jobs on the internet. I had a résumé that I typed and emailed to myself, so I could forward it to anybody who was hiring. I applied to every position I could think of. I didn't even care how much it paid; I just needed to find something.

The two weeks had passed, and I was still unemployed. Rent at Self Help was always due on Sunday night at our weekly "relapse prevention meeting," and I knew I wasn't going to come up with the money in time. I thought about going back to the old neighborhood to flip a couple bundles and make some money for rent. I had no intentions of getting high; I just really needed the money. But, I had been down that road before, and I knew where it would lead me. So instead of going back to dealing drugs, I decided to call my sponsor.

Greg gave me the best advice I could have ever gotten, even if it didn't make sense to me at the time. He reminded me of the difference between my will and God's will. He reminded me that God's will was for me to not sell drugs (who would've thought) but to stay sober and do the right thing. My sponsor told me to trust God's plan, and it would all work out in the end. I was hesitant at first because I could end up homeless if I didn't pay my rent. But there was a part of me that knew Greg was right. Sometimes you just have to let go of the wheel and let God take over.

Sunday finally came, and I still didn't have the rent, so I went to talk to Woody to let him know. Woody was the house manager for the third floor, collecting rent and taking care of any other issues anybody had up there. At the time, I didn't know him too well. I had only met him a couple of times, so I was scared to talk to him about not having rent. I honestly thought he was going to tell me to pack my shit and leave. But when I explained to Woody how I was out every day looking for a job, he completely understood. He told me not to worry about anything and that

176

he would talk to Joe P in the morning. Now, Joe P was on the board of directors at Self Help, so he was the one who was really in charge of the third floor. Woody was just a house manager, so it was up to Joe P to decide if I could stay or not.

Surprisingly, Joe P gave me an extra two weeks to come up with the rent. I felt a huge sense of relief when I heard the good news, but I wasn't out of the woods yet. I still had to find a job! So, I continued my job search but couldn't find anything. I must have applied to well over 100 companies by now. A week and a half went by, and I was still unemployed. I was beginning to get really stressed out. But, I kept reminding myself what Greg told me about the third step. I had to have faith in God and live by his will, not mine. Even if that meant that I would get kicked out of Self Help, I was willing to accept it. Maybe getting kicked out was part of God's plan, and if it was, so be it. I knew by now not to question it because most of the time, we only see God's will in hindsight.

Thursday came, and I was three days away from being homeless. At this point, I had almost given up because I knew that even if I found a job, there was no way I would get a paycheck before Sunday. However, I didn't let that stop me from continuing my job hunt because, either way, I knew I needed to find one. I got up that morning and did my regular routine by saying a prayer and eating breakfast, and then I made my way to the library. On my way to the library, a company named Traction Tire called me about a delivery position they had available and asked if I could come in for an interview the following day. I happily agreed to the interview and hung up the phone with a huge smile on my face. I had a good feeling about this!

The next day, I went to the interview and arrived almost an hour early, but it wasn't so much by choice. The company was located in Bensalem, Pennsylvania, which is right outside of Philadelphia. But, the bus schedules for Bensalem were horrible because they only ran once every hour and a half. So my only choice was to either arrive an hour early or a half-hour late. Obviously, I didn't want to be late, so I had no other choice but to arrive an hour early. Well, apparently, arriving an hour early for a job interview really made a good impression on the company. They explained that because this was a delivery job, being on time was crucial. And I showed them from the start that I could arrive on time, way ahead of schedule.

I left the interview with a very good feeling, and before I could even make it home, the interviewer called to offer me the position. I was ecstatic! When I got back to Self Help, I told Woody the good news, but I also explained how I wouldn't have the rent on Sunday because it would be another two weeks before I got my first paycheck. He brought me to Joe P's office so that I could explain it to him, and Joe P agreed to let me stay as long as I paid the back rent with my first couple of paychecks.

I left Joe P's office feeling like the weight of the world had been lifted off of my shoulders. The day before, it felt like the world was caving in on me, but now I felt like the happiest man on Earth! I immediately realized that Greg was right all along. I did God's will and stayed clean and sober. I did the right thing. I kept my faith. And in the end, God took care of the rest. I felt like God gave me a test, and I passed with flying colors, but this little test was just a small speed bump compared to the roadblock that was waiting ahead for me.

Chapter 29

A lot of people compare their first year of recovery to a roller coaster because of all the ups and downs they go through, and my first year was no different. Just as everything seems to be going perfect, BOOM, life hits you a dose of reality, and your past comes back to haunt you. I was well aware of all this because I had already experienced my first fall on that roller coaster. But after that first dip, the roller coaster began climbing again, and I felt like I was on top of the world. However, I didn't realize that the higher you rise, the farther you fall.

After I started my new job, everything seemed to be going great. It was like all the pieces of the puzzle were fitting into the right places. I had a new job, a new sponsor, and a new girlfriend. I even put on a few pounds, so I began to look and feel healthy again. And to top it all off, I was coming up on three months clean and sober. Life was almost perfect. At this point, Michelle and I had been dating for a few weeks, and I couldn't have been happier. I honestly felt like a little kid again. She even introduced me to her daughter and the rest of her family, so it felt like things were starting to get serious between us.

On my 90-day anniversary of being clean and sober, I had to see my probation officer in Center City, Philadelphia. On my way there, the train stopped at Somerset Station. This was the same stop I would get off at when I was getting high. It was a block away from where I used to hustle on Boudinot Street. But, honestly, it didn't even bother me. I was so happy with my life that the thought of getting high wasn't an option for me. I knew that getting high, even once, would jeopardize everything I had worked so hard for, and I wasn't about to throw it all away.

I made it past Somerset Station with no problem and continued on my journey to the probation office. When I finally got there, the probation officer took one look at me and could tell I was clean. She then spun her computer monitor around to show me my mug shot from when I got arrested. WOW! I looked like fucking shit! I was only 120 pounds in that mugshot, but the person standing before her was 155 pounds. She almost couldn't believe that I was the same person. It's incredible how much of a difference 90 days could make.

After leaving the probation office, I walked toward the Reading Terminal Market to get something to eat. On my way there, I passed by a building with a sign that read "Free HIV test." Things between Michelle and I were getting serious, so I decided to get tested one last time, just in case. But, in the back of my mind, I knew I would pass the test with no problem. Even though my ex-girlfriend had HIV, we were always careful. We never shared needles, and we always used a condom. I even got tested every three months to make sure I didn't catch it. In fact, I had just gotten tested three months earlier, right before I got arrested. And since that test came up negative, I was almost positive that I was in the clear. But, I knew that HIV could sometimes take six months to show up in your system, so I wanted to be 100% sure.

After filling out some paperwork, a young lady brought me to an exam room, poked the tip of my finger with a pin, and smeared my blood onto the test. As we waited for the results, we talked about how great life was. I told her I was in recovery and celebrating 90 days clean and sober. I then explained how I was really getting tested for Michelle's sake and for the peace of mind in knowing that my past decisions wouldn't hurt her in any way. We joked around and talked for a few more minutes until she finally picked up the test and read the results.

"I'm sorry, but you're HIV positive."

You could have heard a pin drop. The atmosphere in that room did a complete 180. The smile on my face instantly vanished. I was fucking speechless. The young lady told me that the test was 99% accurate, but there was always a tiny chance it could be wrong. So she suggested I visit a doctor to get a complete blood exam. She then gave me a list of doctors and phone numbers to call so that I could make an appointment.

After receiving the devastating news, I sluggishly walked around Center City for a while, wandering aimlessly with no real destination. I thought that maybe it was just a bad dream and none of this was really happening, but deep down inside, I knew it was real.

I asked God, "Why? Why now? Why when I try to get sober and do the right thing?" Then, I started to think about Michelle. How was I supposed to break this awful news to her? It wasn't fair. It wasn't fair to me, and it certainly wasn't fair to her. I was so afraid because what if I had already spread it to her? We were careful and used condoms and all, but I was also cautious and used condoms with Tanya, yet I still somehow got it.

I had a thousand thoughts running through my mind at a mile a minute. I really didn't know anything about HIV at the time. All I knew were the horror stories I'd heard over the years. I heard that if you caught HIV, it was considered to be a certain death. I didn't know what to do or who to talk to because I didn't want anyone to know I had it. I was afraid people were going to judge and look at me differently.

I walked around the city with those tormenting thoughts rattling in my brain until I finally decided to talk to someone. But the only person I trusted to keep a secret like that was Marlene. As a drug and alcohol counselor, I knew she had a professional obligation to keep our conversations confidential. So, I knew my secret would be safe with her.

As I rode the train back to Self Help, I felt like a lost soul who finally found his way home, only to find that his home had been destroyed. I just didn't see the point in trying anymore. I mean, what's the point of working so hard for something, only to have it all crumble in the end? As the train continued down the tracks, I stared out the window at the familiar streets below. I was fast approaching dope town, and those little blue bags started calling my name again.

"Next stop, Somerset Station," the automated system stated.

The train slowed to a halt, and the doors quickly opened. I could smell the desperation of Kensington Avenue coming from below the tracks. It reminded me of hot tar or the scent of a skunk. The smell was so nasty, yet I fucking loved it.

"Fuck it! You're going to die anyway. Might as well go out with a bang," the voice inside my head told me.

At that moment, I didn't see the point of staying clean anymore. I felt like I was cursed with HIV, so what difference would it make if I got high or not? So I said, "Fuck it," stood up, and walked toward the door. But right before I got there, that voice inside my head spoke to me again.

"Just pray. God will take care of you in the end."

I stopped dead in my tracks as I began to second guess myself. I didn't know whether I should get off or sit back down, so I decided to do neither. Instead, right there in the middle of the train, I fell to my knees and began to pray. Deep down inside, I knew that getting high wasn't the answer, so I asked my Higher Power to remove those obsessive thoughts.

A couple people on the train looked at me like I was a crazy person, and who knows, maybe I was. But I didn't even care because, at that very moment, it felt like my entire life depended on that prayer. And in a way, it kind of did.

By the time I was done praying, the train had long left Somerset Station. I felt a little better, but the weight of the HIV was still heavy on my mind. A small part of me still wanted to get high, but I knew better than to act on it.

When I finally got back to Self Help, I immediately went to Marlene's office to talk to her. When I told her the bad news, she cracked a half-smile, which threw me off, but I continued the conversation anyway.

"I dunno what to do, man. I'm scared. I was this close to going to get a bag."

Marlene just smiled and let out a sigh as if I were worrying over nothing. She made it seem like everything was going to be alright.

"You know HIV nowadays isn't a death sentence, right?"

"What do you mean? People die from HIV all the time."

"That may have been true 20 years ago, but not anymore. The medicine they have now has come a long way."

"Yeah, but —"

"Brian, you can have HIV and still live a long healthy life."

"Yeah, but I been dating this girl, and I don't know what to do."

"Well, she has the right to know. But don't sweat it. As long as you take your meds, you can't spread it to her."

I began to feel a sense of relief. Even though I was still scared shitless, it was comforting to know that at least I wasn't going to die. There was so much I didn't know about HIV, so I'm glad I came to Marlene because she was definitely the right person to talk to. Marlene seemed to know a lot about HIV, and I began to wonder how she became so educated on the subject.

"You want to know how I know so much about HIV?"

"Yeah, how do you?"

"Because I have HIV too. I had it for many years now."

WOW! I couldn't believe it. I was actually in shock when she told me. Marlene was so full of life. She was one of those people who had a permanent smile glued to her face. It was hard to believe that someone with HIV could walk through life with such a positive attitude. I felt 100 times better when she told me because it meant I wasn't alone. I already viewed Marlene as a motherly figure, but after our conversation, she became my new favorite role model. Not only did she give me information that I needed to hear, but she also gave me hope. Because if she could go

182

through life with that much happiness, even though she had HIV, then I knew I could too!

Shortly after discussing it with Marlene, I shared the news with my three closest friends; Gary, Joe, and Greg. I was afraid of everyone else finding out, so I asked them to keep it a secret for now. Honestly, I wasn't sure how they would react, but they told me the same thing Marlene told me. Greg even put on his sponsor hat and reminded me that HIV could be part of God's will for me. I couldn't even comprehend how HIV was part of God's will, but I knew better than to try to question it. The last time I tried to dispute it, Greg explained how going to jail was part of God's will and that God only reveals his will when I'm good and ready for it. So, for now, I had no choice but to accept it and trust that God would take care of me in the end. But, I knew I had to do the right thing for that to happen, and in this case, the right thing to do was for me to tell my girlfriend the truth.

The next day, I called Michelle and told her I needed to talk to her in person. So she picked me up from Self Help, and we drove to the baseball field down the street. It was a quiet, secluded spot where we could be alone without interruptions. I sat her down on the bench and tried to find the courage to tell her the bad news. At first, I struggled with finding the right words to say, so I just sat there in silence and held her in my arms. I fought with myself for a few minutes and even considered skipping the conversation altogether. My biggest fear was that she would break up with me, but I knew I had to face my fears and tell her the truth, regardless of the outcome. So, I took a deep breath and began the most uncomfortable conversation I ever had to initiate.

"Yo, I gotta tell you something, but--but look, aight, you might not ever want to see me again."

"I don't care what it is, just tell me," Michelle told me as she gently kissed me on my lips.

She was such a sweet girl. I could only assume that she thought I had cheated on her or something. And judging from how she was acting, she was ready to forgive me if that had been the case, if only it were that simple.

"I got an HIV test yesterday, and it came back positive."

She didn't say a word. I mean, what was she supposed to say? We sat there in silence as she held me in her arms. I tried my best to fight back the tears, but it didn't take long for me to lose that fight. It started as a few teardrops but quickly escalated into an uncontrollable, full-on crying fit. I was so embarrassed to cry in front of her like that, but she didn't judge me one bit. She just sat there and hugged me until I ran out of tears.

I told her I would understand if she wanted to leave me because I regretted not leaving Tanya when I discovered she had HIV. In fact, I was now kicking myself in the ass for staying with her. I knew I was at risk of getting it when I was with her, yet I stayed with her anyway; I didn't want Michelle to make that same mistake. But to my surprise, Michelle told me she wanted to stay with me. In my honest opinion, I think she was just trying to be nice because I was going through a hard time. She probably didn't want to add a breakup on top of everything else I was going through.

Even though Michelle agreed to stay with me, things just weren't the same between us after that night. We still got along great with one another, but it felt like the fire between us had died out. She was obviously still happy when we were together, but I could tell she was also scared shitless. After a while, it was evident that our romantic relationship wasn't going to last. I began to feel like I was stuck in the friend zone. I knew a breakup was inevitable, so I prepared myself the best that I could. But being prepared didn't make it any easier.

Two weeks after I told her the truth about my HIV, she told me the truth about how scared she was of catching it. Michelle explained how she thought she could get past it but just couldn't do it. Needless to say, I was heartbroken. And at that moment in my life, I thought I would be single forever. What girl would want to be with a guy who has HIV? I felt helpless, but I wasn't about to let it keep me down.

I just couldn't understand why God would allow this to happen to me. And why would God let it happen just as I tried to get my life back on track? I could understand if I was still getting high, selling drugs, and robbing people. But I was doing the right thing by staying clean and helping others, so it didn't make any sense to me. Even though I knew it was part of God's will, I didn't understand why it was God's will, at least not yet. Instead of questioning it, I continued to pray and lived one day at a time. Because deep down inside, I knew that God's plan was better than mine.

Chapter 30

Shortly after Michelle broke up with me, I started going to an intensive outpatient program, or IOP for short. Honestly, it was a complete waste of time and caused a lot of extra stress in my life that I just didn't need. But, it was a stipulation of treatment court, so if I didn't go, I would have ended up back in jail.

To paint a better picture of IOP and why it was a waste of time, let me start by saying that almost everyone who went to IOP was court-stipulated. And the majority of them did not want to get clean and sober. It was nothing more than mandatory group therapy. I have nothing against group therapy, but when 95% of the group don't take it seriously and are still getting high, it's just a waste of time.

We were required to give urine samples once a week at IOP, which didn't bother me because I had nothing to hide. But I quickly learned that the people in my group found a way to beat the system. See, they tested our urine for drugs but didn't check to see if it was actual urine in the cup. So, many of my group members were secretly filling their cups with lemonade, water, or anything else they could use that looked like urine. At first, I didn't believe it was true, but I watched them all do it week after week without ever getting caught.

When I started going to IOP, I found myself to be in a catch-22. Usually, welfare insurance covers the cost of IOP. But since I had a job, I was ineligible for welfare insurance. And because I didn't work full time, I couldn't get health benefits from my job, either. However, attending the program was mandatory, so my only option was to pay for it out of pocket. It cost $60 per session, and I had to go to three sessions per week. I was only working part-time, making slightly more than minimum wage, so the IOP cost more than my entire paycheck.

The people at the IOP suggested that I quit my job and collect welfare so I wouldn't have to pay a dime. But I had to pay rent at Self Help, so I couldn't just leave my job like that. I didn't know what to do. So I called Mary from treatment court, and she gave me information about another IOP program, which was a little cheaper. The only problem was that it was located in South Philly, the complete opposite side of the city.

As I mentioned in a previous chapter, my new job was located in Bensalem, PA, where buses ran once every hour and a half. And of course, my shift ended 10 minutes after the bus came. So three times a week, I had to wait an hour and a half for the bus, and when I got off that bus, I had to hop onto another bus. When I got off that second bus, I had to jump onto the train, and when I got off the train, I had to take the subway. It took me two and a half hours to get there every day. Then the IOP would last for three hours, and after it was finally over, it would take me another hour and a half to get back home.

When you add all that time up, going to IOP was equivalent to working a full-time job, except I wasn't getting paid for it. In fact, I had to pay them! Not only did I have to pay for IOP out of my own pocket, but I also had court fees I had to pay. Plus, I needed money to eat every day and had to buy transit passes every week. I was barely scraping by, living paycheck to paycheck. And if that wasn't enough, a few weeks later, the government started garnishing my wages!

Remember earlier in the book when I said I went to a computer school? Well, I took out loans to go to that school, and over the years, I spent my money on drugs instead of paying them back like I was supposed to. So as soon as I started earning a paycheck, I must've popped up on the government's radar, and they started taking half of my check every week. It wasn't the government's fault. I was the one who took out the loans and never paid them back, so I couldn't even get mad at them. Besides, it's not like they knew I had court fees or had to pay for IOP and bus fare. Or that I had to pay rent and buy food every week.

Money started getting extremely tight. I couldn't even afford cigarettes anymore and had to bum smokes from people every day. In fact, there were days when I didn't even have money for lunch, so I had to do without it. And for dinner, I ate ramen noodles almost every night because it was the only thing I could afford. You would think I'd be used to this sort of thing from all the years I was getting high and never having money for food, but it was different now that I was clean. When I was getting high, the drugs would suppress my appetite, so being hungry wasn't that big of a deal. But when I got clean, I felt that hunger, and there was nothing I could do about it.

Besides food, I also couldn't afford other basic things, like the washing machine they had at Self Help. It only cost two dollars to use, but even that was difficult for me to come up with every week. So instead, I cleaned my dirty clothes with a bar of soap every time I took a shower.

Self Help's transitional living was supposed to be a stepping stone to the real world. The rent was pretty cheap, plus they provided us with meals every day, although I had to buy my own meals because I was never there to eat lunch or dinner. But the design of this transitional living made it easier for people to save for an apartment and lead successful lives in recovery. However, the situation I found myself in made it impossible for me to save money. In fact, it was almost impossible for me to survive week to week. Sometimes I had to go to a food bank just to have something to eat when I got home from IOP. But there were other times when I didn't have food at all, and that was when I would get temptations to make a quick buck. I knew how easy it would be to stop by the old block, flip a couple of bundles of dope, and walk away with a few hundred dollars in my pocket. But, I also realized the repercussions that came with that pocket full of money. So, as quickly as those thoughts came, is as quickly as they left.

One of the rules of the third floor was that they only allowed us to live there for five months. So it wasn't a surprise when I came home one day and found a letter under my door. The letter stated that my five months were up and I had two weeks to move out. I didn't know what I was going to do. I had absolutely no money saved up and nowhere else to live. So, the next day I talked to Joe P and explained to him my situation. He understood what I was going through and told me I could stay for another five months. I was so grateful that I still had a place to live and relieved to know that I wouldn't end up back on the streets again. It was one thing to be homeless in active addiction, but to live like that while clean and sober seemed ridiculous to me.

That Sunday night, we had our weekly meeting at Self Help, which was mandatory for all third floor residents to attend. The meeting was technically a "relapse prevention meeting." But, it was more commonly known as the "rent collection meeting" because this is where Woody collected the rent every week. He sat at a desk and checked names off a list as people paid their rent.

Usually, these Sunday night meetings were very repetitive in nature. Every week it was the same five or six people who raised their hands to speak, and they always talked about the same thing, over and over again. But this meeting, in particular, wasn't repetitive at all. In fact, it set the stage for something that forever changed my life.

An older guy, whose name I can't remember, had just moved to Self Help from another recovery house, so nobody really knew him yet. When the meeting started, he didn't hesitate to raise his hand to speak.

And when he spoke, it really hit home for me. He shared with everyone how he had just been diagnosed with HIV. I was in shock! I couldn't believe he just told a group of strangers he had HIV! I started wondering if everybody was going to judge him. But then I thought about it again: I wasn't going to judge him for that. So, it made me realize that my fear of being judged was complete bullshit!

When this man shared that he had HIV, it gave me inspiration. Here I was, afraid to tell some of my closest friends, yet this man was able to tell a room full of people he had never met before. I wanted to raise my hand and tell everyone that I also had HIV as a way to help and let him know that he was not alone. I thought back to when I was first diagnosed and how much better I felt when Marlene told me she had it too. I didn't want him to feel that same emptiness I felt that day. I wanted him to know that we were in the same boat. There was also a part of me that, for the last few weeks, wanted to tell everyone that I had HIV but was too much a coward to ever do so. So when this man shared his misfortune with everyone, it gave me the courage I needed to share my deep dark secret that had been bottling up for far too long.

I raised my hand and began to feel my heart beat so fast that I wouldn't have been surprised if it exploded out of my chest right then and there. I could barely get the words out when I opened my mouth, but the more I talked, the more confident I became. I told the man sitting a few chairs down from me that he was not alone, and then I told him, along with 60 other men, that I was also HIV positive. After I was done speaking, I had this indescribable feeling. It felt like the weight of the world was removed from my chest. I finally felt free, as if all of my problems had just vanished into thin air.

After the meeting, everyone shook our hands, hugged us, and commended us for sharing about our HIV. Some of them told me how courageous I was, while others offered their support and told me they were there for me if I ever needed to talk. As everyone offered their kind words to me, I couldn't help but think how wrong I had been. I was filled with so much fear of people judging me that I let this dark secret eat away at me for months, and for what?

To be honest, people did look at me differently after that day, but not in a negative way. People actually looked up to me and viewed me as a strong person and, in some cases, a role model. According to what people told me, one of the main reasons for this is that if they were in my shoes, they wouldn't have stayed clean after being diagnosed with HIV. But whenever people tell me this, I always tell them the same thing: You can stay clean and sober through ANYTHING, as long as you pray, go to meetings, and help others. Sometimes, it really is that simple.

Even though I felt better after that night, I still had some negativity in my life, primarily because of my financial situation. I got to the point where I started complaining about all the stuff I didn't have. In fact, one night at my home group, I raised my hand and complained about how I was tired of living at Self Help and wanted to get my own apartment. Then I complained about needing a car because I was tired of taking the bus and walking everywhere. Then I complained about the old, dirty sneakers I had on my feet and how I didn't have enough money to buy a new pair. After the meeting ended, one of the other home group members approached me.

"Hey Brian, don't worry about the house and the car and all that stuff. It will come with time."

"I know, I know, but I really do need a car. I mean, look at the shoes. They're killing' my feet, man."

He looked down and smiled at my old, worn-out sneakers.

"Ya know, I used to complain about my sneakers, but then I met a man with no legs."

Whoa! When I heard him say that, I got chills up my spine. I knew exactly what he was trying to tell me, and he was absolutely right! A man with no legs would love to be able to walk around in my old dirty sneakers. I immediately thought back to when Snook first gave me these sneakers and how happy I was just to have shoes on my feet, but somewhere along the line, I must've lost that gratitude.

The crazy part was that I didn't even realize I lost it; it just snuck up on me. This whole time, I had been focusing on the things I wanted instead of the things I already had. But after that night, something inside me began to change. I began to look at life from a whole new perspective. I started to become grateful for everything in my life. Instead of looking at the negatives, I started looking at the positives.

So there I was, a 29-year-old man with HIV who had no money, no girlfriend, no car, and no house. Yet, I felt like the happiest man in the world. Sure, yes, I had HIV, but you know what? At least my heart was still beating, and my lungs were still breathing. And yes, OK, I had no money, but so what? I had food to eat every day, which was more than some people had. And even though I didn't have a girlfriend at the time, I had good friends and family who cared about me and were always there when I needed them. And I didn't care about getting a car anymore because I had shoes on my feet. And even though those shoes were old and dirty, at least I could walk around to get where I needed to go. Some people had to use wheelchairs and didn't have the luxury of walking around like I did. And lastly, I didn't have my own house, but oh well! At least I had a bed to sleep in every night, which is more than some people had. Shit, it's more than what I had when I was homeless. So, every morning I woke up and thanked God for all these little things I had in my life, and then I would thank God again at night. I felt like I was on a spiritual high, and life just kept getting better and better.

One day, Greg asked me to speak at our home group. I'm not going to lie: I was nervous as shit, but I did it anyway. I was taught to never say no when AA asked for my help. Even though I always raised my hand to talk at meetings, it wasn't the same as getting up in front of the room and sharing your entire life story. When you raise your hand to talk, you could speak for a few minutes and then pass it off to the next person, but when you are in front of the room, you are expected to tell your entire story. You can't pass it off to someone else if you get too nervous or run out of words.

Most people who shared their story or "experience, strength, and hope" would speak for about 20 minutes or so (depending on the meeting). But the first time I shared my experience, strength, and hope, it only lasted about five minutes. I was super nervous, so I was talking really fast. Plus, I couldn't focus, so I skipped all over the place and missed a lot of parts of my story. I must have sounded like a train wreck, but after the meeting, people told me that I did a good job, even though I think they were just being nice. Either way, it was a gratifying experience.

Meetings became especially helpful when my financial situation started getting tight. When I first started my job, I would go out to the movies or the coffee shop on weekends. But after having my wages garnished and forced to pay for IOP, I couldn't afford to do things like that anymore. So rather than being a hermit crab and sitting in my room all weekend, I just hung out at the meetings instead. Luckily for people like me, there was an AA clubhouse called "Life or Death" in the area. For those who don't know, a clubhouse is basically a meeting place that has meetings all day and night. So, on Friday and Saturday nights, I would go to meetings and hang out until 1:30 a.m., when the last meeting ended.

I will forever be grateful for these meetings. Without them, I would've never survived the weekends without slipping back into my old ways. I always raised my hand to talk at the meetings too, which allowed me to meet many good people who helped me along the way. After the meetings, complete strangers would often approach and help me with whatever issues I was going through.

At one meeting, I shared about how I couldn't even afford cigarettes and had to eat ramen noodles for dinner every night. After the meeting, some guy I had never met before handed me a free pack of smokes. A few minutes later, a group of guys invited me out to eat at the diner and offered to pay for my meal. I never knew there were people like this in the world because I had always hung around selfish drug dealers and junkies who only cared about themselves. So, it felt nice to be around selfless people for a change.

One night after a meeting, I met a guy named Tommy, who gave me some excellent advice. He convinced me to take the coffee commitment for the next week's meeting. All I had to do was get to the meeting a little early, brew a few pots of coffee, and then hand it out to people during the meeting. The coffee commitment was significant for a few different reasons. One, it gave me a sense of purpose. Two, it allowed me to meet and talk with more people. And three, it motivated me to actually go to the meeting. Sometimes I didn't always feel like going, but it was harder to skip if I had the coffee commitment because I knew people were counting on me.

Tom was very knowledgeable about AA, so the more I talked to him, the more I learned. Tom explained that there were two types of people in recovery: those who attend AA and those who are a part of it. He suggested some things I could do to be a part of AA, like taking coffee commitments, chairing/speaking at meetings, or staying afterward to help clean up. Tom also introduced me to the "20/20 Club," a term used to describe people who come 20 minutes before the meeting starts and stay 20 minutes after the meeting ends. Arriving early and staying late allowed me to get to know more people and be more available to those who needed help.

I took Tom's advice and jumped right into it all. I started going to meetings early to make coffee and stayed after the meetings ended to help clean and talk to people. I even started attending business meetings, where I could volunteer to take commitments for the month. At my first business meeting, I offered to chair the 8:00 p.m. meeting every Friday night. Doing so made me feel like I was a part of AA and not just somebody who attended meetings. I quickly learned that it's harder to leave when you feel like you're a part of something. Around the same time that I started diving into the program, Greg began to take me through the fourth step.

"Step 4. Made a searching and fearless moral inventory of ourselves."

This is where the real action takes place. The first three steps are more about understanding and making decisions, but the fourth step is when I had to take a good look at myself in the mirror. Some people struggle with this step, and for a good reason. Nobody wants to take the blame and admit their faults, but for some reason, it didn't really bother me. Deep down inside, I already knew I was a piece of shit. But, I also knew that I wanted to change, and you only get out of this program what you put into it, so I went all in.

Different sponsors will walk you through the steps in different ways, but I really liked the way Greg walked me through them. Greg was pretty laid back about it all. He explained that if I didn't want to put a lot of work into the steps, I didn't have to. But Greg also explained that I would only be hurting myself if I didn't work hard at them. So when it came time for the fourth step, he said I could sit down for a few hours and do it all at once or take my time and be thorough with it.

After explaining this, Greg handed me a worksheet he printed from an AA website. It was multiple pages long, and each page was filled with columns of information I had to write down. To be honest, at first glance, it seemed overwhelming. That's when I decided to take the slower, more thorough approach. I didn't want to feel overwhelmed. When I told Greg my decision, he said I should dedicate at least a few minutes a day to work on it. He then reminded me that if I were serious about it, I shouldn't put it off or skip any days, so I took his advice and worked on it consistently.

The first page of the worksheet is where I listed all my resentments. In each row, I had to write down who (or what) I was mad at, why I was angry, and what role I played in that resentment. That last part confused me because I didn't think I played any role in these resentments. These people screwed me over, not the other way around, so in my mind, I didn't do anything wrong; but that was so far from the truth.

After discussing it with Greg, it became much clearer. I didn't realize it, but I definitely played a role in all of those resentments I had. For

192

example, I had bitterness toward an ex-girlfriend for cheating on me, and my initial thought was, "How am I to blame? I wasn't the one who cheated." But, after giving it some thought, I knew she was a cheater. In fact, that's how we first hooked up. She cheated on her boyfriend to hook up with me. So I went into that relationship, knowing full well that she was a cheater. And that's the role I played.

The next three sections of the worksheet asked me about my fears, sexual conduct, and the people I had harmed. I breezed through the fears and sexual conduct sections with no problems. However, when I made it to the final page, I never realized how many people I had harmed until I started to write them all down on paper. And it seemed like the more people I listed, the more I remembered. Eventually, I ran out of room on the sheet and had to write them on a separate piece of paper.

All in all, it took about a month to finally complete my fourth step. Honestly, it felt great to write it all down and get it out there. It made me take a good look at myself and how my actions affected other people besides just me. But writing it down was only half the battle because now I had to talk about it with my sponsor.

"Step 5. Admitted to God, to ourselves, and to another human being the exact nature of our wrongs."

I had to take everything I wrote in my fourth step and admit it to God and another person. It was a great feeling to finally clean all those skeletons out of my closet. The beautiful thing about doing the fifth step with my sponsor was how it made me realize that I was not unique. Almost everything I had written, Greg was able to relate to in one way or another. Greg stole from his friends and family, just like I did. Greg also committed crimes to feed his habit, just like I did. Greg even treated his ex-girlfriends like shit, just like I did. For years I thought there were things I did that nobody else had ever done, but it turns out I was not alone; I was not that special.

When we went over the resentment section of my fourth step, Greg told me that if I absolutely wanted to be free, I would have to try to forgive them all. Honestly, most of my resentments were from so long ago that the forgiveness part was pretty simple. But there were a few resentments on that list where forgiveness didn't come so quickly. Greg told me that forgiveness wasn't always for the person I was mad at but instead was meant to benefit myself. By forgiving someone, I no longer had to hold onto that anger or let them live rent-free in my head. It made a lot of sense to me, but he could see that I still wasn't ready to forgive some people.

"Resentment is like drinking poison and waiting for the other person to die."

What Greg meant by this was holding onto that anger was only hurting me. They continued to live their lives, whether I had resentments or not. But even after Greg told me this, I still wasn't ready to forgive them. I wanted to, but I just couldn't do it. So, he recommended that I pray for them instead. Greg said I should pray for something good to happen to them. He suggested that I pray for them to have a nice day, hit the lotto, find their soulmate, or something along those lines. It didn't make sense to me, but it definitely worked.

After a few weeks of praying for people I had resentments toward, I ran into this guy I knew, Pat, on the bus. You might remember Pat from earlier in the book, as he was the one who stole my unemployment money while I was locked up. It was about $900 that he stole from me, which was supposed to be my bail money. So in a way, he also stole my freedom. But, I had been praying for Pat for the past few weeks. I prayed that he would get clean and live a happy life. And throughout those weeks of praying, I slowly came to forgive him. I also realized that losing that money was part of God's will because if Pat had never stolen that money, I could have bailed myself out of jail. And if I bailed myself out, I would have never made it to rehab. So, when I saw Pat on the bus, I walked over and sat down next to him.

"What's up, Pat?"

He was in shock. He probably thought I was going to beat his ass right there on the bus, and honestly, if I was still getting high, I probably would have. But I wasn't that person anymore. I was clean and sober now, working the steps and praying every day. However, Pat didn't know any of this at the time. All he knew was that he had stolen $900 from me. I decided to show him I was there on peaceful terms by shaking his hand. But when I extended my hand, he flinched. I guess he thought I was going to punch him. When he realized I wasn't going to hit him, he confusingly reached out and shook my hand.

"Thanks for stealing that money from me."

"Wha-wha-wha-what money?"

"The $900. Ya know, from when I was booked."

194

"I dunno what you're talking about. It wasn't me."

He tried to play it off like he didn't steal the money, but we both knew that he did. Instead of arguing, I told him I forgave him and explained how the stolen money was a blessing in disguise. I even tried to offer him help with getting clean, but he had no intention of changing his ways. I honestly felt bad for him because he looked like fucking shit and smelled like Kensington's ass crack. But, all I could do was continue to pray for him.

A few days later, I had the chance to thank another person from my past. I was delivering tires to an auto shop when I noticed a police officer standing in the lobby. He looked familiar, but it took me a couple seconds to realize who he was. He was the same cop that arrested me a few months earlier. This was the same arrest that ultimately landed me in rehab. If this cop had never put me in handcuffs that day, I don't know if I would have ever gotten clean. So I walked right up to him and thanked him for arresting me.

He didn't recognize me at all. It was probably because the last time he saw me, I was strung out on dope. And now that I was clean and sober, I looked like a totally different person. I put on 35 pounds, was clean-shaven with a fresh haircut, and wore nice clean clothes. Honestly, there were days I barely recognized myself when I looked in the mirror. I reminded him of how he arrested me on Boudinot Street for selling dope, and as soon as I said "Boudinot Street," he remembered who I was. I explained how he basically saved my life, and before I left, I thanked him again and shook his hand. I could see how he was moved by my simple words of gratitude. If that officer wasn't aware of it before, on that day, he was made aware of the impact he had on other peoples' lives, and I could tell he felt good about helping me.

I never in a million years thought I would shake hands with a police officer who arrested me, but I did, and to be honest, it felt great to do so. This gave me the idea of how to make amends to other police officers, as I couldn't track down every officer I listed on my fourth step.

The following week I saw a police officer in a parking lot who looked to be having a bad day. So, for no reason whatsoever, I shook his hand and thanked him for risking his life every day. I told him how even though cops often get a bad rep, there are still some people in the world who appreciate them. A smile ran across his face as he thanked me for my kind words. I could tell he was proud of his job, just as every police officer should be. I know that I gave the cops a lot of problems in the past, and I wanted to make up for it by doing little things like this. Doing this sort of thing for police officers became part of my amends process for my ninth step. However, in making these amends, I had accidentally skipped steps six, seven, and eight.

When I told Greg what I did, he told me two things. One, the good deed I did for that officer didn't count because I went and told everyone about it. He explained that I shouldn't tell anybody when I do a good deed. Otherwise, I would only be doing it for selfish reasons, such as looking for praise and feeding my ego. And that led to the second thing Greg told me, which was why I shouldn't be skipping steps. He explained that the 12 steps were in a specific order, and there was a reason why we do them in this particular order. He continued to explain that my selfish behavior of blabbing my good deeds to the world fell right in line with the following two steps I had yet to complete. Steps six and seven dealt with God removing my character defects and shortcomings. Even though I was doing well in recovery, I still had a lot to learn.

Chapter 31

"Step 6. Were entirely ready to have God remove all our defects of character."

"Step 7. Humbly asked God to remove our shortcomings."

These two steps had me confused since day one because "defects of character" and "shortcomings" sounded like they had the same meaning. But they were different steps, so they must mean different things, right? Wrong. After going through steps six and seven in the big book, Greg explained that these two phrases actually did mean the same thing. However, they were worded differently so it wouldn't sound repetitive, which confused me even more.

"But if they have the same meaning, why list it twice?"

"Because they're two different steps."

"That makes no sense. It's asking me to do the same thing twice."

"Read them both again, very carefully."

I reread each step, word for word. I even read them a third time, and I still didn't see the difference. But this was a perfect example of why I needed a sponsor to help me through the steps. Steps six and seven both sounded the same but were, in fact, different. It turns out that step six is a preparation step, and step seven is a step of action.

For some, this may have been self-explanatory, but not for me. I needed Greg to draw it out with crayons so that I could understand exactly what it meant. He pointed out the keywords in each step. In step six, it was the word "ready," and in step seven, it was the word "asked." So, step six basically made sure I was ready to remove my character defects. But to remove them, I first had to know what they were.

Greg handed me a sheet of paper with examples of different shortcomings a person may have so that I could better understand them. He then asked me to list all of my character defects, forcing me to look in the mirror once again to see what type of person I really was. After writing my list, Greg asked if I was ready to let go of my character defects. I told him I couldn't find one good reason to hold onto them, so he instructed me to ask my Higher Power to remove them from my life. But asking my Higher Power to remove them just once wasn't going to do the trick. It's not like I would pray for God to remove them, and then they just all vanish the next day. It took time and patience, and I had to ask God every day to remove my shortcomings. Praying to remove them on a daily basis was a constant reminder that I, in fact, still had them.

After a while, I realized how these character defects affected my everyday life. This awareness allowed me to stop myself whenever they came into play and change how I was thinking and living. It allowed me to change myself as a person and be able to help more people too. I didn't want to be the same person I used to be. Any asshole can stop doing drugs, but until they change how they think and behave, they will still be an asshole. So, I started doing everything I could to become a better person.

Greg knew I wanted to become a better person. But to become a better person, I would need to have virtues, and character defects were the opposite of virtues. So basically, I had to remove the bad to make room for the good, and that's precisely what steps six and seven dealt with. After completing steps six and seven, we wasted no time moving on to steps eight and nine.

"Step 8. Made a list of all persons we had harmed, and became willing to make amends to them all."

The first half of this step was easy because I had already written a list of people I had harmed in the fourth step. But the second part of this step had the keyword "willing" in it. Luckily for me, I had no problem with that part. I was more than willing to make amends with the people I had harmed, but Greg had to teach me the proper way to make those amends.

"Step 9. Made direct amends to such people wherever possible, except when to do so would injure them or others."

When I first read the ninth step, I thought I just had to call everyone from my past and say, "I'm sorry," but it wasn't quite that simple. First, Greg told me I should use the words "I was wrong" instead of saying "I'm sorry." This is because addicts and alcoholics, like myself, had told people "I'm sorry" a million times in the past, but how many times did we really mean it? How many times did I say sorry for something, only to do it over and over again? Over time, the words "I'm sorry" can lose meaning, not only to myself but also to the people I hurt. However, saying "I was wrong" shows how I am admitting to the wrongs that I had done.

Greg also taught me about the other part of the amends process, where I asked if there was anything else I may have done to hurt them. This allows the other person to air out any grievances they may have. There is always a chance I have hurt them in other ways, without realizing it, or in ways I had forgotten about.

198

The final part of the amends process was the act of trying to make things right. Most of the time, common sense will tell you how you can make things right. For example, if I stole money from someone, then the best way to make things right with them would be to pay them back the money I stole. But even if I wasn't sure how to make things right with someone, I learned that asking them, "How can I make this right?" was a pretty good starting point.

I thought that biting my tongue would be the most challenging part of making amends. This was about cleaning up my side of the street and nothing else. So, I couldn't blame the other person for anything, no matter what they did. What I mean is, if I punched someone in the face because they stole something from me, I had to make amends for hitting them. I couldn't bring up the reason why I punched them. But, once again, I made it more complicated than it actually was. Every time I made amends to someone for something like that, they also apologized for their role in the situation.

Whenever I made amends and asked how I could make things right, nine out of 10 times, they would say, "You don't have to do anything," or "Just stay clean and sober," or something along those lines. It was a great feeling to make amends with people, especially my family members, who I know I put through hell. Honestly, I thought my dad would have trouble forgiving me for some of the things I had done to him, but he stopped me before I could even get halfway through.

"Brian, I forgave you a long time ago."

Even though most of my amends went smoothly, the person I felt I hurt the most, Penelope, was unwilling to talk to me. Not only did I start fights because of my jealousy, but I also stole from her and even robbed her house after we broke up. But, the worst thing I did happened after I started dating Tanya. One night, Tanya and I were drunk, and Tanya thought I still had feelings for Penelope. So, to prove Tanya wrong, I called Penelope to tell her I was in love with Tanya. But, it was 3:00 a.m., and Penelope was sleeping, so I left a message on her voicemail. The next day I woke up and realized it was Penelope's birthday. So, Penelope woke up on her birthday and got a message saying I was in love with another girl.

It was an awful thing that I'd done, and I wanted to make amends for it, along with everything else I did to her. But, when I reached out to Penelope, she refused to hear what I had to say. I had no choice but to respect her wishes. I will never be able to make amends to her, and that's my fault. I have to live with my regrets, and I have no one to blame except myself.

There were also other amends I couldn't make because I had no way of getting in touch with the people on my list, so I had to come up with creative ways to make those amends. One example of this was the police officers I mentioned earlier. That's why I began thanking random cops on the street; that was my way of making amends to those I created trouble for. Another example was some of the people I robbed at knifepoint. I had no way of tracking these people down, so I bought meals for homeless people as a way of paying back the money I stole.

Out of all the amends I made throughout the years, the most difficult one I ever had to do was for my mom. I wanted to make amends to her, but that was difficult considering how she had passed away 10 years earlier. Greg suggested I write her a letter and leave it at her gravesite. This was right around Mother's Day, so the timing worked out perfectly since I wanted to visit her anyway. But Mother's Day that year was the first time I had to deal with my mom's death while clean and sober.

When I visited my mom's grave, I started talking to her as if she was right there with me. I remember joking with her and asking how the weather was up in heaven. But, it wasn't long until those smiles turned to tears. I pulled the letter out of my pocket and began to read it to her. Tears leaked from my eyes as I told her how I was wrong for everything I had done. I was wrong for the money I stole from her. I was wrong for all the times I made her cry. I was wrong for the times I kept her up all night worrying about me. I was wrong for the times I got arrested and brought shame and embarrassment to her.

By the time I finished reading the letter, the paper was drenched with tears. I was a terrible son to her, which wasn't fair because she was the best mother I could have ever asked for. The worst part about it all was that she was not there to see how I turned my life around. I kept telling myself that she was looking down from heaven and saw everything I was doing, but even though I knew she was proud of me, it still didn't take away my pain.

I placed the letter on her grave, told her I loved her, and wiped the tears from my eyes. I walked away from her grave feeling so depressed. It felt like I lost my mom all over again because it was the first time I had to actually deal with these emotions while sober. Usually, I would get drunk or high to bury those feelings deep down inside me, but I knew that getting high wasn't an option. Now, even though I knew it wasn't an option, that didn't stop the little voice inside my head from trying to convince me otherwise.

"Dude, fuck it! Just go get yourself a bag," the voice inside told me.

Deep down inside, I didn't want to get high. I knew what the consequences would be if I did, but I couldn't stop the tormenting thoughts from speaking to me.

"C'mon, you've been working so hard. You deserve this."

I tried to ignore the voice. But it seemed like the more I ignored it, the louder it got.

"It's Mother's Day, and your mom is dead! C'mon, man, people in AA would understand."

The voice had a good point, and it was hard not to listen. I mean, it spoke to me in my own voice. Thankfully I was going to enough meetings to know that the voice speaking to me was not actually me; it was my alcoholism/addiction. And the disease of alcoholism/addiction is cunning, baffling, and powerful! So, for once in my life, I decided to stand up for myself and talk back to it.

"NO! My mom wouldn't understand!"

That single thought was what kept me clean and sober that day. Sure, I could have used the whole "Mother's Day is a rough day for me" excuse to go and get high. But deep down inside, I knew my mom wouldn't want that, and that was the only thing that mattered. THAT was my amends to my mom; staying clean and sober! And it has been my amends to her every day since.

A few weeks after Mother's Day, I had to see the doctor about my HIV. The doctor told me I discovered HIV early, so my health was still in good shape. However, they also found that I had Hepatitis C. My doctor said that the Hep C was caught very early too, so I didn't need to start treatment right away if I didn't want to. But she wanted me to start on the HIV medicine as soon as possible, so I told her I'd just start taking them both immediately. I didn't see the point of postponing the Hep C treatment; I just wanted to get it over and done with.

The doctor gave me some valuable information about HIV medicine that made me feel a lot better. She told me that the medication virtually eliminates HIV from my bloodstream, making it much harder to spread to others. So, as long as I took my medicine like I was supposed to,

I would be "undetectable," which means that even an HIV test won't be able to detect that I have it. She even explained that I could have a child one day if I wanted to. But I didn't understand because I was under the impression I could never have unprotected sex. The doctor explained that even if I had unprotected sex, there was virtually no chance of spreading it to others as long as I was undetectable. It's not like I was thinking about having kids anytime soon, but it was good information to have.

There is a definite stigma in society regarding HIV, but I don't understand why. It's not nearly as bad as I thought it would be. Sure, HIV can kill me if I don't treat it, but I can live a pretty normal life as long as I take my medicine. It's not like I'm always sick or constantly in and out of hospitals. In fact, the worst part about having HIV was its effect on my love life, and the only reason it impacted my love life was because of the stigma. Whenever I met a new girl, I always did the right thing and told them about it. But doing the right thing didn't always have the positive outcome I expected. I thought they would appreciate the honesty and give me a chance, but it didn't always work out like that.

At first, I didn't know how to tell girls about my HIV status. In fact, I scared a few girls away by telling them about it on the first date. After telling them, they didn't care about how the medicine worked or how they could never catch it. All they heard was "HIV," and then they would start running for the hills. But, like everything else in my life, HIV was part of God's will and was actually a blessing in disguise.

Before I caught HIV, I always met girls and tried to sleep with them as soon as possible. But, being HIV positive made me realize that I should take my time in relationships so that we could get to know each other first. My theory was this: if a girl got to know me, she would see that I was a good guy. And if she saw that I was a good guy, the HIV might not scare her away so easily.

For me, finding a girlfriend was never a problem, but keeping one was. Sometimes I would meet a girl, and after a week or so, I'd tell them about my HIV. Some of the girls stayed with me, while others did not. Some even freaked out and got super mad because I "put her at risk" by sharing a funnel cake with her. Yes. You read that correctly. We didn't sleep together or even kiss each other. All we did was share a funnel cake, and she thought she was at risk because of it. But the mentally sound girls who decided to stay with me and start a relationship never stayed for long. Usually, the relationship would last for a few weeks, and then we would break up, and I'd move on to another girl a week or two later. It was very unhealthy for me to be in and out of relationships like this, especially early in sobriety.

When I first got to AA, it was suggested that I not get involved in any relationships until I had at least one year sober. I obviously didn't listen to this suggestion at first. I figured as long as I didn't date girls who drank or got high, then I would be OK. But the more girls I dated, the more that this suggestion started to make sense. Alcoholics and addicts use drugs and alcohol to deal with emotions, and let's face it, relationships can be incredibly emotional, especially during a breakup. After going through a couple of breakups, I thought I was incapable of making a girl happy. But then a close friend pointed something out to me: I needed to learn how to make myself happy before I could make someone else happy. So, for the next few months, I stopped chasing girls and started chasing that happiness. Sometimes, being single was hard because I was so used to having a girlfriend. At first, I felt very lonely, but I was determined to stay single and learn how to make myself happy. So, I tried to help as many people as possible to fill that lonely void. Fortunately, between Self Help and AA, there was no shortage of people who needed help.

I started taking newcomers from Self Help to AA meetings as often as I could. But there were some nights when I didn't feel like going to a meeting, so I had to push myself to go. I didn't do it for myself, though. I did it for the newcomers because I knew it was helping them. When I first got to the third floor, people like Greg took me to meetings, so I wanted to do the same for others. Besides, everyone could use a little motivation from time to time.

This was around the same time when I first realized that I had changed as a person because the weirdest thing started to happen: people started asking me for advice. Asking me for advice seemed inconceivable. A few months earlier, I was selling drugs, robbing people, and shooting dope in my arms. But, now people were asking me for guidance in their life. Before long, Self Help even put me in charge of the Sunday night relapse prevention meeting. It was a little hard to wrap my head around it at first, but it felt good to know that people could rely on me when they needed a shoulder to lean on. For the first time in my life, people actually trusted me.

Chapter 32

After I finished my ninth step, I moved on to steps 10, 11, and 12, commonly known as the "maintenance steps." They call them this because these steps prevent you from slipping back into your old ways by taking personal inventory, staying in touch with your higher power, and helping other alcoholics/addicts. In fact, people in recovery never really "complete" these steps because they are meant to be done continuously.

"Step 10. Continued to take personal inventory and when we were wrong promptly admitted it."

"Step 11. Sought through prayer and meditation to improve our conscious contact with God as we understood Him, praying only for knowledge of His will for us and the power to carry that out."

"Step 12. Having had a spiritual awakening as the result of these steps, we tried to carry this message to alcoholics, and to practice these principles in all our affairs."

The 10th step was pretty much a continuation of some of the other steps. This meant that I would have to continue to be aware of my resentments, shortcomings, people I harm, etc. Greg told me that if I should ever harm someone or do something wrong, I should immediately do the ninth step and make amends. It wasn't hard to figure out why this was important. I had just finished making amends to everyone, so I felt like I had a clean slate. But that didn't give me the green light to go out and be an asshole to everyone again. That sort of behavior would've caused me to fall back to my old ways.

The 11th step was also pretty easy to understand, but Greg explained it in his own words anyway. He taught me that the closer I was to God, the farther I was from the Devil. And since I was already praying every day and night, it wasn't a hard step to continue doing. The only thing that really changed for me was one part of my prayers. Before I made it to this step, I always asked God, "let me do your will today," but Greg taught me that I should instead ask, "let me know what your will is for me today." By asking it like this, it allowed me to make the decision myself instead of God making it for me. God gave us all a conscience, so I had to use that conscience and make the right decisions.

When Greg and I discussed the 12th step, it turned out that I had already been doing this the whole time; I just didn't realize it. In simple terms, the 12th step is about helping other alcoholics/addicts. Speaking at a meeting, for example, is considered to be working the 12th step. Another example would be bringing newcomers to meetings. But, most importantly, doing the 12th step involves helping other alcoholics/addicts who are still suffering. Doing this step keeps people like me clean and sober, so in my opinion, it's one of the most important steps.

As I continued to do these steps, my life continued to improve. It didn't take long for my family to invite me back into their lives again. It felt great to see my nieces again, and luckily they were all young enough that they wouldn't remember seeing me all strung out on drugs. However, I never tried to hide my past from them. Even today, I am very open with them about my addiction, hoping that they can learn from my mistakes and never walk the same path as me.

With my family back in my life, I felt like the pieces of the puzzle were finally connecting. That year, while Christmas shopping, I realized something. As I was looking for a gift for my sister Kim, I realized I had already given her the gift she wanted. I remembered the previous year when she sent me that letter, explaining how all she wanted for Christmas was her little brother back in her life. Well, that year, I gave her exactly what she wanted. She finally had her brother back, clean and sober. I think I also give her a frying pan, but I can't remember.

Shortly after the holidays, on February 19th, 2011, I celebrated one year of sobriety. I couldn't believe I went a whole year without drinking or using drugs, not even once. I was so happy and grateful. I was high on life, and everything was going great!

It's an unwritten tradition in AA to speak whenever someone celebrates an anniversary. The main reason for this is to offer hope to the newcomers and show them that the program really does work. So when I reached that one-year milestone, Greg asked me to speak at one of the regular meetings we attended. While speaking at the meeting, I got to the part of my story about when I had 90 days sober. Usually, I would leave out what happened on my 90-day anniversary, but not this time. This time, I told everyone how I was diagnosed with HIV and almost got high because of it. I had already shared my HIV status at the Self Help meeting, but this was the first time I did it at an outside AA meeting.

While telling my story, I explained that if I had stayed at Self Help the first time I was there and not climbed out the window in the middle of the night, I would have never contracted HIV. That six-month period, after I left Self Help and before I went to jail, is when I caught it. I would have been fine if I had just stayed, but I escaped from rehab to get high, only to come back six months later with HIV and more felony drug charges.

When I finished my story, people started to raise their hands to talk. Almost everyone in the room was shocked, not only because I had HIV but because I stayed clean and sober through it all. They were incredibly amazed at how happy I was and how I always walked around with a smile, even though I had HIV. I truly felt like God had blessed me, and that night, God answered a question that I had been asking him for the past nine months:

"Why did I get HIV just as I'm trying to get my life together?"

I never understood how something like that could be part of God's plan for me until that night. I think I caught HIV because God knew I was strong enough to deal with it and wanted me to warn others that they could also catch HIV if they didn't stay clean. It was also part of God's plan to inspire others and use it as proof that alcoholics and addicts can remain clean and sober no matter what life throws at them.

After the meeting, a guy I had known for a while pulled me aside to talk privately. He told me that he had just discovered he had HIV and wanted to know how I got through it without getting high, so I told him my entire experience with it. I educated him on the medications and how they could help him to live a perfectly healthy life. It seemed to relieve a lot of his stress and worries, and he was incredibly grateful for me taking the time to talk to him. Not only did it feel great to be able to help someone, but it also reassured me that it was part of God's will for me to talk about it at meetings.

After that night, I felt like nothing could stop me. I already had a permanent smile on my face every day, but now I was able to take my happiness to a whole other level. I began to feel like every day was a celebration. Every day felt like a holiday, so I wanted to spread that joy to everyone around me. I had always heard that smiles were contagious, so it only made sense that positive thinking was also contagious. I walked around that following Monday, telling everyone I saw, "Happy Monday!" Some people looked at me like I was crazy, but it still put a smile on their faces, so I kept with it. The next day I said "Happy Tuesday!" to everyone I came in contact with. This became an everyday thing for me, and most people absolutely loved it. But, there was always that one person who would ask, "What's so fucking happy about Tuesday?"

Whenever someone asked me this, I explained how I had millions of reasons to be happy. For one, I didn't have to wake up dope sick anymore. I didn't have to steal money or rob somebody to get high. I didn't have to run from the cops or wake up in a cold jail cell. I had a bed to sleep in. I had food to eat. I had good friends and family who cared about me. I had everything in my life that I needed to survive another day.

After explaining it the way I did, most people could relate and understand why I was so damn happy. It even helped some of them realize that being happy isn't about how much money you have, how many friends you have, or how hot your girlfriend is. It's about having everything you need to survive and being able to help others.

I soon earned the nickname "Happy" at Self Help and found myself saying "Happy (whatever day of the week it was)" a couple hundred times a day. Every time someone saw me, they would say it to me, so it instantly became my catchphrase. Over the years, countless people told me how I helped them whenever they were having a bad day and how I probably didn't even realize it. They said sometimes hearing those two words really put things in perspective for them. It helped them to remember that they had everything they needed in their life, and everything else was just a luxury.

Chapter 33

I've been known as a jokester for most of my life. I just love playing practical jokes and making people laugh, so on April Fool's Day of 2011, I played a joke on my supervisor at Traction Tire. I walked into his office and told him I had found another job. He was so disappointed and said he was sad to see me go. That's when I blurted out "April Fools!" and everyone in the office started to laugh.

A few days later, while eating breakfast at Self Help, Timmy from the kitchen sat down to talk with me. Timmy was the supervisor, so he knew I had a strong work ethic from when I used to volunteer there, which is probably why he sat down to talk to me that day.

"Would you be interested in working at Self Help?"

"Yeah, of course!"

"OK, walk with me."

I followed Timmy into the back office to meet his boss, Jeff, the director of food services at Self Help. Jeff said he wanted to hire me for a new position that was opening up. The job was for a vegetable gardener, which confused me because I literally had no experience in that field.

"Look, I don't know anything about growing vegetables, though."

"Oh, it's not hard. We can teach you."

I would have been stupid to say no to the job. It paid $12 an hour, plus benefits. Not to mention it would be full-time, plus I would be able to live at Self Help for as long as I wanted to because employees are exempt from the five-month rule. This was perfect because I had just gotten another letter, which stated I had two weeks to find a new place to live. So, without hesitation, I agreed to take the position but told Jeff and Timmy that I had to give my current job two weeks' notice.

When I got to Traction Tire that day, I walked into my supervisor's office to talk to him again.

"Hey Joe, listen, man, I found another job and –"

"Yeah, right. I'm not falling for that one again."

I felt like an asshole because I literally just played that joke on him a week ago, but I was dead serious this time. I was sad that I was leaving, but it was time for me to move on. All of my co-workers were sorry to see me go too. They told me they would miss hearing me say "Happy Monday" every week. They even got me going away cards and said I was welcome back anytime. It was weird to experience all of this because I had never in my life given two weeks' notice to a job before. I would typically just get fired or quit on the spot and leave. But this only proved the 12 steps were working because my character defects were no longer running the show.

Two weeks later, I started my new job at Self Help. I thought taking care of a vegetable garden would be easy, but it was much harder than I thought. I wasn't allowed to use pesticides or weed killers because Jeff wanted an organic garden. I didn't even know the definition of the word organic. Yet, there I was, growing organic vegetables, where everything had to be done by hand. This wasn't a tiny garden like you would see in someone's backyard. It was almost the length of a football field, so keeping up with the weeds was a very daunting task. I had to load up a wheel barrel with weeds and dirt, which can get pretty heavy at times, and unload it on the other side of the property, 300 yards away. I had to do this multiple times a day just to keep up with the weeds; it was very strenuous work, but it felt good at the end of the day.

Working in that garden helped me to become both physically and spiritually fit. It felt like I was working with God every day. It helped me to appreciate the little things in life, like watching tiny seeds grow into food and then watching that food being used to feed hungry people recovering from drugs/alcohol. I know it sounds corny, but every morning when I heard the birds chirping, it brought a smile to my face. Life just seemed to get a little easier after working at Self Help; I finally felt at peace with the world.

When I got my first paycheck from Self Help, I realized that the government didn't garnish my wages! So, not only did I get paid more per hour, but I worked 40 hours (instead of 20) and received an entire, ungarnished paycheck. I started bringing home triple the amount of money I did when I worked at the tire company. But, I knew it would only be a matter of time before they started garnishing my wages again. So instead of waiting for that to happen, I called the student aid office and tried to work out a deal with them. It was actually a lot easier than I thought it would be. They put me on a payment plan and promised they would not garnish my wages as long as I stayed up to date with my payments; I haven't missed a payment since.

One night, a few weeks after starting my new job at Self Help, I brought a newcomer to a meeting at Life or Death. We got on the bus and started walking down the aisle to find an open seat.

"Yo Brain," a familiar voice spoke.

I looked behind me and saw my brother Shawn sitting in one of the seats. He looked like fucking shit. I'm talking about the "He's my own brother, and I didn't even recognize him" type of shit. He was wearing old, filthy clothes, and his face was covered in dirt. It looked like he had forgotten how to use a razor, and his hair hadn't seen a comb in years. And to top it all off, he had a trash bag full of clothes that smelled like raw sewage. To be honest, Shawn resembled the person I used to see in the mirror before I made it to Self Help.

I sat down next to him and asked where he was headed to. He told me he was just wasting time until he had to go to work. One look at him, and I could tell he was lying. I knew he didn't have a job. I knew he was homeless. I knew he was just wandering around with no destination. I knew all of this because I used to do the same shit. But, I also knew that he needed help, so I asked him to come to a meeting with me. To my surprise, Shawn agreed to go to the meeting. After we got off the bus, I told him how much better my life had gotten now that I was clean and sober. Being the pathological liar that he was, Shawn tried to tell me that he was also clean and sober, but even Stevie Wonder could have seen that he wasn't.

After the meeting, I bought Shawn something to eat and thanked him for coming to the meeting with me. I wanted him to turn his life around, so I convinced him to meet me the next day and go to another meeting. But when the next day came, he never showed up. I probably could have tracked him down, but it would have been pointless. He just wasn't ready to get clean and sober yet, and I knew it was impossible to help someone who didn't want to be helped. All I could do was pray for him and keep doing what I was doing. I was hoping that if I continued to stay sober, then maybe one day he would come find me when he was ready.

A few weeks later, someone from Self Help asked me to be their sponsor. I happily agreed and began to take them through the steps, but I again had to learn that I couldn't save everyone. The following week he relapsed, and I had not seen him since. He was the first person I ever sponsored, so I felt horrible when he relapsed. At first, I thought it was my fault. I felt I did something wrong or didn't help him enough; maybe I wasn't very good at explaining the steps or something. I blamed myself for a long time, but I learned no matter how hard I tried, some people only pretended to want help. All I could do was be available for those who did want the help, but I couldn't force anyone to actually put the work in.

Right around this time, a lot of people close to me started dying. It all began when my uncle Bill passed away. He was sick for a while, so we all knew it was coming, but knowing in advance didn't make it any easier. He was a great man, always smiling, laughing, and joking around with everyone. He was filled with life, the kind of person who lit up the room just by walking in it. The whole family was sad to see him go, but we knew he was in a better place, up in heaven with my mom smiling down on us.

A short while later, my cousin's wife, Debbie, passed away. She was Uncle Bill's daughter-in-law. Her husband Billy, my first cousin, passed away a few years prior. I know this can be confusing because my family has so many Bills and Billys. On this side of my family, there were three generations of Billys. The oldest was my Uncle Bill, who had just passed away. Then, his son, Cousin Billy, passed away a few years ago. Finally, my cousin's son, Billy, was my second cousin and the one I used to paint with.

I felt so bad for my second cousin Billy and his siblings Eric, Greg, and April. They had just lost their father a few years earlier. Then they lost their grandfather and, shortly after that, their mother. I knew there was nothing I could say to make any of them feel better. All I could do was pray for them and tell them I was there if they needed anything.

A few months after Debbie passed away, I was listening to the radio when the DJ said someone was killed by a hit-and-run driver while out celebrating his birthday. Then the DJ said the guy's name was Billy McCue. I thought it was weird because my cousin's name was Billy McCue. But, no, it couldn't be him. I would have heard about it by now. But then I realized that Billy's birthday had just passed, so I immediately called my sister, and she confirmed that it was our cousin. I was in a state of shock. I mean, out of all my cousins, he was probably the one I was closest with.

In fact, I had just talked to him a few weeks earlier, and he told me that he had stopped getting high and was only drinking now. I actually tried to convince him to go to a meeting with me, but he said AA just wasn't for him. I later learned that his drinking played a role in how he died. He was walking home after drinking and celebrating his birthday when a hit-and-run driver killed him.

This really fucked my head up and made me feel terrible for my cousins. They lost their dad, their mom, their grandfather, and now their oldest brother, all in a short period. I couldn't even imagine the pain they were going through. I prayed for them every day. I just wanted God to give them the strength to overcome these difficult times. I didn't understand why everyone was dying, but I knew that I wouldn't drink or use over it. My connection to AA was too strong to even consider that as an option. Besides, I knew getting high or drunk wouldn't bring anybody back or make anything better. If anything, it would have made things worse.

It wasn't just family members who were dying on me, though. At Self Help, people were dying left and right. Of course, most of these deaths were caused by overdoses. People would successfully complete the program, go out and find their own place, and then end up dead a few weeks later. I wasn't super close to any of the people who died or anything, but it still sucked to hear about it, especially when it happened every other week.

With everyone around me dying, I got scared when it came time for my two close friends, Gary and Joe, to move out of Self Help. After they moved out, we still hung out here and there and went to meetings for a while, but then suddenly, I stopped hearing from them. That shit scared me. I honestly feared for their lives. A few weeks later, I heard through the grapevine that they both had relapsed and were stuck back in Kensington, hooked on that dope again. It seemed like everything in life was hitting me all at once, and I didn't know how much more I could take.

Next, I found out that my boy Jerry had died from an overdose. Last time I saw Jerry was when he came to Self Help, only to leave a few hours later. I've known Jerry for years and got high with him on the streets. In fact, he was the one who introduced me to heroin, so when he died, it really hit home for me. I realized just how lucky I was, not only to be alive but to be clean and sober on top of it.

When Jerry died, it made me grow even more concerned about Gary and Joe. I didn't want them to end up like Jerry, but there wasn't much I could have done except to put it in God's hands. So, I prayed for them every chance that I got. One of the weekly meetings I attended was held at a church, and in the back of that church was a prayer garden. Every week I arrived at the meeting early to sit and pray for them in that garden. I wasn't sure if God was going to answer my prayers or not, so I had no choice but to hope for the best and prepare for the worst.

212

Chapter 34

After what seemed like an eternity, I finally finished my IOP, which really helped me out financially. With the extra money, I quickly paid off my court fees, just so I could get it over and done with. With no more financial burden and wasted time going to IOP, I felt like a great deal of stress had been lifted off my shoulders. The following month I graduated from treatment court, which meant I was also finished with probation. So, within a month's time, all of my financial and legal issues completely vanished; everything was starting to look up for me.

Now that I had more money in my pocket, I could go back to my ninth step to make some financial amends. See, when I first started the ninth step, I had to skip a couple of people on the list because I wasn't financially able to repay them at the time. But, now that I was getting back on my feet, I wanted to make those financial amends. The first person I approached was my brother, Mike, but he wouldn't accept any money from me. All he wanted me to do was to stay clean and sober.

The second person on my list was my old boss, Ralph, from the dry cleaners. This is the same boss who gave me a second chance after I was caught stealing but ultimately had to fire me for always being late. I probably stole close to $1000 from him but was ready to make weekly payments until I paid him back in full.

I walked into the dry cleaners and immediately saw Ralph, but he didn't recognize me now that I was clean and sober. I started the amends process by telling him I was wrong for everything I'd done. Then, I handed him $100 and promised to pay back the rest of the money I stole from him. But just like my brother, Ralph wouldn't accept my money. He told me he was happy to see I was doing better and just wanted me to stay clean and sober.

Even though I was doing better now, I couldn't help but think about the people who weren't doing so well, especially my brother Shawn and my good friends Gary and Joe. So, I continued to pray for them until one day, God answered my prayers, and I found Gary sitting in the Self Help meeting room. Then, a few days after that, Joe also returned to Self Help. About a month later, they completed their inpatient program and moved back to the third floor. Once they were back upstairs with me, it was just like old times, and we all started to go to meetings again. Gary even asked me to sponsor him, which I happily agreed to do.

Shortly after Joe and Gary made it back to Self Help, I bought myself a cheap computer and microphone to record some new songs I had written. There was this dude on the third floor named Chango, who made some dope ass beats. He knew I was a rapper, so he gave me some free beats so that I could start recording. And these weren't some basic, generic beats, either. These beats were off the hook! Chango had a true gift, and he could have easily made it in the rap game if only he could have stayed clean. But unfortunately, this disease got the best of him, and he is no longer with us.

The first time I recorded a song while sober, I wasn't sure how it would turn out. When I was getting high, I always thought that smoking weed made me a better rapper, but in reality, it was the complete opposite. After recording my first sober track, I compared it to the ones I recorded while I was high. I could immediately tell the difference. The songs I recorded while sober were far superior; my voice was more precise, my flow was on point, and the quality was a hundred times better. On top of all that, the lyrics just made a lot more sense. I was talking about real-life shit instead of just throwing two sentences together that rhymed.

One of the songs I recorded, titled "The Struggle," seemed to be a good hit with people in recovery. So shortly after recording it, I made a music video for it. The video didn't go viral, but it got about 1,500 views, which was way more than I expected it to get. People in recovery really seemed to like it. And once the word got around, I began to feel like an AA celebrity.

After receiving positive feedback from the music I was putting out, I started to perform at some open mic spots with my boy Billy, aka "Ruflis Lucas." Ruflis and I met a few years earlier at the methadone clinic but had lost touch until we ran into each other at the coffee shop one night. He seemed to be doing well and was hanging out with other people in recovery, so I assumed he was clean too. A few weeks after we ran into each other, we recorded a song with our mutual friend, Eddie, who had just gotten out of prison. The song came out a lot better than anyone had expected. In fact, it was so good that Ruflis kept begging me to do some shows with him so that we could perform it together. I was hesitant at first because I had never performed live on stage before. But, I figured it would be no different from doing karaoke at the coffee shop, so I went for it.

When I met Ruflis at the open mic spot, it was nothing like I expected it to be. It was held outside in some old, dirty-ass abandoned lot,

214

a few blocks from where I used to sell dope. Hanging out in the middle of Kensington and being surrounded by the life I was trying to escape probably wasn't a good idea. Looking back in hindsight, I probably should have just left. But I figured I would be fine since I was there with Ruflis, who was also clean and sober.

I'm not sure why, but when Ruflis first asked me to perform at the open mic, I imagined hundreds of people would be in the crowd. But, when we showed up, only about 25 people were there. The small crowd was a disappointment, but it didn't bother me that much. What did bother me, though, was how almost everyone there was either smoking weed or drinking, including Ruflis, who I thought was clean and sober.

Against my better judgment and for my love of Hip-Hop, I stayed so that Ruflis and I could perform our song, "Second Chances." The song was about having a second chance at life and how we were using that second chance to stay out of trouble. Yet, there I was, hanging around people who were getting drunk and high. I tried my best to not let it bother me, but the truth is, I was super uncomfortable. After the show, Ruflis apologized for not warning me about the drugs and alcohol. Then he explained how he was clean from the hard drugs but still drinks and smokes weed here and there.

I went back to the open mic once or twice after that, hoping that the weed smoke wouldn't bother me, but it always did, so I stopped going after a while. A few weeks after I stopped going, someone else told me about a rap competition at this place called "Lyrics Lounge." I signed up for the competition but didn't realize that Lyrics Lounge was actually just a bar. When I got there and realized I would be surrounded by alcohol, I thought about leaving. But I figured it was better than the last open mic because at least there weren't dope dealers on the corner and people smoking weed in the crowd. So, I thought I would be OK, but by the end of the night, I began to feel really anxious, and there was even a moment when I thought about drinking.

When the thought of drinking crossed my mind, I immediately stepped outside and called a friend from AA. I wasn't seriously entertaining the idea of drinking, but the idea was still there, and it scared the shit out of me. After that night, I had a choice to make. I could continue to chase my dream of being a famous rapper, performing at bars and venues surrounded by drugs and alcohol, or I could just stop rapping. I felt like giving up hip-hop was my only choice.

It was a difficult choice to make, but my sobriety depended on it. How was I supposed to stay clean and sober by hanging out in bars every weekend? What if one night I slipped up and did have a drink? I didn't want to risk it. Besides, what were the chances I would've made it big time? As much as I loved hip-hop, I loved being clean and sober even more. Even though I continued to spit rhymes for people in recovery, I gave up on the dream of being famous and decided to put down the mic.

Chapter 35

Because of the climate here in Philadelphia, I couldn't work outside and grow vegetables all year round. Once the weather started to change, I had to go inside and work in the kitchen. That first winter, while working indoors, I formed some tight bonds with my co-workers. Now, I became close with quite a few people in that kitchen, but there are two in particular who I am still close with to this day, and I consider them to be my best friends.

Ryan, Steve, and I have a unique bond, and even though we have some things in common, we couldn't be any more different from one another. For instance, I'm a white guy who listens to hip-hop music and wears baggy clothing. Ryan, on the other hand, is a black guy with a shaved head and glasses who listens to headbanger music. In fact, we always joke about how I am blacker than him, and he is whiter than me.

And then there is Steve. Steve is a few years younger than Ryan and me, but he is wise for his age, perhaps wiser than both of us. He is the outdoors type, completing the look with a long reddish beard, chewing on tobacco, and listening to country music. One look at him, and you would think he was a lumberjack or something. So when you put the three of us together, we are nothing alike. Yet, we have a very close relationship, with lots of "yo mamma" jokes and deep discussions about recovery.

When I started working at Self Help, Ryan rented a condo with another co-worker, Pete, and a third guy we all knew from Self Help, but I can't remember his name. About a year later, that third roommate relapsed and got kicked out of the condo. It just so happens that I was looking for a new place to live at the time. Living at Self Help was great and all, but I had two years clean at this point and just felt like it was time for me to move on. So, when Ryan and Pete asked if I wanted to take his place, I didn't even have to think about it. It was the perfect spot. It was only a mile away from Self Help. Plus, I could carpool with Ryan to work every day.

A year after I moved into the condo, I decided to get a car. I didn't mind carpooling to work with Ryan every day but was tired of taking the bus everywhere else. So, with my income tax return, I bought a hoopty from an old friend from the neighborhood, Joe. The car had a few cosmetic issues, but it ran pretty good, which was all I really cared about. One of the reasons I got that car was because I was tired of taking the bus to meet girls every time I had a date. I thought getting a car would make dating easier, but it didn't change anything. I still had the same girl problems I had early on in recovery. I would meet a girl, date her for a few weeks, and then break up. This time, the only difference was that I didn't try to find a new girl immediately after a breakup. Instead, I would take some time to focus on myself and see where I went wrong in the relationship.

My dating life continued like this until sometime in 2013 when our landlord kicked us out of his condo. Maybe I shouldn't use the term "kicked out" because that makes it sound like we did something wrong, which isn't the case at all. See, our landlord split up with his wife and needed his condo back so that he had a place to live. So, it's not like he was mad at us, or we didn't pay the rent or anything like that. In fact, I could tell he felt awful about doing it, but we completely understood.

I needed to find a new place to live, so I posted on Facebook, asking if anybody knew of any rooms for rent. Later that day, my cousin Emma reached out to me. She had just split up with her boyfriend and was having trouble paying the rent at her apartment. So she asked if I wanted to stay with her to help out with the rent. I gladly accepted her offer and moved in the following week.

I remember feeling bad for Emma because, on top of going through a breakup, her father had also recently passed away. Uncle Jim was one of my favorite uncles. He was one crazy dude, one of the funniest people I had ever known, in fact. He reminded me of a Vietnam vet who took one too many hits of LSD. And considering how he actually did fight in Vietnam, there could be some truth to that. On the other hand, it could've just been the war itself that made him that way.

After I got clean, Uncle Jim told me how proud he was of me for turning my life around. He lived right on Kensington Avenue, so he saw firsthand how drugs destroyed people's lives. Although he's no longer with us, I still think about him and am grateful he saw me make it out of that neighborhood.

I felt weird bringing girls home after I moved in with Emma, so I slowed down with online dating for a while. However, it took no time at all for me to start feeling lonely again. So, I decided to give the dating apps another shot. I went on a few dates here and there, but nothing ever came out of it. As the holidays approached, my loneliness worsened, but every girl I met just wasn't a good match for me. I began to lose hope and accepted the fact that I may have to be single for the rest of my life. But just as I was about to give up, God gave me a Christmas miracle.

Christmas Day was always a lonely one for me. Don't get me wrong, I love Christmas and was fortunate to spend time with my family, but we always exchanged gifts on Christmas Eve. So, when Christmas morning came, I always woke up alone with nobody to enjoy the day with. It's not like I had children to watch open gifts or anything, and all my friends were always busy with their families. So I really had nobody to hang with or nothing to do on Christmas Day.

Christmas of 2013 was no different; if anything, it was worse. I had already been feeling lonely in the weeks leading up to the holiday, so when the day came, I felt even more alone. I hit a meeting during the day to prevent myself from going insane, but that night when I got home, the lonely void began eating away at me. So, I opened the OK Cupid app on my phone as a last Hail Mary attempt at finding love.

It had been a while since I used the app because I had lost all hope for online dating. I was tired of coming across the same profiles, day in and day out. But that Christmas night, I felt so lonely that I wanted to log in just to see if I had any messages; I didn't have any. Since I was bored and already had the app open, I decided to look through the profiles to see if I could find anyone interesting. I swiped through a couple photos, but none of the girls were really my type. But then, I came across one that was 100% my type, so I gave her five stars. As soon as I gave her five stars, a notification appeared on my app: I had a new match!

I clicked on the notification and saw that the match was for the girl I had just rated five stars. As soon as I saw her profile, I felt hope pouring back into my heart again. Her name was Monica, and she was cute as shit; plus, she didn't drink or do drugs. I messaged her that night and got an immediate response, so we exchanged numbers and began texting back and forth. It was the best Christmas gift I could have ever received.

Two days later, on December 27th, we met outside the movie theater for our first date. I was afraid that the date wouldn't go well or that she wouldn't look like her profile picture because that happens very often with online dating. But when I saw Monica standing outside the theater, she looked even more beautiful than she did in her picture. I couldn't believe my eyes. More importantly, I couldn't believe that a girl this cute wanted to go on a date with me.

We decided to see "A Wolf on Wall Street," which, in retrospect, wasn't the best choice for a first date. But it didn't matter, because we were both happy to be in each other's company. After the movie, I drove Monica home, but when it came time to drop her off, I didn't want her to leave. At the time, I wasn't sure if she felt the same way I did because she was kind of quiet on the way home. But after texting with her the next day, I learned that she did feel the same way; she was just shy. For the next couple of weeks, I was in a super good mood because I felt like I was really hitting it off with Monica. I got a smile on my face every time I thought about her. However, in the back of my mind, I was worried because I knew I still had to tell her about my HIV.

Monica invited me to her house one night to watch a movie, and I figured that would be the best time to tell her the unfortunate news. I knew it would go either one of two ways. Either she would be totally cool with it or would act like she was totally cool with it and then start acting weird.

"Listen, there's something about me that you need to know."

"What is it?"

"Well, I have HIV."

"Wait...Like, for real, for real? This ain't a joke?"

Me being the prankster that I was, she thought I was pulling her chain. But after reassuring her that I was serious, she didn't seem to mind at all. She just shrugged it off like it was no big deal. It was the one thing that could have prevented our relationship from moving forward, and she was perfectly OK with it. I also got to meet Monica's son for the first time that night too. His name is Jimmy, and he was 12 years old at the time. He was really shy, just like his mom, but seemed like a really good kid.

The next few months seemed to be going great for me. I upgraded my wheels and bought a used Mustang, which put my mind at ease because I no longer felt like my piece-of-shit car would break down at any given moment. Around this same time, I also managed to quit smoking cigarettes. Monica was a non-smoker, so she became my support system and motivated me to stop. It was difficult at first, but there were little things I did that made it more manageable. For one, I used these cherry-flavored nicotine lozenges, which tasted almost like candy, except they were a little harsher. The thing I liked about them was I was able to break them into pieces. So, I slowly weened myself off by eating smaller and smaller pieces over time.

I also cut a drinking straw down to the size of a cigarette, and whenever I had an urge to smoke, I would puff on the straw just like I would a real cigarette. See, the lozenges helped me overcome the physical addiction to nicotine, and puffing on the straw helped me overcome the mental aspect of it. Before I knew it, I stopped craving cigarettes altogether. At the time of writing this book, I haven't smoked a cigarette in over eight years.

A couple weeks later, Monica asked me to move in with her. We were only dating for probably about three or four months at the time, but it doesn't take a whole day to recognize sunshine. When you are happy, you're happy, and nothing else matters. So, I happily agreed to move in with her, but I had to break the bad news to my cousin, who I knew would struggle financially if I moved out.

God works in mysterious ways. When I told Emma that I was moving in with Monica, she was actually relieved. Emma's lease on the apartment was coming up, and she decided not to renew it. So, she was going to tell me to look for a new place anyway. It's funny how things always work out in the end. The only bad part about moving in with Monica was that she lived in South Philly, on the opposite side of the city. Everyone and everything that I knew was in Northeast Philly: my job, my friends, my meetings, my family, etc. But, I was in love with Monica, so I was willing to make sacrifices for her. I knew I wanted to spend the rest of my life with her, so even though I felt like I was leaving my old life behind, I was creating a new one with her.

In starting my new life with Monica, I began to think about the future. Working at Self Help was a great stepping stone, but it wasn't something I wanted to do for the rest of my life. The thought came to me one day as I kneeled in the cold mud and began to feel a pain in my knees. Not to mention the backaches I had every day from all the bending and heavy lifting I had to do. It was never severe enough to prevent me from working, but I was only 33 years old. What would I do in 10-15 years when my knees and back started giving me real problems? It's not like Self Help had a pension plan or paid enough money for me to create a retirement account. They offered a 401K, but I barely contributed anything to it because I couldn't afford to; they just didn't pay enough.

Around this same time, my best friends, Steve and Ryan, both left Self Help to pursue other careers, so that's when I knew it was time for me to move on as well. Don't get me wrong, I loved working at Self Help; I really did. Over the years, I met a lot of good people there. I've seen guys who were utterly defeated as they walked through the front door, beaten down by life, and caught in the grips of drug addiction. I watched those same guys grow into honorable men and become productive members of society. Sometimes, I may have even played a small part in helping them along their way. Working at Self Help was an unforgettable experience. I witnessed miracles happening every day, but miracles don't pay the bills.

Even though I was doing much better financially, money started getting tight now that I had new expenses. I had car payments I had to make now, plus I was spending a lot more on gas because I had to drive to work every day from South Philly, and that mustang was a gas guzzler. Living expenses also got more expensive when I moved in with Monica. She had quite a few animals because she's heavily involved in animal rescue. And since I also love animals, I happily shared the expense of food, litter, and vet bills. It might not sound like much, but when you add it all up, it was really straining my wallet. So even though I loved working at Self Help, I wanted something more. I needed something more. What I needed was a career.

I started seeking a career that not only paid more but also didn't involve hard manual labor. One application I filled out was for a clerk position with the City of Philadelphia. I didn't even know what a clerk was, but it sounded like some sort of office job that would be easy on the knees and back. After filling out the application, I had to take a test, which I didn't do too good on. But I didn't do too bad, either. My score was somewhere in the mid-80s, which is mediocre at best. So I didn't have high hopes of being picked for the position because hundreds of people took the test with me.

A good year and a half went by, and I still hadn't found a new career yet, but I kept trying because I knew I would find one eventually. I went on a couple of interviews, but nothing ever came out of them. Then one day, out of the blue, the Free Library of Philadelphia called and asked if I was interested in interviewing for a position as a library assistant. I agreed to go on the interview but was baffled because I never filled out an application for the library. During the interview, I discovered they got my information when I took the test for the clerk position. When I took that test, I had no idea that the Free Library of Philadelphia would be contacting me. But I'm glad they did because a job at the library sounded much better than some boring clerk position.

The interview went very well, so well in fact that I received a phone call a few days later and was offered the position. I was sad yet excited when I put my two weeks' notice in at Self Help. I was excited because I couldn't wait to start my new career at the library. But I was sad because I was going to miss Self Help. I spent five and half years there, four and half in which I was an employee. The place literally changed my life. When I first walked into the building, sheriffs escorted me with handcuffs and shackles on my feet. But now, I was leaving to pursue a career at the Free Library of Philadelphia. If that's not a complete 180-degree turnaround, then I don't know what is. Over the years, I formed some close bonds with my co-workers, along with a countless number of clients. So, I was going to miss a lot of people there, but I had to do what I had to do.

On my last day at Self Help, my boss and co-workers threw me a surprise going-away celebration. It wasn't a full-on party or anything like that. It was more like a small gathering and only lasted for a few minutes. My boss, Jeff, was a certified chef with a true talent for baking. So, he baked this really fancy cake for us all to enjoy. The CEO and CFO of the company also attended the gathering. The CEO even gave a small speech and talked about how much my "Happy Mondays" would be missed. He then asked me to say a few words, which really threw me off guard.

"I just want to say how much this place changed my life. When I walked in these doors, I mean, I didn't even have a pair of sneakers on my feet. But I met a lot of good people along the way and --"

I got too choked up. I couldn't even finish my sentence because I was trying to hold back the tears, but I fought through it the best I could.

"This place saved my life...I just want to say thank you. Thank you for saving my life."

I couldn't fight the tears any longer. They got the best of me. At that moment, I realized just how much I was going to miss that place, but no matter how far away I get from Self Help, it will forever be in my heart.

Chapter 36

As I'm sure you can imagine, working at a public library is much different from working at a rehab. For one, the rehab was an all-male facility, so there was a lot of ball-busting, cursing, and "That's what she said" jokes. Basically, I didn't have to filter myself at all. But working at the library was the complete opposite. I had to be very careful about what I said. I was used to interacting with addicts who came from the streets. But now, I was working around children and elderly bookworms. It was a drastic change, and in the beginning, I slipped up a couple times by dropping an F-bomb while talking to my co-worker. However, over time, I learned how to control myself, and before I knew it, I began talking more professionally.

Working at the library was pretty much what I expected it to be. Most of my day is spent putting books back on the shelves, helping patrons find books, and checking them out. Sometimes I even help with the afterschool program and assist kids with their homework. Even though the library can get busy at times, the majority of the day is slow. There is a good amount of downtime, and it took me a while to get used to it. I was accustomed to having jobs that required me to constantly be doing something. At Self Help, there was no such thing as downtime. In the summer, there were always weeds to be pulled and vegetables to be picked. In the winter, there was always food to be chopped and dishes to be washed. It was one of those "If you got time to lean, you got time to clean" types of atmosphere.

Another thing that I had to get used to was how the library didn't have addicts and alcoholics for me to help on a daily basis. Don't get me wrong, the library definitely has its fair share of addicts. But, it's not like I can approach them about their drug and alcohol problems. As a library employee, I have to keep things professional, and confronting someone like that could jeopardize my career.

Luckily I found another passion that helped fill the void, which my girlfriend Monica introduced me to. Monica is heavily involved in animal rescue, so after I met her, I also became involved in animal rescue. I had always been an animal lover, but I never really got into rescuing them until I met Monica. She worked at an animal shelter and fostered kittens until we could find them a good home. She especially loved to foster feral kittens, which would hiss, scratch, and bite anybody who got too close to them.

But Monica had a gift for turning these young, angry kittens into the most friendly, loving cats you would ever meet.

After I learned how to socialize feral kittens, I discovered that it gave me the same satisfaction I felt when I helped other addicts/alcoholics. These feral kittens were, in some ways, similar to the clients at Self Help; terrified and miserable when they first walked through the doors. But after a couple of weeks, their demeanors would change, and they will have no problem jumping on my lap to snuggle with me. I'm talking about the cats. The cats snuggle on my lap, not the clients; that would just be weird.

Monica's passion for animals is one of the many reasons I fell in love and wanted to spend the rest of my life with her. So, I decided to ask her something that had been weighing on my mind for quite some time. We ordered Chinese takeout for dinner, and after we finished eating, Monica left the room for a minute. That's when I put my plan in motion. I used a pair of tweezers to remove the little paper fortune from one of the fortune cookies and slipped my own little piece of paper inside. A few moments later, Monica came back and opened up her fortune cookie. As she began to read her fortune, I got down on one knee and opened a box to display a diamond ring.

Her fortune read: "Will you marry me?"

"Wait, is this another one of your jokes?"

"It's not a joke. I'm serious."

"Then yes!"

We got engaged in December, but we both wanted a spring wedding. So, we set a date for the following year. That way, we wouldn't be scrambling to come up with enough money in time. It also gave us an entire year and a half to plan it out. Doing it this way made things a lot less stressful, and we never argued or had a difference of opinion over anything. That's probably because I learned long before we ever got married that Monica is always right!

On May 21st, 2016, I married my soulmate, my best friend. It was pouring rain that day, and I mean it was an absolute drenching downpour, but other than that, the wedding was perfect. All of our friends and family celebrated with us, and it was a night that I will never forget. She made me the happiest man in the world when she said, "I do."

Not long after Monica and I got married, many people in my life started dying; again. It all started when I received a phone call from Greg's sponsor, Frank. Frank told me that Greg had been diagnosed with cancer and that he wasn't doing too well. Steve and I went to the hospital to visit him as soon as I found out.

When we got to Greg's room, he didn't seem as bad as I thought he would be. I mean, he lost a lot of weight, so physically, he didn't look great. However, he seemed perfectly coherent and could get up and move around with no problems. Honestly, he was acting like his regular self, so mentally, he was in great spirits. He even told Steve and me that it wasn't as bad as it sounds. He seemed to have a lot of hope; to me, it sounded like he expected to beat cancer with no problems.

I left the hospital feeling much better because I thought Greg had a fighting chance at beating cancer. But a few weeks later, I received another phone call from Frank; Greg had passed away. I was heartbroken. Greg was taken from us way too early; he was too young. He had one of the most gentle, loving souls I had ever witnessed in a person. He was like an AA role model who taught me everything I needed to know to stay sober. This man was constantly helping people. He would stop at nothing to help a newcomer, a selfless trait that helped pave my road to recovery. Greg helped me in so many ways that I could probably write an entire book about it, but every time I tried to thank him, he would always say the same thing:

"You helped me more than I helped you."

I will never forget those words. Early in sobriety, I didn't quite understand it. But as I followed in Greg's footsteps and started helping other addicts/alcoholics, I understood what Greg was trying to tell me. In fact, we would always joke around and playfully argue about who helped who more. I'm just glad that Greg was clean and sober when he passed because I know that was something he was genuinely proud of.

A few months after Greg passed away, I got a phone call from an old friend who told me my boy Chris had died. Chris was my headbanger friend, who I used to get high with before I went to detox for the first time. I've known and hung out with Chris for years, so when I got clean and sober, I reached out and offered to help him, but he just wasn't ready to change. The last time I talked to Chris, he said he wasn't using heroin anymore but was still drinking and smoking weed. I didn't know whether to believe him or not, but in the end, there was nothing I could have done to change his mind unless he wanted to get help.

Shortly after Chris passed away, I saw on Facebook that my friend Ruflis had passed away. He was the one I used to rap with at the open mic shows. This one cut deep, too, because I had just seen him a few weeks beforehand. When I saw him, he looked high as shit, so I wanted to talk to him about trying to get clean again, but he was with a friend of his, so I never brought it up. I often wonder what if I did try to convince him; could I have helped him? But, I learned a long time ago that I had to take the fireman hat off because I couldn't save everyone.

After Ruflis passed away, I found out that my ex, Tanya, had died from an overdose. This one hit home, not because I still had feelings or anything like that, but because it made me realize just how lucky I was to be alive. I lived the same lifestyle as Tanya, so if I had never gotten clean, I would have died too. In fact, we probably would have bought our dope at the same spot; the same dope that killed her would have also killed me.

Just when I thought these clusters of deaths were over and done with, I received a phone call from Gary. He told me that our good friend Joe had passed away. We haven't really seen each other in a while, but it didn't make it hurt any less. After Joe and Gary left Self Help, they were both doing pretty well. Gary met a girl from AA, Bree, who he settled down and started a family with. They now have four kids and are living life beyond their wildest dreams. I couldn't be any happier for them. And after Joe left Self Help, he continued attending meetings and was doing pretty good. As far as I know, Joe died clean and sober.

A few years later, my uncle, Bernie, passed away due to health complications. He was one of my closest uncles because he lived so close to me growing up. He was one of the funniest people I had ever met, so he always brought a smile to my face every time I saw him. I used to work at McDonald's near his house, and when he came in every morning, I'd slip him his coffee for free when the manager wasn't looking. I will never forget the look on his face whenever I did this. He always looked around first to make sure nobody was watching and then scurried out the door with a guilty look on his face as if he had just robbed a bank or something.

A year after Uncle Bernie's death, Uncle Tom passed away. Uncle Tom had the kindest soul you could ever imagine. He was a perfect gentleman too. I never knew anyone who spoke as proper as Uncle Tom did, and he did so with one of the most soothing voices I have ever heard. He could have easily worked in radio with the way that he spoke. I will never forget how Uncle Tom always offered valuable advice. Before I wrote this story, I told him how I would love to write a book someday.

"Well, Brian, they say you should write what you know."

His advice is part of the reason why I wrote this book. What subject do I know better than my own life experiences with drugs, alcohol, and recovery?

Most recently, my aunt Kathleen passed away. She was one of the kindest people I have ever met. I honestly can't remember her ever saying anything negative about anybody in my entire life. She always made me feel so welcome at family gatherings and just had a warm presence about her. She will surely be missed, as well as all my other family members and friends I lost along the way. But just because they are gone does not mean they are forgotten.

Over the years, I've lost so many people in my life. My old counselor, Marlene, passed away due to health complications. Ricky, who took me to my old house to get my clothes while I was in rehab, and who I became close with over the years of working at Self Help, died from a drug overdose. Woody, from Self Help, also passed away, although I'm not exactly sure what caused his death. Then there was my estranged cousin, Adam, who had been a drug addict his entire life. I wrote letters to Adam while he was in prison and told him how the 12 steps changed my life. Through the letters we wrote to one another, he expressed interest in recovery and planned on getting the help he needed once he got out. He even called me when he was released but abruptly ended the phone call mid-conversation and said he would call me back. I never heard from him again; a few months later, he passed away.

It always hurts to lose someone close to you, some more than others. It doesn't matter how far away we drifted over the years, even the ones still living, because I have great memories that I will cherish for the rest of my life. I continue to think about the ones I've lost along the way, and every once in a while, life throws me a little reminder that they are still smiling down on me. All I can do is look up and smile back; I know I'll see them again, someday.

Chapter 37

A few years after I started working for the library, I got an email from my union that really sparked my interest. The email told me about a new program called the "Free College Benefit," which paid 100% tuition for any union member who wanted to obtain their associate degree. Before receiving this email, I considered going back to school, but the high cost of tuition was the one thing that stopped me. If you remember from earlier in my story, I made the mistake of taking out school loans for a computer school that got me nowhere in life. I was still paying those school loans off and didn't want to add to my debt by taking out more loans.

When I saw the email about the free college tuition, I immediately clicked on the link and applied for the program. Before I knew it, I was a student at Eastern Gateway Community College, which offers online courses for people who live out of state. I didn't know what I wanted to major in, so I decided to get my Associate of Arts.

I was nervous about going back to school. I was never really a school person back in my high school days. However, it turns out that my dependence upon mind-altering substances held the contributing component to the analysis regarding my previous educational experience. See what I did there? I sounded all smart and shit, didn't I? You can thank my college education for that!

Seriously though, the first course I took was Psychology 101, and I absolutely loved it! I scored a perfect A in my first-ever college course, and I couldn't have been more proud of myself. At first, I thought it was a fluke and was going to be a one-time thing. But then, I finished my second course with straight A's. Then my third course with straight A's. Then my fourth, and my fifth, and so on and so on. Before I knew it, I had enough credits to get my associate degree with a perfect 4.0 GPA.

While earning my associate degree, a promotional opportunity presented itself at the library, and I decided to go for it. It was for a supervisor position where I would oversee the other library assistants. To get the job, I had to take a competitive exam. The results of that competitive exam determined who would be considered first to fill the available positions. Being a college student definitely helped with the exam because it exercised my brain and made me a better test taker.

A few weeks after taking the exam, I got called in for an interview and was chosen to fill one of the positions at a nearby library. The pay was slightly more, but I was more concerned with gaining the extra responsibilities. The extra responsibilities meant additional experience. Additional experience would be beneficial when it comes time for the next promotion. I am slowly climbing the ladder of success, but just like recovery, I have to take it one step at a time.

Even though I was doing better for myself, I couldn't help but think about my brother Shawn, who was still getting high. Shawn had been in and out of mental facilities for most of his adult life. He never told me what his diagnosis was, but one day I came across some of his release papers, which stated he was a schizophrenic. Part of me believed it to be true because Shawn had always exhibited the behavioral symptoms of a schizophrenic. But, part of me also thought it was one of Shawn's attempts to get his hands on some drugs. I still, to this day, don't know if Shawn was born with a mental issue or if it stemmed from his drug use, but either way, he definitely had mental problems.

I mentioned a few chapters back how I ran into my brother Shawn on the bus one night and took him to a meeting. After that meeting, I gave Shawn my phone number so he could call me the next day, but my phone never rang. Over the years, I occasionally ran into him while he was pushing a shopping cart down the street and collecting cans. It killed me to see him like that, but there was little I could do except buy him some food and offer support if he wanted to get clean.

Even though Shawn never called me the day after that meeting, he eventually did call me, five years later, from Friend's Hospital, a mental facility. The next day when I visited him, he told me he had been living in a tent under the highway. He then told me that he started panhandling at Princeton Avenue and State Road, down the street from the house we grew up in. Shawn explained that collecting cans just wasn't cutting it anymore because he recently began using heroin. Shawn's drug of choice had always been crack, so I was surprised to learn about his transition to heroin. But, Shawn surprised me again by telling me he was ready to get clean. In fact, he even told the staff at Friend's Hospital that he wanted help with his drug addiction. I was so happy that Shawn was finally getting the help he needed. But a few weeks later, I drove by Princeton and State Road and saw him panhandling with a sign that read "Anything helps."

I pulled the car over and talked to him for a little while, and he told me he was going back into rehab the following week, but we both knew it was a lie. I gave him a few dollars and told him to call if he needed anything, but he never picked up the phone. Over the next few months, I periodically drove by the corner where he panhandled so that I could stop to talk to him for a few minutes. I wanted him to know that I still cared about him and that I was just a phone call away if he ever wanted to get clean. But like always, I waited for a phone call that would never come.

The holidays were fast approaching, and I wanted to give Shawn a Christmas gift, but I knew better than to give him something he could sell for drugs. So, instead, I got him something that he could really use; a nice pair of gloves and a warm hat to protect him from the cold. I also wrote him a letter that told him how much I cared about him. It also explained how much my life has changed since I got clean and sober and how I believed he could do the same if he wanted to. I went looking for him that Christmas Eve, but he wasn't out panhandling on the corner. So, I went under the highway to try and find his tent, and sure enough, it was right there like he described. I walked toward the tent and called his name, and his head popped out to see who it was. He invited me into his tent to get out of the cold, and as soon as I stepped inside, I started coughing because it was filled with smoke. This mother fucker had a campfire burning inside the tent, with no ventilation.

"Dude, what are you doing? You're gonna kill yourself."

"Nah, Brain, I do this all the time."

I still couldn't believe that my brother was living like this. The part that killed me the most was how he had actually grown accustomed to it. Shawn had been living on the streets for so long that he didn't think anything was wrong with it anymore; it was his norm. I tried my best not to let the smoke get to me, but it was difficult, so I knew I wouldn't be able to stay very long. I hurried up and gave him his Christmas gift along with the letter I had written to him. It was really dark in the tent, so I told him to read the letter in the morning when it would be easier.

The next day, Shawn called me. I was surprised to hear his voice. I was even more surprised when he said that he had read my letter and was ready to get clean. But of course, he decided this on Christmas Day when most detoxes weren't open for walk-ins. I googled a few places to see where I could bring him; our only option was a crisis center. I will never forget watching him walk through those doors and thinking to myself, "At least he'll be safe for the next 72 hours."

I much rather had brought him to an actual detox, but to do that, I would've had to wait until the next day. When it comes to helping an addict/alcoholic, it's best to get them the help immediately. An addict/alcoholic's mindset can easily change day to day. They may want to get clean today, but tomorrow when they get their hands on some drugs, they might change their mind. Once they get that fix, they say, "This isn't that bad. I'll be OK." I only know this because I told myself that lie many times throughout my addiction.

I'm going to be 100% honest here: I didn't have high hopes for Shawn staying clean, but that's only because of his track record. I thought that Shawn would maybe last for a few weeks and then leave the rehab like he had numerous times before. But, a few weeks later, Shawn shocked me again when he called from the rehab on Spring Garden Street, asking if I could bring him some cigarettes. I was happy to learn that he not only made it to rehab, but he actually stayed too.

Two months later, when Shawn graduated from rehab, I talked him into living at a recovery house. Luckily, working at Self Help over the years allowed me to meet many good men who pursued careers in the recovery field. One of those men was a good friend, Kevin, who volunteered in the garden when he was an inpatient client. After Kevin left Self Help, he got a job at a recovery house called "Joy of Living."

I called Kevin and asked if he could get my brother into the recovery house, and sure enough, Kevin was able to help. A few days later, my brother moved into Joy of Living and continued his journey to a better life. Shortly after Shawn moved in, he asked me to be his sponsor. I told Shawn I could only be his temporary sponsor because of a conflict of interest. I explained to him how it could be awkward if I was listed anywhere on his fourth step. Luckily Kevin had a close friend in AA who agreed to sponsor my brother.

A few weeks later, I shared some bad news with Shawn; our grandmom had passed away. She was 90 years old and lived a long, happy life. She had been sick for a while, so it wasn't a big surprise to any of us. But I wasn't sure how Shawn was going to handle it. It's not like they were super close at the time or anything. I mean, she moved down to Florida 20 years earlier, and I don't think Shawn had seen her since she moved. Nevertheless, that doesn't mean he wouldn't be upset by the sad news. She was still his grandmother, and I'm sure he had lots of great memories of her.

When I told Shawn the bad news, he seemed to take it pretty well. I asked Kevin to keep a close eye on him, just in case. But much to my surprise, it didn't affect his recovery at all. He actually managed to get six months clean and seemed to be doing well for a while. He was attending meetings and working with his sponsor, so it gave me hope that Shawn would be OK.

A few weeks later, Kevin called and asked if I had seen Shawn. Apparently, he left two days earlier to look for a job and never came back. So, the following day I drove by Princeton and State Road, and sure enough, my brother was out there panhandling. Shawn told me he had a moment of weakness and how one bag led to another, which led to another, and then to another. He had now been gone from the recovery house for three days and was afraid to go back. I told him I would bring him back, but he just didn't want to go. It's not like I could've forced him, so I had no choice but to accept his decision.

A few months later, I was in the area with my stepson, Jimmy, when I saw my brother Shawn panhandling once again. He looked horrible. Don't get me wrong, he had always looked awful, but he looked way worse this time than he usually did. I pulled the car over and pointed him out to Jimmy.

"Jimmy, see that guy over there?"

"Yeah."

"That's my brother, and that's what happens when you do drugs."

Being a typical teenager, Jimmy just rolled his eyes at my attempt to use my brother as a cautionary tale. I never suspected Jimmy of using drugs or anything like that. He's actually a good kid, but I figured it wouldn't hurt to at least point out what drugs can do, just in case.

When I got out of the car to talk to Shawn, it was evident that he was dope sick. I tried to speak to him about going back to rehab, but he swore up and down that he had talked to someone already, and they were just waiting for a bed to open up for him at the detox center. I didn't know whether to believe him or not, but my instincts told me he was lying. I told him how I hoped he was serious, then gave him a few dollars to get his fix; I couldn't stand to see my brother dope sick like that. As I walked away, I turned around and told Shawn something we usually never said to each other.

"Yo Shawn…I love you, bro."

Those were the last words I ever spoke to my brother. Two weeks later, he was found in Pennypack Park with a bullet in his head.

My brother Mike was the one who told me the bad news. Honestly, when he said that Shawn had passed away, I wasn't really surprised. It's something that I had been expecting for a while, but when I heard the words "passed away," I just assumed that he had overdosed. I was shocked when Mike told me that Shawn was found with a bullet in his head. He then told me that he and the detective both thought it could have been self-inflicted.

After I hung up the phone, I thought about Shawn committing suicide, but it didn't add up. Don't get me wrong, I knew that Shawn was fully capable of suicide; there was no question in my mind about it. But, the fact that he was found in Pennypack Park really baffled me. Shawn never hung out in Pennypack. He always stayed around the Tacony neighborhood, where we grew up. So, why walk two miles away just to kill himself? If anything, he would have done it in his tent, where he felt most comfortable.

The other question I thought to myself was, "Where did he get the gun from?" I initially thought that he could've stolen it from someone. Perhaps he broke into a car and found it in a glove box? But even if that was the case, he could have easily gotten a couple hundred dollars for it on the street. I'm speaking from experience when I say that no addict in their right mind would ever turn down an opportunity to get that much money. Even if Shawn was suicidal and came across a gun, he most likely would've sold it for drugs. The ideal way for an addict to go out would be to overdose so they could get high one last time.

Another thing that made zero sense to me was how they couldn't find the gun at the scene. If Shawn killed himself, then where was the firearm? It would have been in his hand, right? But it wasn't. The only thing in his hand was his crack pipe and a couple empty bags. Mike thought that maybe a homeless person had found the gun and taken it, and because Pennypack Park is filled with homeless people and addicts, it didn't seem like that much of a stretch.

With these questions in mind, I decided to reach out to the detective. When I called, I asked him if there was anything else he could tell me. He said two shots were fired, and one skimmed across Shawn's face. He told me that sometimes this could be considered a "hesitation shot," where a suicidal shooter pulls the trigger, but the gun slips, and the bullet skims their face instead. I then asked the detective another question.

"What side was the bullet fired from?"

"It was from Shawn's left side."

I knew right then and there that Shawn didn't kill himself. Shawn was right-handed, not left-handed! During the autopsy, they checked Shawn's hands for gunshot residue. When the results came back, they verified what I knew all along: Shawn did not pull that trigger. This left one question: Who did?

The detectives who worked the case ended up getting to the bottom of it, and they caught the guys who were responsible. About a year later, at the trial, I learned what really happened. Here is a short version of the story:

One of the neighborhood dealers, Hafiz Myrick, who I mention by full name because, well, fuck him, kept his stash hidden in a bush located near Shawn's tent. So, one day when Hafiz couldn't find it, he assumed that Shawn had stolen it. So Hafiz met up with his boy, whose full name I can't remember. All I remember was his nickname was "Meatball." So Hafiz met up with Meatball and went out looking for Shawn. They must have found him at Princeton and State Road and somehow made him get in the car. I'm not sure if they forced him or maybe tricked him, but one way or another, Shawn got in the car.

Hafiz and Meatball then drove Shawn to a parking lot next to Pennypack Park, where Shawn's body was found. We think the first shot, which skimmed Shawn's face, was fired inside the car because Hafiz's car was found with the back windshield shot out. After that first shot, Shawn must've taken off and ran into the woods, where Hafiz and Meatball chased after him. Once they caught him, Hafiz put a bullet in his head and left him in the woods. The fucked up part about this story is how Hafiz found his drug stash later that day. Shawn didn't steal it! Hafiz just misplaced it. So my brother died for no reason at all!

After hearing all of this at the trial, I was confident that the jury would find Hafiz guilty. But I wasn't sure about Meatball since he wasn't the one who actually pulled the trigger. Even Meatball's lawyer argued that it was Hafiz's drugs, Hafiz's car, and Hafiz's gun. But the prosecutor said something that will always stick with me.

"You don't bring a witness to a murder."

The jury deliberated pretty quickly. It only took a couple hours for them to reach a verdict. You could have heard a pin drop when they came back into that courtroom. The tension in that room was one of the most intense things I had ever witnessed. My heart was pounding so hard and fast that I thought people on the other side of the room were able to hear it. It felt like time had slowed down, and my heart grew louder and louder with each pounding beat. The judge finally broke the silence by asking the jury to read the verdict.

"We, the jury, find the defendant, Hafiz Myrick, guilty of murder in the first degree."

You couldn't believe the relief that I felt at that moment. It was comforting to know that this monster would be locked away forever. But, when it came time to read the verdict for Meatball, they found him not guilty on all charges. It was bittersweet because even though Meatball got off scot-free, at least the one who actually pulled the trigger was going to spend the rest of his life in prison.

I'm not going to lie. I still have resentments against Hafiz and Meatball. I know I talked a lot about forgiveness earlier in this book, but I can't bring myself to forgive them for murdering my brother. Deep down, I want to forgive them because I know it will bring me peace, but I just can't do it. Maybe one day in the future, I will be able to forgive them, but until then, I will continue to pray for them because that's what AA has taught me to do.

I wish there was more I could have done for Shawn. If I could have convinced him to go back to rehab when I saw him, he might still be here with us today. I know I'm being hard on myself, and his death is not my fault, but I just wish things had turned out differently. No matter how bad Shawn got, I always had hopes of him turning his life around. I knew that if I could do it, then he, too, could have done it. But I learned over the years that you can't force anybody to get clean and sober. I could have talked to Shawn until I was blue in the face, and it wouldn't have made a difference. I could have kidnapped him and brought him to rehab, but the next day he would have been climbing out the window to escape the same way I once did.

I shed a lot of tears for my brother after he died, but the thought of getting drunk or high never once crossed my mind. Throughout my recovery, I learned how to deal with emotions without mind-altering substances, so I don't even think about using or drinking anymore when something tragic happens. I'm not saying that the thought NEVER crosses my mind, but on the rare occasion it does, it usually leaves quicker than it came. Over time I have learned that drugs and alcohol weren't really my problem but were the solution to my problems. I'm now fortunate enough to have other solutions, such as my Higher Power and the 12 steps. I just wish Shawn could have stayed clean long enough to realize the same thing. Nevertheless, I know we will see each other again, someday. Until then, I will continue to live one day at a time.

Chapter 38

Shortly after Shawn got murdered, my dad was diagnosed with lung cancer; my family just couldn't catch a break. I didn't understand how he even got lung cancer because I never once saw him smoke a cigarette. I know he used to smoke but quit years before I was born, so it didn't make sense to me.

Dad was living in Florida at the time. When he retired years earlier, he moved down there to be closer to my grandmom (his mother). He moved right before I started doing heroin, so I never really saw him until after I got sober. I made it a point to visit him at least once a year. During my visits, we would always take day trips to the beach, eat at local restaurants, or just hang out at the pool together. But after he started his treatment, he didn't have the energy to do any of that. In fact, when I went to visit him that year, he had lost a lot of weight and spent half the week just lying around and taking naps. I felt so bad for him and wished I could have helped somehow, but there was little I could have done.

A few months after my dad began his treatment, his cancer went into remission. Needless to say, we were overjoyed to hear the good news, as it gave our family a lot of hope for the future. But a few months later, my dad had a lot of trouble keeping his balance, so he was admitted back into the hospital. After running some tests, we learned that the cancer had spread to his spinal fluid, which explained why he was suddenly losing balance.

My brother Mike flew down to Florida to visit our dad while he was in the hospital. A few days after he got there, Mike told me that Dad wasn't doing too well and that I should get down there soon. For the next couple of days, I kept trying to call my dad, but he never answered his phone. Mike told me that Dad probably didn't answer because he had been sleeping a lot, but part of me thinks it's because my dad didn't want to admit to me, or himself, what was really happening; he was dying.

Mike initially thought our dad had some time left, so I planned to come down in a few weeks. But as the days went on, Dad got worse and worse, so I decided to go sooner than I had planned. I wanted to get a flight out the next day, but it was expensive, so I booked a flight that left a few days later to save some money.

My sister arrived a couple days before I did, and when she got there, she called to let me know that I should get down as soon as possible.

But by this time, I had already booked my flight, which was scheduled to leave in two days, so there was little I could have done. Part of me began to worry because what if my dad died before I got there? But I doubted that would happen because he was absolutely fine a week ago. Besides, my flight was only two days away.

I landed at Tampa airport on March 28th, 2019, around 8:00 a.m. After I got my rental car, I called my brother Mike. He told me they were already at the hospital and I should just meet them there. When I got there, Mike and Kim came down to meet me in the lobby. I thought it was weird how they both came down to meet me but didn't think much of it at the time. What really seemed strange to me was how quiet they both were being. We got on the elevator and rode it to the third floor, and nobody spoke a single word for the entire ride.

When we got off the elevator, Mike stopped me before we made our way down the hall.

"Hold on, bro, before we go down there."

I thought he was going to tell me to be prepared for what I was about to see. I thought he was about to warn me how our dad looked like shit and was hooked up to tubes or something along those lines. But what he told me completely threw me off guard.

"Look, there's no easy way to say this, but Dad passed away this morning."

I couldn't believe my ears; I was too late. If I wasn't so fucking cheap, I would have caught that earlier flight and made it on time. My siblings told me I shouldn't blame myself, but I did. In fact, I continue to blame myself to this day. Maybe I am being too hard on myself, but I can't help it. That's just how I feel.

Mike and Kim gave me a few minutes alone with our dad to say my goodbyes. As I sat and talked to my dad for the last time, I couldn't help but think about how much our relationship had changed over the years. As a teenager, I feared my father because he was a cop, and I was an addict/drug dealer, so we were natural enemies. Then, through most of my 20s, we barely spoke a word because we resented each other so much. But when I got clean and sober at age 29, everything changed. After making amends, we became really close. Even though he lived a thousand miles away, we were able to strengthen our relationship.

There were many things about my dad that I never knew until after I got clean. For example, I never noticed how funny my dad was. Throughout my teenage and young adult years, I always viewed my dad as this strict, militant type of father who rarely ever spoke to me. But that's not who my dad really was. After I got clean, I got to know the real him, and he was a good, kind-hearted person who was quick to crack a joke and have the entire room rolling with laughter.

I had a great relationship with my dad for those nine years after I got clean and sober, and I owe it all to the AA program. Without the 12 steps, I would have never been able to form that close bond with him. And even though I arrived too late, at least I was there. If I was still getting high, I wouldn't have shown up at all. For one, I wouldn't have been able to afford it. But even if I could afford a plane ticket, the fear of being away from heroin for too long and getting dope sick would have been enough to stop me.

That first night after my dad passed away was especially difficult. I slept on my dad's couch but barely slept at all; I kept thinking about him. I dozed off here and there, only to wake up believing that his death was nothing more than a bad dream. But after a few moments, I snapped back to reality and realized that it wasn't a dream; he was really gone, and I already missed him.

The next day, I desperately needed a meeting. Luckily for me, no matter where you are in the world, an AA meeting is never far away. I could have easily searched the internet for nearby meetings. But my good friend, Bob, had just moved to Lakeland, Florida, a year before my dad passed, so he was only an hour's drive away. When I arrived at Bob's house, he made me feel right at home. Bob offered me his condolences, but a few minutes later, he had me cracking up. Bob had always been a funny mother fucker who could make just about anybody laugh, so I was grateful for his company that day. He really helped to take my mind off of things and brought me to a great meeting. Thank God for Bob and people like him in AA. Because of people like him, I got through some of the most challenging times of my life.

After I left Bob's house, my brother and sister started to call and text me repeatedly. I think they were afraid that I went out drinking or something, even though it was actually the opposite. In their defense, it was getting kind of late, they hadn't heard from me all day, and my dad had just passed away, so I understood why they could have thought that. But when

I got back home, I assured them everything was OK, and I was just hanging out with a good friend from AA.

Honestly, the thought of drinking or getting high didn't even cross my mind. Even though dealing with my dad's death was not easy, I was well prepared with the tools AA gave me over the years. I knew to go and hit a meeting BEFORE the thought of drinking even had a chance to form inside my head. I also knew that drinking wouldn't bring my dad back, and it sure as hell wouldn't make me feel any better. But most importantly, I knew that my dad wouldn't want me to drink.

By remaining clean and sober, I could be there for my family when they needed me the most. My dad didn't have a will, so the next few months were a hassle trying to deal with his estate and all the legal stuff that goes along with it. Since I worked at the library and had a lot of downtime, it was easier for me to handle it, so I volunteered to take charge.

My dad left us all a little chunk of money. It wasn't enough to quit my job and retire or anything even close to that, but it was definitely more than expected. Most of the money he left us was in the form of an IRA. I had the option of cashing out the IRA, but I decided against that. I can't help but think about what would have happened if I was still getting high. With that much money, I would have ended up dead by the end of the week.

After transferring my dad's IRA and setting up my own IRA, I looked into other retirement options available through my job with the city. I already knew about the pension plan, but after doing a little research, I learned that they also offered a deferred comp plan. So, I set up the account and started contributing five percent of my paycheck, which really wasn't that much. After a while, I decided to bump it up by a few more dollars. Then, I bumped it up a little more, and then a little more after that. I am now contributing 14% of my paycheck, and every time I get a raise, I contribute more so that I don't even see that extra money.

After setting up these retirement accounts, I began to think about other ways to plan for my future. So, I started to invest in the stock market. At first, I wasn't really making any money. In fact, I think I may have even lost a little bit. But eventually, I did make some money, but then I lost it, and then I made it back again. That's the thing with the stock market; you never know which way it will go. I'm still learning, and maybe one day, I'll have enough for early retirement. But just being financially stable enough to invest money like this was beyond my wildest dreams at one point in my life.

Look, I'm not telling you this to try and brag or anything like that. I'm just trying to show you how much I changed as a person throughout my recovery. For example, when I first got clean and sober, my credit score was around 550, which is pretty bad. But by making financial amends and learning about how credit scores work, I slowly improved my score. Today my credit score is 816, which is almost perfect. I could easily go out and get a $20,000 loan if I wanted to. This just seems crazy to me because I remember back when people wouldn't even loan me $20, let alone $20,000.

When I had eight years clean and sober, my wife and I got a car loan and treated ourselves to a nice, certified pre-owned car. Three years later, we refinanced our home with a new mortgage. We even got some cash back on that mortgage, so we could make some major home improvements. Most recently, in 2022, my wife and I traded in our used vehicle to get a brand new car that only had 11 miles on it. These are not things I could have done if I were still getting drunk and high.

If you had told me 12 years ago that I would one day be a homeowner with a nice car, college degree, beautiful wife, multiple retirement accounts, nearly perfect credit score, and money invested in the stock market, I would have looked at you like you had 17 heads. There was a time when I couldn't hold onto $10 for more than a couple of minutes, so my money situation today seems surreal at times. Don't get me wrong, I am not rich or anything even close to that. I still have to work for a living and will have to continue to work for at least another 15 years before I'm ready to retire. But, I know I will retire much earlier than I would have if I wasn't the responsible adult I am today; and I owe that all to my dad and AA.

Chapter 39

As I'm sure you already know by now, I had no problem getting honest while writing this story, so I'm not going to stop now. The truth is, there was a five to six-year period where I didn't attend meetings on a regular basis. But to explain this, I have to back up to when I first moved in with my wife, Monica.

Before I met Monica, I went to meetings almost every day. Where I lived in Northeast Philadelphia, there were meetings everywhere, and they had them at all times of the day. But when I moved to South Philly, my meeting attendance slowly started slipping, which happened for several different reasons. The main reason was that there weren't nearly as many meetings in South Philly as there were in the Northeast.

I found two meetings that fit into my schedule, but honestly, I didn't like them that much. This sometimes happens with AA meetings. You're not always going to enjoy every meeting you go to, and that's OK. But when I lived in Northeast Philly, I had plenty of other meetings to choose from, so it was never really a problem. However, now that the meetings in my area were limited, it was a problem. So, instead of going every day, I only went to four or five meetings a week, which were all located in Northeast Philly. And I only went to those meetings because I was still working in the Northeast at the time.

Every day after work, I would leave Self Help and go to one of the many meetings in the area before I headed home. But, in 2015, when I started my job at the library, that all changed. The library I worked at was in South Philly, so I was never in the Northeast anymore. However, I found an early morning meeting near the library that I started going to before work. I really liked the meeting, but they only held three meetings a week, so I just went to all three of them.

A few months later, my wife got a new job and needed to use the car to get there, which made it harder for me to get to my meetings, so I slowly drifted away. Even without the car, I tried to make that morning meeting at least once a week because I still wanted to be a part of AA. But after a while, I found myself skipping a week here and then skipping a week there. Before I knew it, I wasn't going to the meeting at all anymore. It all boiled down to my laziness. I would rather sleep in for that extra hour than get up and go to a meeting.

As my meeting attendance slowly dwindled, I kept pushing myself to go to one of the other meetings near my house, even though I didn't really like them. The one meeting was a half block away from my home. I could literally pick up a rock from my backyard and hit the building, yet I couldn't bring myself to go. And once again, it all came down to pure laziness. There were many times I told myself, "I'm going to this meeting tonight, no matter what!" But when it came time to leave, I'd be chilling on the couch watching TV and just didn't feel like leaving the house.

So, by this point, I pretty much stopped going to AA on a regular basis. But, don't get me wrong, it's not like I never went to meetings at all. At first, I was still meeting up with Ryan and Steve every couple of weeks to go hit a meeting here and there. But eventually, every couple of weeks turned into every couple of months. Before I knew it, I was hitting one or two meetings a year, which really scared the shit out of me.

I have been to enough meetings to know what happens to people who stop attending them. I heard those stories way too often. Someone will get a few years sober, stop going to meetings, and then end up relapsing. I didn't want that to be part of my story. But no matter how much I wanted to go back to AA, I just couldn't bring myself to do it, and I don't know why. I guess I lacked the motivation I had when I first got clean and sober.

Now, here is the part when I get very honest. As I was re-writing this book, I started to feel like a hypocrite. How could I stand behind this book, talking about the importance of meetings, if I didn't even go to meetings anymore? I also thought about how embarrassed I would be if I did an interview for my book and someone asked me what meetings I go to or if I had a sponsor. So, my hypocrisy and fear of embarrassment motivated me to return to AA. I know this is a selfish reason to go back, but it didn't matter to me. I look at it like this: it doesn't matter how you get to AA, or in my case, how you get back to AA, as long as you get there.

I finally made it back to AA in January 2022. However, the Covid-19 pandemic drastically changed AA meetings since I last attended them, as I could now participate in Zoom meetings from the comfort of my own home. This was perfect because I could no longer use my laziness as an excuse. I literally did not have to leave my house to go to a meeting.

For the first few days, I randomly attended Zoom meetings across the country until I found one I liked. On day 3, I lucked out and found one of the best meetings I have ever attended. It was a beginners' meeting, and

244

since I was just coming back to AA and felt like a beginner again, it was almost as if this meeting was calling my name. A few minutes into the meeting, I started getting some really good vibes. I could instantly tell there was a lot of good recovery in the room, and it gave me back the AA motivation I had lost over the years.

I decided to dive right back into the program. I started raising my hand to share at every single meeting, just like I did when I first started going to AA. I also started using the chat feature to help others and motivate them to keep coming back. A week later, I volunteered to share my story at a speaker meeting. The next day, I found a sponsor and started re-working my steps. I even put myself on the sponsor list so that I could begin sponsoring newcomers again.

As I fully immersed myself back into the AA program, I couldn't help but feel guilty for how selfish I had been for the past few years. When I first got clean and sober, AA was there for me and helped me every step of the way. But, as time passed, I drifted away because I thought I didn't need AA anymore. I forgot that maybe AA needed me. The whole purpose of this 12 step program is to help others, especially newcomers. But I hadn't been doing that for the past few years. See, I took the help when I needed it, but I never gave it back to the newcomers like I was supposed to.

I am so lucky that I didn't relapse. I think the only thing that kept me sober during that period was how I continued to do steps 10, 11, and 12. I tried my best to be a good person, and if I did something wrong, I would immediately make amends for it. I also kept praying to my Higher Power as often as I could. I'd be lying if I said that I prayed every day because there were plenty of days when I just simply forgot, but I did pray on most days, as long as I remembered to do so.

As far as step 12 goes, I tried to carry the message of AA to others, although it wasn't nearly as often as it was when I was going to meetings. Working at the public library, we get a lot of addicts, many of whom are homeless, and visit the branch pretty often. But I never wanted to jeopardize my career by talking to them inside the library about their addiction. So I would wait until I saw them around the neighborhood and then share my experience, strength, and hope with them. I would also offer them guidance on where they could turn if they ever wanted to get help.

One other thing that kept me sober during those years was helping animals. When I first started going to AA, I learned that helping others is what helped me to stay clean and sober. But, as I got farther away from AA, I dove deeper into animal rescue. So, instead of helping people, I was just helping animals now. And I truly believe this is what helped to keep me on the right path.

Now, I may be completely wrong. Maybe helping animals isn't what kept me clean and sober. Perhaps I just got lucky. All I know is I'm not going to press my luck any further. Now that I've made it back to AA and have a second chance at recovery, I'm staying for good this time. I'm not going to be selfish because what if everyone in AA became selfish and left the program after they got some sober time? Who would be there to help the newcomers? Who would have been there to help me when I needed it? See, I came back to AA for selfish reasons, but now that I'm back, I'm sticking around for selfless reasons.

Chapter 40

My story isn't over yet. Just because I'm clean, sober, and living life "beyond my wildest dreams" doesn't mean I don't have plans for the future. I will continue to strive in recovery and help others as much as possible. Life doesn't stop just because I achieved everything that I ever wanted.

I recently graduated from community college with an Associate of Arts Degree. Although it is quite a milestone for me, I'm not going to stop there. My education is not finished yet. When I first enrolled in school, I didn't know what I wanted to be. But after working at the Free Library of Philadelphia for the past seven years, I decided I wanted to become a librarian instead of just the library assistant I am now. To do this, I would need a Master of Library Science Degree, and you know what? I'm going to get it! I will earn one degree at a time, just like I take my recovery one day at a time.

My education and career are not the only part of my future that I have plans for. As I mentioned in the previous chapter, I am also planning for my retirement so that I will be financially stable and not have to worry about money later on in life. When we retire, Monica and I will be moving to Florida. After visiting my dad and grandmom every year, we fell in love with the place. Not only do they have crystal clear beaches, but the wildlife down there is simply incredible. So, as animal lovers, it is our dream location to retire.

Even though I have plans for the future, I still have to live one day at a time. I continue to do steps 10, 11, and 12 on a daily basis, or at least try my best to. I'm still human and make mistakes, but by continuing to do step 10, I can admit to those mistakes and immediately make amends when I am wrong. By continuing to do step 11, I keep myself in close contact with my Higher Power and remain thankful for the food I eat, the bed that I sleep in, the air that I breathe, the shoes on my feet, etc.

I also continue to do the 12th step in my daily life by carrying the message of AA and helping other alcoholics/addicts. I might do this when I see a homeless addict begging for change outside a store. Instead of giving them money and enabling their addiction, I buy them something to eat. Then I sit down and talk to them for a few minutes. In those few minutes of talking, I tell them about my experience with drug addiction and the strength that AA has given me as a way to offer them hope in their own lives.

It doesn't always work, but you'll be surprised at how much you can help somebody by sparing just five minutes of your day. Most people just walk by and ignore them, refusing to even acknowledge their existence. So talking for a few minutes can help reassure them that there are still people in the world who care about them. And by explaining how I overcame my addiction, I am planting the seed of recovery, which could sprout at a later date.

When I was going through the struggle of addiction, I thought the Devil lived in Kensington, but after I got sober, I learned the truth. The Devil lives all around us. It doesn't matter where you live, how poor you are, or who your family is. This mental disease of addiction/alcoholism can affect anyone. The sad part is that it usually hurts the addict's family and friends more than it hurts the addict themselves. Sure, I have been through a lot of pain, but it doesn't compare to the pain I put my family through.

Even in sobriety, I have stared eye to eye with the Devil himself. But throughout the years, I have learned that the closer I am to God, the farther I am from the Devil. That doesn't mean that I am a perfect person. I am still human and fall short constantly. There are many things I have done in sobriety that I am ashamed of. There have been times I have lied or been dishonest. I am not a saint, but I can honestly say that I no longer have to hide behind a bottle of booze or a bag of dope.

It doesn't matter what happens in life because I know I can get through anything without taking a drink or getting high. Drugs and alcohol will not solve any of my problems, no matter how big or small. For example, if my dog dies today, drinking or using is not going to help. In fact, if I go out and get drunk, then tomorrow morning, I'm going to wake up with a dead dog, plus a hangover. And that's not to mention the repercussions of the stupid decisions I make while under the influence, especially financial and legal ones. But, if I stay sober through it, I may be able to help someone else stay sober when their dog dies.

I'm not much of a gambler, but I like to compare life to a game of poker. I wasn't dealt a bad hand. I didn't have it that rough as a child; I just played my cards wrong. Sometimes when you play poker, you just have to fold, and when you fold, you get dealt a new hand. However, sometimes the new hand you're dealt turns out to be a shitty one, but that doesn't even matter. You can still win if you play your cards right, and I'm living proof of that. Like most addicts and alcoholics, I was dealt a shitty hand when I got clean and sober, but I kept playing anyway. There were a couple times when I wanted to cash in my chips, but God was there to save me, and for that, I will forever be grateful.

God saved me that night on the train tracks when I tried to kill myself and on that Christmas morning when I almost overdosed. God saved me again when I found out I had HIV and wanted to get high. I have been given so many chances, and now it's my turn to help others who have been given a second chance at life. That's God's true plan for me.

I don't know if I will be clean and sober tomorrow, but I know I will be today. That's all I can ask for. I can't change my past, and I can't predict the future; that's why I live one day at a time. If I live to see tomorrow, then I know it will be another "happy" day.

For anyone reading this who may struggle with alcoholism or drug addiction, please know there is a better way of life. If I could do it, then I know you can too. My story is not unique. It's not a "one out of a million" type of story but is just one story out of millions. If this book helps just one person to get clean and sober, then it was well worth the time and effort I put into writing it. Drugs and alcohol may be hard to overcome, but remember that the struggle will not last forever.

Dope Sick Hip-Hop

I had dreams of living life on white sandy beaches,
But fiending for those drugs shattered my dreams into pieces…
My family couldn't trust me or even let me see my nieces,
But I'm still writing rhymes like a student writing a thesis…
I need this, just like I used to need those drugs,
I got this Dope Sick Hip-Hop breathing from my lungs…
I feel like shit when I'm not spitting lyrics out my tongue,
And I miss my microphone, cause hip-hop is my love…
And after everything in life I been through,
Hip-hop has been right there, helping me get through…
See, I been through more than you could even imagine,
Fighting demons with this pen like a sword to a dragon…
I spent plenty of nights when I fell to my knees just,
Praying to God like "O Lord help me, Jesus"…
I grabbed myself a pen, cause yo, I'm going to need this,
To re-write my life like a born-again fetus…
Addiction is a disease….Hip-hop? That's my medicine,
God's my new dealer, my friends are the Excedrin…
But every day's getting better with the direction that I'm heading in,
But let me shed some light like my name was Thomas Edison…
I was in a dark place, where the scum of the earth dwell,
I was trying to find Heaven in the darkest parts of Hell…
I needed money for drugs, so drugs are what I sell,
Until they locked me up and threw me in a cold prison cell…
Well, that opened my eyes…it opened them real quick,
I realized I had a problem…Ay yo, I was real sick…
But life is no game, no! This is some real shit,
I still have lots of problems that I still have to deal with…
But sometimes I can't deal with all these problems in my hand,
So I'm juggling this shit to the best that I can…
But instead of running away when shit hits the fan,
Now I'm able to stand tall…like a real fucking man!

Acknowledgements

First and foremost, I would like to thank my Higher Power, whom I choose to call God, for, without him, I would have never survived the struggle I had to go through. Secondly, I would like to thank the 12 step program, for, without it, I would have eventually fallen back into my old ways. I would also like to thank everyone who helped me along the way, those in the program and those who are not. I would also like to thank everyone who I mentioned in my story. Whether you've affected my life negatively or positively, you helped pave the way for me to become the person I am today.

I would like to give a special thanks to my family. Not only for putting up with my shit for so long but also for loving me unconditionally and offering your full support when I needed it the most. I would like to give extra thanks to my sister, Kim, for helping me edit this book and pointing out the numerous mistakes I made in the original version. You have always been my favorite (and only) sister.

I want to give a special thanks to my wife, Monica, for loving and accepting me just the way I am, offering her full support in everything I do. You are my soulmate, and without you, I would be lost in this world.

I would like to thank all of those I've lost along the way. Although I am sad that you are gone, your deaths have only made me stronger and served as a reminder that I'm only one poor decision away from death. I thank you all for the memories, both good and bad, for without them, I wouldn't have had much of a story to tell. I would also like to thank everyone else I have failed to mention. It would be impossible for me to name everyone, but you have all impacted my life in one way or another.

Thank you to all the beta readers who have submitted reviews and given me honest criticism as I rewrote this memoir. I appreciate each and every one of you for helping me along my writing journey.

Last but definitely not least, I would like to thank you, the person reading this right now. I thank you for allowing me to share my story with you. Whether or not you are an addict, I hope this story has helped you in one way or another. It means so much to me that you would take the time to read about my life. I am incredibly grateful for you, and I wish you nothing but the best in life.

Resources for Addicts/Alcoholics

Alcoholics Anonymous
www.AA.org

Narcotics Anonymous
www.NA.org

Cocaine Anonymous
www.ca.org

SAMHSA
(Substance Abuse and Mental Health Services Administration)
1-800-662-HELP (4357)
www.samhsa.gov

Suicide Prevention
1-800-273-8255
www.suicidepreventionlifeline.org

Resources for Loved Ones
of Addicts/Alcoholics

Al-Anon (Support Group for Family & Friends of Alcoholics)

www.al-anon.org

Nar-Anon (Support Group for Family & Friends of Addicts)

www.nar-anon.org

About the Author

Brian Storm grew up in Philadelphia, PA, where he discovered a passion for writing at an early age. However, a drug addiction took priority over Brian's life, as he spent the next 15 years selling drugs to support his habit. Eventually, Brian turned his life around with the help of a 12 step program, where he discovered a passion for helping other alcoholics and addicts. This passion led Brian to write his memoir, "The Struggle," to share his experience, strength, and hope with others. Years later, Brian pursued a career at the Free Library of Philadelphia and went back to school to obtain his Associate of Arts Degree. In 2016, Brian married his soulmate, Monica, who helped him realize his love for rescuing animals.

Ingram Content Group UK Ltd.
Milton Keynes UK
UKHW020208160323
418650UK00019B/244/J